On Common Ground

Jerry George · Don Stone · Faye Ward

Toronto
OXFORD UNIVERSITY PRESS

Oxford University Press
70 Wynford Drive, Don Mills, Ontario M3C 1J9
http://www.oupcan.com

Oxford New York
Athens Auckland Bangkok Calcutta Cape Town Chennai Dar es Salaam Delhi
Florence Hong Kong Istanbul Karachi Kuala Lumpur Madrid Melbourne Mexico City
Mumbai Nairobi Paris Singapore Taipei Tokyo Toronto Warsaw
and associated companies in
Berlin Ibadan

Oxford is a trademark of Oxford University Press

Canadian Cataloguing in Publication Data

On common ground

ISBN 0-19-541020-3

1. Canadian literature (English).   I. George, Jerry.
II. Stone, Don, 1938-   III. Ward, F.C., 1949-

PS8233.05   1994   C810.8   C93-095246-4
PR9194.4.05   1994

Editor: Dianne Horton
Editorial Assistant: Micaëla Gates
Design: Marie Bartholomew
Composition: Ibex Graphic Communications

Illustrators: 3 in a Box (*artists*): Kathryn Adams, Andrée Chevrier, Glen Hanson, Paul Hotrum,
Peter Lacalamita, Tadeusz Majewski, Pierre-Paul Pariseau, Scot Ritchie, David Rolfe, Leo Scopacasa,
David Shaw, Riccardo Stampatori, Susan Todd, Jeremie White, Russ Willms

3 4 5 6 - 02 01 00 99

This book is printed on permanent (acid-free) paper ∞.
Printed and bound in Canada by Tri-Graphic Printing.

Acknowledgements

Special thanks to the following educators for their constructive comments in reviewing and class-testing the manuscript:

DAI ANN BAYNES, Burnaby North Secondary School, Burnaby School District, British Columbia; KAREN BRUST, Louis
St-Laurent High School, Edmonton, Alberta; MIKE BUDD, English Consultant, Essex County, Ontario; ROSALIND
EDMONDSON, Cardinal Carter Secondary School, Leamington, Ontario; TERRY FRANKS, Shoreline Secondary School,
Victoria, British Columbia; SUE HARPER, John Fraser Secondary School, Mississauga; CAROL MAYNE-OGILVIE, St. Francis
Xavier High School, Edmonton, Alberta; ARTHUR MILAN, Mount Carmel School, Edmonton, Alberta; STEFAN SIERAKOWSKI,
Pearson Collegiate Institute, Scarborough, Ontario; ELAINE SNADEN, Riverside Secondary School, Windsor, Ontario;
NOLAN TAGGART, Pine Ridge Secondary School, Pickering, Ontario; GARY WILSON, Cedar Hill Junior Secondary School,
British Columbia.

Many thanks also to students in the following schools for class-testing the material:

Burnaby North Secondary School, Burnaby, British Columbia; Louis St-Laurent High School, Edmonton, Alberta; Mount
Carmel School, Edmonton, Alberta; St. Francis Xavier High School, Edmonton, Alberta; Pearson Collegiate Institute,
Scarborough, Ontario; Riverside Secondary School, Windsor, Ontario; Cedar Hill Junior Secondary School, Victoria,
British Columbia.

Contents

The Me You See

On The Inside

Side by Side

Our World

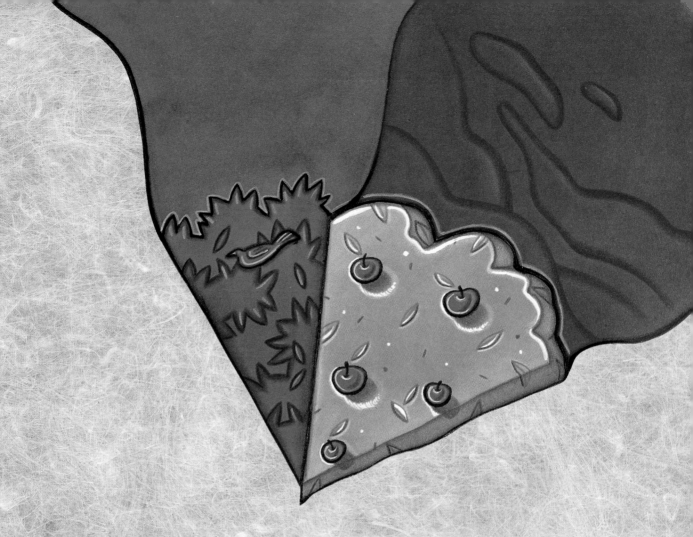

The Me You See

Flowers and Freckle Cream

Elizabeth Ellis

When I was a kid about 12 years old, I was already as tall as I am now, and I had a lot of freckles. I had reached the age when I had begun to really look at myself in the mirror, and I was underwhelmed. Apparently my mother was too, because sometimes she'd look at me and shake her head and say, "You can't make a silk purse out of a sow's ear."

I had a cousin whose name was Janette Elizabeth, and Janette Elizabeth looked exactly like her name sounds. She had a waist so small that men could put their hands around it . . . and they did. She had waist-length naturally curly blonde hair too, but to me her unforgivable sin was that she had a flawless peaches-and-cream complexion. I couldn't help comparing myself with her and thinking that my life would be a lot different if I had beautiful skin too—skin that was all one color.

And then, in the back pages of Janette Elizabeth's *True Confessions* magazine, I found the answer: an advertisement for freckle-remover cream. I knew that I could afford it if I saved my money, and I did. The ad assured me that the product would arrive in a "plain brown wrapper." Plain brown freckle color.

For three weeks I went to the mailbox every day precisely at the time the mail was delivered. I knew that if someone else in my family got the mail, I would never hear the end of it. There was no way that they would let me open the box in private. Finally, after three weeks of scheduling my entire day around the mail truck's arrival, my package came.

I went to my room with it, sat on the edge of my bed, and opened it. I was sure that I was looking at a miracle. But I had gotten so worked up about the magical package that I couldn't bring myself to put the cream on. What if it didn't work? What would I do then?

I fell asleep that night without even trying the stuff. And when I got up the next morning and looked at my freckles in the mirror, I said, "Elizabeth, this is silly. You have to do it now!" I smeared the cream all over my body. There wasn't as much of it as I had thought there would be, and I could see that I was going to need a part-time job to keep me in freckle remover.

Later that day I took my hoe and went with my brother and cousins to the head of the holler to hoe tobacco, as we did nearly every day in the summer. Of course, when you stay out hoeing tobacco all day, you're not working in the shade. And there was something important I hadn't realized about freckle remover: if you wear it in the sun, it seems to have a reverse effect. Instead of developing a peaches-and-cream complexion, you just get more and darker freckles.

By the end of the day I looked as though I had leopard blood in my veins, although I didn't realize it yet. When I came back to the house, my family, knowing nothing about the freckle-remover cream, began to say things like, "I've never seen you with that many freckles before." When I saw myself in the mirror, I dissolved into tears and hid in the bathroom.

My mother called me to the dinner table, but I ignored her. When she came to the bathroom door and demanded that I come out and eat, I burst out the door and ran by her, crying. I ran out to the well house and threw myself down, and I was still sobbing when my grandfather came out to see what was wrong with me. I told him I'd sent for the freckle remover, and he didn't laugh—though he did suggest that one might get equally good results from burying a dead black cat when the moon was full.

It was clear that Grandpa didn't understand, so I tried to explain why I didn't want to have freckles and why I felt so inadequate when I compared my appearance with Janette Elizabeth's. He looked at me in stunned surprise, shook his head, and said, "But child, there are all kinds of flowers, and they are all beautiful." I said, "I've never seen a flower with freckles!" and ran back to my room, slamming the door.

When my mother came and knocked, I told her to go away. She started to say the kinds of things that parents say at times like that, but my grandfather said, "Nancy, leave the child alone." She was a grown-up, but he was her father. So she left me alone.

I don't know where Grandpa found it. It isn't at all common in the mountains where we lived then. But I know he put it in my room because my mother told me later. I had cried myself to sleep that night, and when I opened my swollen, sticky eyes the next morning, the first thing I saw, lying on the pillow next to my head, was a tiger lily.

How to Hide a Pimple

Delia Ephron

Drawings by Edward Koren

While casually playing with hair, pull strand across face at pimple level. Secure hair in mouth.

If pimple is on forehead, wear bangs.

Apply Band-Aid.

Press hand against cheek as if punctuating the expression, "Oh my!"

Camouflage with
make-up, patting it on
with index finger.

If pimple is on chin, rest elbow
on table top, chin in hand.

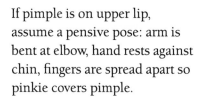

If pimple is on upper lip,
assume a pensive pose: arm is
bent at elbow, hand rests against
chin, fingers are spread apart so
pinkie covers pimple.

Make the following calculation: If pimple is on my left side, my date should
always be on my right side. Conversely, if pimple is on my right side, my
date should always be on my left side.

"I Want To Be Beautiful So Bad, It Makes Me Sick"

Mary Walters Riskin

Everywhere you look, "thin is in." Television and magazine ads feature beautiful, thin models. With a few exceptions like Roseanne Arnold and William Conrad, only thin people seem to appear in television shows and movies. Sometimes it looks as if all the successful and happy people in the world are thin.

Magazines offer a new diet every month and everyone's got a new weight-loss program. The weight-loss industry is booming: nearly 80 percent of females have been on a diet by the time they turn 18. Most people go on a diet, lose a few kilograms, go off the diet and gain the weight back. Then they repeat the cycle, in a strange and frustrating concession to "body image." But for some, the desire to be thin can turn into a real obsession—one that can rob them of their friends, their health and even their lives.

When Alison was 13, she hated the way she looked. She thought she was fat and ugly, so she quit eating. Not for a day or a week, but for three months. "I didn't really care if I had a heart attack or died. I just wanted to be skinny," she says. She was hungry all the time, but she ate as little as possible. She'd eat half an egg or half a piece of toast. Some days, all she had was an apple. She began to jog, even though she felt tired and weak all the time. Her weight dropped from 59 kg to 39 kg and she looked terrible—like one of those starving kids in Africa. But she didn't see how thin she was. She thought she was still fat. She felt proud of the way she could stop herself from eating.

Jody, 18, was 168 cm and "stodgy" at 68 kg. She didn't like her body either.

Kids teased her a bit about her size, but she couldn't stick to a diet and she couldn't stop thinking about food. At her boarding school, there was lots of food available at every meal, and there was always something around if she were hungry for a snack. "When I got depressed over something like an argument or a bad mark on a test, the only way to console myself was with food. I'd turn into a zombie at times. I'd inhale food. Then I'd make myself vomit."

This cycle is called "bingeing and purging," and sometimes, Jody binged and purged five or six times a day. Yes, she lost weight. Alison was anorexic, and Jody was bulimic. Both of them were so obsessed with being thin that they were prepared to put their bodies—and their lives—in danger. They're not alone. Eating disorders have become almost an epidemic in North America in the last twenty years.

"I wanted to be perfect." Monika Schnarre, one of Canada's most successful models, is a recovered bulimic. Jane Fonda binged and purged in the early years of her acting career. Karen Carpenter, a popular singer in the 1970s, died of complications from anorexia when she was 32.

It's mostly females who become victims of these disorders, but males can develop them too. Even Elton John has revealed his years-long bout with depression and bulimia. Both anorexia and bulimia are behavioural disorders, not diseases. They are a way in which some people respond to stress and to problems in their lives. When they feel like everything else in their lives is out of control, they control their eating habits.

"I just wanted to be perfect," Alison says. "I thought life would be wonderful if I could just be thin."

Our society has to take a lot of the blame for the recent increase in eating disorders. Studies show that more than 80 percent of females and 20 percent of males in North America want to be thinner than they are right now. In societies where thinness is not seen as such a big part of being attractive, eating disorders are rare. The problems often start with sensible diets which become obsessions. Anorexics and bulimics are usually perfectionists. They're usually intelligent, and they always lack self-esteem. Jody says, "I always compared myself to others and I was never good enough."

"I began to gain weight like any normal girl going through puberty, but I didn't look at it as normal," Alison says. "I didn't like my body. I wanted everyone, mostly guys, to appreciate me. I thought, I'll just quit eating for two weeks. But then I was so scared of getting fat again, I'd just keep on not eating.

My normal weight is about 52 kg, but I went down to 39 kg and I couldn't see any difference in the way I looked."

In addition to being so thin her bones showed, Alison's skin looked yellow and her hair got dry and began to fall out. Her periods stopped and she couldn't sleep more than four or five hours a night. When her friends told her she looked sick, she wouldn't admit she had a problem. Anorexics and bulimics become sneaky: they don't want anyone to know what they're doing to themselves. They are obsessed with food. Yet all they care about is being thin. No matter how much weight they lose, they don't see how awful they look. Whenever they eat anything, they feel guilty and they get more and more depressed.

"When I went home at Christmas," Jody says, "my mother noticed my eating habits were strange. My sister and my dad both commented. But it wasn't until a month after, when I binged and purged nine times in one day, that I saw what I was doing to myself."

Both anorexia and bulimia can be fatal. Malnutrition can cause irregular heartbeats and cardiac arrest. As many as 10 percent of anorexics die. Half literally starve themselves to death; the others become so depressed that they commit suicide.

"I didn't want to get help." "My friends said I turned into a completely different person," Jody says. "I realized I was getting more and more unhappy. Now I know it's one of the side effects of bulimia when it gets this severe. I just kept on thinking if I can lose a few more kilos, I'll be happy. I'll be the same old person again. But it never happened."

Before teens with eating disorders can get help, it's best if they recognize that they have a problem, and admit it to someone. That can be really hard to do.

"I didn't want to get help because then I'd be forced to gain weight. I'd lose control," Alison says. Many anorexics and bulimics refuse to believe they have a problem until something really serious happens to their bodies. "I remember falling onto the floor and crying," Alison says. "Blood was coming from my throat. I never realized what I was doing to myself until that moment. I went and told my brother."

"Another time I was taking an exam," Alison says. "I studied a lot, no matter how lousy I felt. It was hot in the classroom, and I got dizzy and felt really sick, and I passed out." When her teacher couldn't revive her, Alison was rushed to hospital. She was there for over a month, recovering from malnutrition and a stomach ulcer, and starting therapy.

Other people don't need to hit bottom before they look for help. "I just got tired of being obsessed with my body like all women in my family." Cathy, 17, says, "I wanted to change that." Kids with anorexia and bulimia need to get help from therapists who specialize in eating disorders. School counsellors and other people can point them in the right direction, but they need to work with someone who really understands the problem before they can get better.

"Don't be ashamed." The good news is that both anorexia nervosa and bulimia can be overcome and the earlier a person gets help, the speedier the recovery.

Alison's weight is now stabilized at 51 kg. "Therapy is helping a lot," she says. I always knew there were other girls out there, I guess. But the girls and guys in the group are so incredibly normal." Her advice for other kids who are suffering from eating disorders? "Don't be ashamed. It's a problem that a lot of people have." Jody adds, "It's hard to believe, and everyone tells you this—what's on the inside is a lot more important than what's on the outside. Once you're happy with who you are inside, the outside just comes automatically. And one day you realize that you do like your body and there's not much you can or want to do to change it."

Note: Weights and measures have been converted to metric.

How Much Does It Cost?

Mary Fong

"You should be a poet," someone said.
"A traditional Chinese poet."

In grade school
I told my friends
I don't even speak the language
and we use spoons all the time
at home.

Walking in a shopping mall
in downtown Vancouver
a squat Chinese woman
holds a green sweater.
Gae doh chin? she asks.

I look at the tag
count to ten on my Chinese fingers.
Three, eight, nine, five.
"It costs $38.95,"
I say in English.

I try again
say each number in Chinese
one by one.

Finally I tell her
M'gee ah.

Gae doh chin: How much is it?
M'gee ah: I don't know.

11

The Case for the Defence

Graham Greene

It was the strangest murder trial I ever attended. They named it the Peckham murder in the headlines, though Northwood Street, where the old woman was found battered to death, was not strictly in Peckham. This was not one of those cases of circumstantial evidence in which you feel the jurymen's anxiety — because mistakes *have* been made — like domes of silence muting the court. No, this murderer was all but found with the body; no one present when the Crown counsel outlined his case believed that the man in the dock stood any chance at all.

He was a heavy stout man with bulging bloodshot eyes. All his muscles seemed to be in his thighs. Yes, an ugly customer, one you wouldn't forget in a hurry — and that was an important point because the Crown proposed to call four witnesses who hadn't forgotten him, who had seen him hurrying away from the little red villa in Northwood Street. The clock had just struck two in the morning.

Mrs Salmon in 15 Northwood Street had been unable to sleep, she heard a door click shut and thought it was her own gate. So she went to the window and saw Adams (that was his name) on the steps of Mrs Parker's house. He had just come out and he was wearing gloves. He had a hammer in his hand and she saw him drop it into the laurel bushes by the front gate. But before he moved away, he had looked up — at her window. The fatal instinct that tells a man when he is watched exposed him in the light of a street-lamp to her gaze — his eyes suffused with horrifying and brutal fear, like an animal's when you raise a whip. I talked afterwards to Mrs Salmon, who naturally after the astonishing verdict went in fear herself. As I imagine did all the witnesses — Henry MacDougall, who had

been driving home from Benfleet late and nearly ran Adams down at the corner of Northwood Street. Adams was walking in the middle of the road looking dazed. And old Mr Wheeler, who lived next door to Mrs Parker, at No. 12, and was awakened by a noise — like a chair falling — through the thin-as-paper villa wall, and got up and looked out of the window, just as Mrs Salmon had done, saw Adams's back and, as he turned, those bulging eyes. In Laurel Avenue he had been seen by yet another witness — his luck was badly out; he might as well have committed the crime in broad daylight.

"I understand," counsel said, "that the defence proposes to plead mistaken identity. Adams's wife will tell you that he was with her at two in the morning on February 14, but after you have heard the witnesses for the Crown and examined carefully the features of the prisoner, I do not think you will be prepared to admit the possibility of a mistake."

It was all over, you would have said, but the hanging.

After the formal evidence had been given by the policeman who had found the body and the surgeon who examined it, Mrs Salmon was called. She was the ideal witness, with her slight Scotch accent and her expression of honesty, care and kindness.

The counsel for the Crown brought the story gently out. She spoke very firmly. There was no malice in her, and no sense of importance at standing there in the Central Criminal Court with a judge in scarlet hanging on her words and the reporters writing them down. Yes, she said, and then she had gone downstairs and rung up the police station.

"And do you see the man here in court?"

She looked straight at the big man in the dock, who stared hard at her with his Pekingese eyes without emotion.

"Yes," she said, "there he is."

"You are quite certain?"

She said simply, "I couldn't be mistaken sir."

It was all as easy as that.

"Thank you, Mrs Salmon."

Counsel for the defense rose to cross-examine. If you had reported as many murder trials as I have, you would have known beforehand what line he would take. And I was right, up to a point.

"Now, Mrs Salmon, you must remember that a man's life may depend on your evidence."

"I do remember it, sir."

"Is your eyesight good?"

"I have never had to wear spectacles, sir."

"You are a woman of fifty-five?"

"Fifty-six, sir."

"And the man you saw was on the other side of the road?"

"Yes, sir."

"And it was two o'clock in the morning. You must have remarkable eyes, Mrs Salmon?"

"No, sir. There was moonlight, and when the man looked up, he had the lamplight on his face."

"And you have no doubt whatever that the man you saw is the prisoner?"

I couldn't make out what he was at. He couldn't have expected any other answer than the one he got.

"None whatever, sir. It isn't a face one forgets."

Counsel took a look round the court for a moment. Then he said, "Do you mind, Mrs Salmon, examining again the people in court? No, not the prisoner. Stand up, please Mr Adams," and there at the back of the court with thick stout body and muscular legs and a pair of bulging eyes, was the exact image of the man in the dock. He was even dressed the same—tight blue suit and striped tie.

"Now think very carefully, Mrs Salmon. Can you still swear that the man you saw drop the hammer in Mrs Parker's garden was the prisoner—and not this man, who is his twin brother?"

Of course she couldn't. She looked from one to the other and didn't say a word.

There the big brute sat in the dock with his legs crossed, and there he stood too at the back of the court and they both stared at Mrs Salmon. She shook her head.

What we saw then was the end of the case. There wasn't a witness prepared to swear that it was the prisoner he'd seen. And the brother? He had his alibi, too; he was with his wife.

And so the man was acquitted for lack of evidence. But whether—if he did the murder and not his brother—he was punished or not, I don't know. That extraordinary day had an extraordinary end. I followed Mrs Salmon out of court and we got wedged in the crowd who were waiting, of course, for the twins. The police tried to drive the crowd away, but all they could do was keep the road-way clear for traffic. I learned later that they tried to get the twins to leave by a back way, but they wouldn't. One of them—no one knew which—said, "I've been acquitted, haven't I?" and they walked bang out of the front entrance. Then it happened. I don't know how, though I was only six feet away. The crowd moved and somehow one of the twins got pushed on to the road right in front of a bus.

He gave a squeal just like a rabbit and that was all; he was dead, his skull smashed just as Mrs Parker's had been. Divine vengeance? I wish I knew. There was the other Adams getting on his feet from beside the body and looking straight over at Mrs Salmon. He was crying, but whether he was the murderer or the innocent man nobody will ever be able to tell. But if you were Mrs Salmon, could you sleep at night?

Lose Now, Pay Later

Carol Farley

I think my little brother is crazy. At least I hope he is. Because if his looney idea is right, then all of us are being used like a flock of sheep, and that's a pretty gruesome thought. Humans just can't be that stupid. My brother has a dumb idea, that's all. It's just a dumb idea.

This whole situation started about eight months ago. That's when I first knew anything about it, I mean. My best friend, Trinja, and I were shopping when we noticed a new store where an old insurance office used to be. It was a cubbyhole, really, at the far end of the mall where hardly anybody ever goes. We were there because we'd used that entrance as we came home from school.

"Swoodies!" Trinja said, pointing at the letters written across the display window. "What do you think they are, Deb?"

I stared through the glass. The place had always looked dim and dingy before, full of desks, half-dead plants, and bored-looking people; but now it was as bright and glaring as a Health Brigade Corp office. There weren't any people inside at all, but there were five or six gold-colored machines lining the walls. Signs were hung everywhere.

SWEETS PLUS GOODIES = SWOODIES, one said. Flavors were posted by each machine; peanut-butter-fudge-crunch . . . butter-rum-pecan . . . chocolate-nut-mint . . . Things like that. The biggest sign of all simply said FREE.

I have to admit that the place gave me the creeps that first time I saw it. I don't know why. It just looked so bare and bright, so empty and clean, without any people or movement. The glare almost hurt my eyes. And I guess I was suspicious about anything that was completely free. Still, though, there was a terrific aroma drifting out of there—sort of a combination of all those flavors that were listed on the signs.

"Let's go in," Trinja said, grabbing my arm. I could see that the smell was getting to her too. She's always on a diet, so she thinks about food a lot.

"But it's so empty in there," I said, drawing away.

"They've just opened, that's all," she told me, yanking my arm again. "Besides, machines and robots run lots of the stores. Let's go inside and see what's in there."

Do you know that wonderful spurt of air that rushes out when you first open an expensive box of candy? The inside of that store smelled just like the inside of one of those boxes. For a few seconds we just stood there sniffing and grinning. My salivary glands started swimming.

Trinja turned toward the nearest machine. "Coconut-almond-marsh-mallow." She was almost drooling. "I've got to try one, Deb." She pressed the button, and a chocolate cone dropped down, like a coffee cup from a kitcho machine. Then a mixture, similar to the look of soft ice cream, filled it. "Want to try it with me?" she asked, reaching for the cone. We both took a taste.

It was absolutely the neatest sensation I've had in my whole life. Swoodies aren't cold like ice cream or warm like cooked pudding, but they're a blending of both in temperature and texture. The flavor melts instantly, and your whole mouth and brain are flooded with tastes and impressions. Like that first swoodie I tried, coconut-almond-marshmallow; suddenly, as my mouth separated the individual tastes, my brain burst into memories associated with each flavor. I felt as if I were lying on a warm beach, all covered with coconut suntan oil—then I heard myself giggling and singing as a group of us roasted marshmallows around a campfire—then I relived the long-ago moments of biting into the special Christmas cookies my grandmother made with almonds when I was little.

"Wow!" Trinja looked at me, and I could see that she had just experienced the same kind of reactions. We scarfed up the rest of that swoodie in just a few more bites, and we moved on to another flavor. With each one it was the same. I felt a combination of marvelous tastes and joyous thoughts. We tried every flavor before we finally staggered out into the mall again.

"I'll have to diet for a whole year now," Trinja said, patting her stomach.

"I feel like a blimp myself," I told her, but neither one of us cared. We both felt terrific. "Go ahead in there," I called to some grade-school kids who were looking at the store. "You'll love those swoodies."

"It's a publicity stunt, we think," Trinja told them. "Everything is free in there."

In no time at all the news about the swoodie shop had spread all over town. But days passed, and still everything was absolutely free. Nobody knew who the new owners were or why they were giving away their product. Nobody cared. The mall directors said a check arrived to pay for the rent, and that was all they were concerned about. The Health Brigade Corp said swoodies were absolutely safe for human consumption.

Swoodies were still being offered free a month later, but the shop owners had still not appeared. By then nobody cared. There were always long lines of people in front of the place, but the swoodies tasted so good nobody minded waiting for them. And the supply was endless. Soon more shops like the first one began opening in other places around the city, with machines running in the same quiet, efficient way. And everything was still absolutely free.

Soon all of us were gaining weight like crazy.

"It's those darn swoodies," Trinja told me as we left the mall after our daily binge. "I can't leave them alone. Each one must have a thousand calories, but I still pig out on them."

I sighed as I walked out into the sunshine. "Me too. If only there was some easy way to eat all the swoodies we want and still not gain any weight!"

The words were hardly out of my mouth when I noticed a new feature in the mall parking lot. Among all the usual heliobiles there was a tall white plastic box, sort of like those big telephone booths you see in old pictures. A flashing sign near the booth said THE SLIMMER. A short, thin woman was standing beside it. She was deeply tanned and her head was covered with a green turban almost the same color as the jumpsuit she was wearing.

Trinja looked at the sign, then glanced at the woman. "What's that mean?"

"It means that this machine can make you slimmer," the woman answered. She had a deep, strange-sounding voice. "Just step inside and you'll lose unwanted fat."

She seemed so serious and confident that I was startled. In the old days people thought they could lose weight in a hurry, but those of us who live in 2041 aren't that gullible. No pills or packs or wraps or special twenty-four-hour diets can work. There isn't any easy way to get rid of fat, and that's all

She overcame her shyness, and crept from her hiding place to approach Narcissus. But he, satisfied now that he had solved the mystery of the voice, roughly pushed her away and ran.

"I would die before I would have you near me!" he shouted mockingly over his shoulder.

Helpless, Echo had to call after him, "I would have you near me!"

The nymph was so embarrassed and ashamed that she hid herself in a dark cave, and never came into the air and sunlight again. Her youth and beauty withered away, and her body became so shrunken and tiny that eventually she vanished altogether. All that was left was the pathetic voice which still roams the world, anxious to talk, yet able only to repeat what others say.

Poor Echo was not the only one to be treated brutally by Narcissus. He had played with many hearts, and at last one of those he had scorned prayed to the gods that Narcissus would some day find himself scorned by one he loved. The prayer was heard, and granted.

Tired and thirsty from his hunting, Narcissus threw himself down beside a still, clear pool to drink. As he leaned over the shining surface, he saw reflected the most beautiful face he had ever seen. His heart trembled at the sight, and he could not tear himself away from it—his own image.

For a long time Narcissus remained there beside the pool, never raising his eyes from the surface, and from time to time murmuring words of love. At last his body withered away and became the stem of a flower, and his head the lovely gold and white blossom which still looks into quiet pools, and is called the narcissus.

Thank You, M'am

Langston Hughes

She was a large woman with a large purse that had everything in it but hammer and nails. It had a long strap, and she carried it slung across her shoulder. It was about eleven o'clock at night, and she was walking alone, when a boy ran up behind her and tried to snatch her purse. The strap broke with the single tug the boy gave it from behind. But the boy's weight, and the weight of the purse combined caused him to lose his balance so, instead of taking off full blast as he had hoped, the boy fell on his back on the sidewalk, and his legs flew up. The large woman simply turned around and kicked him right square in his blue jeaned sitter. Then she reached down, picked the boy up by his shirt front, and shook him until his teeth rattled.

After that the woman said, "Pick up my pocketbook, boy, and give it here."

She still held him. But she bent down enough to permit him to stoop and pick up her purse. Then she said, "Now ain't you ashamed of yourself?"

Firmly gripped by his shirt front, the boy said, "Yes'm."

The woman said, "What did you want to do it for?"

The boy said, "I didn't aim to."

She said, "You a lie!"

By that time two or three people passed, stopped, turned to look, and some stood watching.

"If I turn you loose, will you run?" asked the woman.

"Yes'm," said the boy.

"Then I won't turn you loose," said the woman. She did not release him.

"I'm very sorry, lady, I'm sorry," whispered the boy.

"Um-hum! And your face is dirty. I got a great mind to wash your face for you. Ain't you got nobody home to tell you to wash your face?"

"No'm," said the boy.

"Then it will get washed this evening," said the large woman starting up the street, dragging the frightened boy behind her.

He looked as if he were fourteen or fifteen, frail and willow-wild, in tennis shoes and blue jeans.

The woman said, "You ought to be my son. I would teach you right from wrong. Least I can do right now is to wash your face. Are you hungry?"

"No'm," said the being-dragged boy. "I just want you to turn me loose."

"Was I bothering *you* when I turned that corner?" asked the woman.

"No'm."

"But you put yourself in contact with *me*," said the woman. "If you think that that contact is not going to last awhile, you got another thought coming. When I get through with you, sir, you are going to remember Mrs. Luella Bates Washington Jones."

Sweat popped out on the boy's face and he began to struggle. Mrs. Jones stopped, jerked him around in front of her, put a half nelson about his neck, and continued to drag him up the street. When she got to her door, she dragged the boy inside, down a hall, and into a large kitchenette-furnished room at the rear of the house. She switched on the light and left the door open. The boy could hear other roomers laughing and talking in the large house. Some of their doors were open, too, so he knew he and the woman were not alone. The woman still had him by the neck in the middle of her room.

She said, "What is your name?"

"Roger," answered the boy.

"Then, Roger, you go to that sink and wash your face," said the woman, whereupon she turned him loose—at last. Roger looked at the door—looked at the woman—looked at the door—*and went to the sink.*

"Let the water run until it gets warm," she said. "Here's a clean towel."

"You gonna take me to jail?" asked the boy, bending over the sink.

"Not with that face, I would not take you nowhere," said the woman. "Here I am trying to get home to cook me a bite to eat, and you snatch my pocketbook! Maybe you ain't been to your supper either, late as it be. Have you?"

"There's nobody home at my house," said the boy.

"Then we'll eat," said the woman. "I believe you're hungry—or been hungry—to try to snatch my pocketbook!"

"I wanted a pair of blue suede shoes," said the boy.

"Well, you didn't have to snatch *my* pocketbook to get some suede shoes," said Mrs. Luella Bates Washington Jones. "You could of asked me."

"M'am?"

The water dripping from his face, the boy looked at her. There was a long pause. A very long pause. After he had dried his face and not knowing what else to do dried it again, the boy turned around, wondering what next. The door was open. He could make a dash for it down the hall. He could run, run, run, run, *run!*

The woman was sitting on the day-bed. After a while she said, "I were young once and I wanted things I could not get."

There was another long pause. The boy's mouth opened. Then he frowned, but not knowing he frowned.

The woman said, "Um-hum! You thought I was going to say *but*, didn't you? You thought I was going to say, *but I didn't snatch people's pocketbooks.* Well, I wasn't going to say that." Pause. Silence. "I have done things, too, which I would not tell you, son—neither tell God, if he didn't already know. Everybody's got something in common. So you set down while I fix us something to eat. You might run that comb through your hair so you will look presentable."

In another corner of the room behind a screen was a gas plate and an icebox. Mrs. Jones got up and went behind the screen. The woman did not watch the boy to see if he was going to run now, nor did she watch her purse, which she left behind her on the day-bed. But the boy took care to sit on the far side of the room where he thought she could easily see him out of the corner of her eye, if she wanted to. He did not trust the woman *not* to trust him. And he did not want to be mistrusted now.

"Do you need somebody to go to the store," asked the boy, "maybe to get some milk or something?"

"Don't believe I do," said the woman, "unless you just want sweet milk yourself. I was going to make cocoa out of this canned milk I got here."

"That will be fine," said the boy.

She heated some lima beans and ham she had in the icebox, made the cocoa, and set the table. The woman did not ask the boy anything about where he lived, or his folks, or anything else that would embarrass him. Instead, as they ate, she told him about her job in a hotel beauty shop that stayed open late, what the work was like, and how all kinds of women came in and out, blondes, red-heads, and Spanish. Then she cut him a half of her ten-cent cake.

"Eat some more, son," she said.

When they were finished eating she got up and said, "Now, here, take this ten dollars and buy yourself some blue suede shoes. And next time, do not make the mistake of latching onto *my* pocketbook *nor nobody else's*—because shoes come by devilish like that will burn your feet. I got to get my rest now. But I wish you would behave yourself, son, from here on in."

She led him down the hall to the front door and opened it. "Goodnight! Behave yourself, boy!" she said, looking out into the street.

The boy wanted to say something else other than, "Thank you, m'am," to Mrs. Luella Bates Washington Jones, but he couldn't do so as he turned at the barren stoop and looked back at the large woman in the door. He barely managed to say, "Thank you," before she shut the door. And he never saw her again.

The Boxing Champion

Roch Carrier

By April I knew it would happen again.

The rink was becoming soft. Our skate blades sank into the ice. The girls laughed when they saw us floundering around. The snow was gray. It was spring.

The street was a canal filled with water. Our ice forts were melting like cheese. Our snowmen were collapsing like fat drunken men.

The girls liked spring. They dreamed about the flowers they would soon be gathering in the grass. They strutted around in their coats and bright-colored berets.

The cows were waiting for our rink to turn into a pasture again.

The boys hated spring. There was nothing to do. Except school— and boxing . . .

The world champion was Joe Louis, the "Brown Bomber." His big swollen face often appeared in the newspaper. I didn't like the sport enough to put his picture on my bedroom wall next to one of Maurice Richard, the famous Number 9 of the Canadiens, our favorite hockey team.

And so when the rink was nothing but a big puddle, there we were in the Côtés' summer kitchen. There were twelve Côté children, perhaps thirteen. When the weather turned warm, the family emigrated from the winter kitchen to the summer kitchen, which was roomier, airier and brighter. In the spring it was a big empty space.

One of the Côtés had borrowed a piece of chalk from school. He drew a big square on the wooden floor. That was the ring. Another Côté struck a big nail against a bottle. The bell! And then two pugilists tore each other apart. I applauded as hard as the others, but I hated boxing.

I always did my best to be the last to climb into the ring. My adversary would face me, skipping and threatening me with his big fists. I danced about, head down, I rolled my gloves. Wham! I picked myself up on my rear end and my nose was bleeding. The match had lasted as long as a single punch. It wasn't me who administered it.

Some of the girls at school used to come to our fights. If one of the Côtés was hit, they would coo. When I walked out of the ring, stunned, my face bleeding, they didn't even see me. I tried hard to bleed as much as possible. They hadn't the slightest interest in me. Yet deep down I knew I was a champion.

My friends were the sons of farmers, truckdrivers or loggers. Since their earliest childhood they had been doing the work of men. My nose knew that they punched like men.

Their bodies were stocky. They had broad shoulders and short arms and bowlegs. They were as tough as the wood of a maple. They wolfed down pork and pea soup. I should have fled, but I didn't want to be alone so I followed my friends.

My mother lit into me.

"Why on earth," she asked, "did you have to get mixed up with boxing again?"

And that was how things happened in the spring, in my village.

I had my tenth birthday, and then, the next winter, an ad in the newspaper drew my attention. "I'll make you a world champion," said a man with muscles like the Greek statues that illustrated our dictionaries. "In 33 days I became a champion who will represent Canada at the Olympic Games. Be like me. Send me five dollars and I'll reveal my secret."

Exactly what I needed! Along with a letter that didn't have a single mistake, I sent five one-dollar bills to the address mentioned. That same week I received a reply from the *Miracle Muscle Center*: "I can tell that you're the stuff of champions. Unfortunately, you must abandon hope unless you train with my very excellent 'Miracle Muscle Exercisers', as well as my 'Miracle Muscle Barbells'. To obtain them just send thirty dollars to the *Miracle Muscle Center*." I had thirty-two dollars in the bank.

My mother didn't want me to spend all my savings. She thought bank interest was as important as my muscles. Finally I told her:

"*Maman*, do you want your boy to have skinny little arms like a girl?"

She looked at me and said:

"If you don't have enough money, Roch, I'll give you a couple of dollars."

Soon I received my champion's arsenal. To surprise the Côtés, I must keep my strategy a total secret. First I obtained my sister's silence. That was easy. If she said one word about my training, I threatened to put a mouse in her bed. As for my brothers, if they kept my secret I promised them I wouldn't tell our mother that they got sick from smoking our grandfather's pipe.

Deep in my heart I knew I was a champion. Unfortunately, I'd never been able to prove it.

Secretly, I set to work. When I got up in the morning, instead of my prayers I repeated one hundred times: "I'm a champion."

I ran to school, chanting: "I'm a champion! I'm a champion!" During classes, I wrote over and over and over: "I'm a champion." According to my *Miracle Muscle Guide*, this was motivational auto-suggestion.

After school, when my homework was finally done, I raced to my exercisers. Fifty times, I spread my arms to pull open a single spring. Then I added a second one and struggled till I was exhausted. Sweating breathlessly, I whispered: "I'm a champion."

After supper I raced up to my room. To develop my calves I took the stairs three at a time.

"Roch!" exclaimed my mother. "Do you have to tear the house apart?"

I splashed some soapy water on my muzzle and launched into round one of my boxing match. It wasn't the biggest Côté boy, but I punched away. He was tough. I punched again: his nose, his ear, chin, belly, plexus, jaw.

Finally, I threw the definitive hook that would slam the biggest Côté to the floor. I trod on his earthly remains and got back into bed, triumphant. I lay there motionless and listened to the music of my muscles, which were developing as predicted in the *Miracle Muscle Guide*.

On other days, I took up my Miracle Muscle barbells. My hands were blistered. My shoulders creaked like rusty hinges. Instead of removing discs to lighten the load, I added more. My backbone cracked. My dorsal muscles burned like fire. I pulled. The flesh of my arms seemed to tear. My chest seemed to be descending into my stomach.

One day I would conquer adversaries far superior to the Côtés. I'd become the first French-Canadian boxing champion in the world! I was a champion. I knew it deep in my heart.

In the mirror I gazed at my biceps. They contained as much power as a cannon. My fists were as hard as cannonballs. My chest was as solid as the foundations of the church.

When I went to school I piled sweater upon sweater to disguise my new athlete's body. I had so many muscles now, it was almost impossible to hide them. That would be a surprise for the Côtés!

Now the winter was not so cold. I felt hot under my layers of sweaters. Water dripped from the icicles that hung from the roof. The rink was getting softer. It was spring!

Boxing season was starting up again. The boys and a few of the girls were in the Côtés' summer kitchen. We pushed back the table. Against the wall we piled skis, ski-poles, skates, snowshoes. Carefully, the oldest Côté traced the official limits of the ring in chalk.

"Who wants to fight?" asked the youngest Côté, leaping into the center.

"Get ready!" I cried.

Solemnly, I peeled off all my sweaters to show off my new muscles. My heart was pounding.

The youngest Côté burst out laughing.

"Where'd the plucked chicken come from? There isn't even enough for a sandwich."

A champion doesn't lose his head if he's insulted.

"Côté," I threatened between clenched teeth, "you'd better concentrate."

The bell rang. I attacked like a champion.

When I opened my eyes again I realized that I was stretched out in the ring. My nose was bleeding.

A young girl smiled at me and tossed me some wildflowers.

She was the prettiest girl in the whole class.

I'd never dared to talk to her.

What a wonderful spring it was!

Warning

Jenny Joseph

When I am an old woman I shall wear purple
With a red hat which doesn't go, and doesn't suit me.
And I shall spend my pension on brandy and summer gloves
And satin sandals, and say we've no money for butter.
I shall sit down on the pavement when I'm tired
And gobble up samples in shops and press alarm bells
And run my stick along the public railings
And make up for the sobriety of my youth.
I shall go out in my slippers in the rain
And pick the flowers in other people's gardens
And learn to spit.

You can wear terrible shirts and grow more fat
And eat three pounds of sausages at a go
Or only bread and pickle for a week
And hoard pens and pencils and beermats and things in boxes.

But now we must have clothes that keep us dry
And pay our rent and not swear in the street
And set a good example for the children.
We must have friends to dinner and read the papers.

But maybe I ought to practise a little now?
So people who know me are not too shocked and surprised
When suddenly I am old, and start to wear purple.

from Lyn Cowan, *Ruby at the Fair*

Bald Is Beautiful

Peg Kehret

Did you ever think about how important hair is? It's the first thing mentioned when anyone describes another person. She's blond, they'll say; or, he's a redhead.

Shampoo ads make it seem like a person's hair is the *only* important thing about them. As long as your hair is shiny, bouncy and free of dandruff, you have no problems.

With so much emphasis on hair, it's small wonder that I came unglued when I found out I was going to lose mine.

I didn't cry when I had the CAT scan. I didn't cry when the doctor told me about the brain tumor. But after I found out I had to have my head shaved, I cried.

My mom said my hair would grow back and my dad said I could buy a wig and my little brother, Syd, said think how much time I would save in the bathroom every morning.

My sister, Janie, was the only one who understood. She said it was terrible that I had to be bald and she didn't blame me one bit for crying.

The surgery went even better than expected. The tumor was small and it was not malignant. When I woke up, I was weak and woozy, but for the first time in months, I didn't have a headache.

But when I looked in the mirror, I almost threw up. I looked like one of those mannequin heads that beauty shops display wigs on. I was smooth and white and round. And ugly. I never saw anything so ugly as me with no hair.

At my second checkup, the doctor removed the stitches and said I could go back to school half days. I was scheduled to start the next Monday afternoon.

I didn't want to go. I looked like a freak. How could I go back to school, looking like a freak? Even if I wore a wig, everyone would know it was a wig and stare at me. What if the wig fell off? What if some creepy boy pulled it off? I said I would rather dance barefoot in a barrel of thistles than go back to school without any hair on my head.

I told my parents that if I had to go back to school bald, I would run away and sleep in a cave and eat wild berries. They said I couldn't sit around and feel sorry for myself and do nothing but wait for my hair to grow out. My mother said if I didn't want to wear a wig to school, I could wear a turban. I said a turban would be even worse than a wig and I refused to get either one. My father said I should be thankful I was alive and to quit complaining about my lack of hair.

Syd asked me to go to his homeroom on my first day back, because he'd bet some kid fifty cents that his sister was bald and he wanted to collect his money.

Janie didn't say anything.

I said I would be a freak for the next six months and I would never be happy again until I got my hair back.

My dad said to quit calling myself a freak and I said one bald girl in the whole school was most definitely a freak.

When Janie and Syd left for school on Monday morning, Syd started to remind me about his fifty-cent bet, until Janie poked him and told him to be quiet.

The minutes dragged by that morning. I dreaded walking into the school and having everyone stare at me. I dreaded being different from all the other kids. I never felt more alone than I did that morning while I waited until it was time to go. I was miserable and I knew when I got to school, I'd be even more miserable.

I couldn't eat any lunch. I sat at the table, staring at my cheese sandwich and waiting for Janie. I had asked her to come home at noon and go back with me, so I wouldn't have to walk into the school that first time alone. Maybe she wouldn't come. She probably decided she didn't want to be seen with a freak. Who could blame her?

I tried not to cry. It was bad enough to be bald; I didn't want my eyes to be all red and swollen, too.

I heard the front door open.

Behind me, I heard Janie say, "Are you ready to go?"

I swallowed hard, trying to get up my courage.

"The way I figure it," she went on, "Syd's friend owes him a dollar."

I started to say there was no way I was going to parade my bald head around in front of Syd's friends, and then I turned and saw her.

Janie had skipped class that morning. Instead of going to school, she went downtown and got her head shaved. She was smooth, and white, and round, just like me.

I sat still as stone, while the full impact of what she had done sank in.

"One bald girl might be a freak," she told me. "Two bald girls could start a new fashion."

Although the words were joking, her lip quivered as she spoke.

When we got to school, everyone stared, just like I knew they would. But I wasn't miserable. I wasn't miserable at all. I was happy! As I marched down the hall with my head held high, and my beautiful sister beside me, I knew that some things are way more important than hair.

The Pinch-Hitter

Michael Parent

By late August of my 13th year, I'd had my Social Security card for more than three years, won the junior checkers championship at the neighborhood playground twice, and ridden my bike the seven miles to Martin's Point Beach a few times. But I'd never once gotten a base hit off Billy Boudreau.

School was about to start again in a few days. So if I didn't do it real soon, I'd probably have to wait until next year. I'd spend the whole endless winter watching my friends play that other game, the one all of us Canuck kids in Lewiston, Maine, were supposed to be good at and that I had barely begun to play 'cause I couldn't skate very well. And I'd have to take crap from Pete Poliquin, who'd never even touched one of Billy's fastballs but didn't seem to care about it like I did. I'd see Billy around in the winter, but he never said anything. Nobody could hit him, and he wasn't the bragging type anyway. All the other pitchers at the neighborhood ball field threw fastballs that looked like grapefruits, while Billy threw Bayer aspirins, but he never pointed that out. He didn't have to.

We gathered early on what I hoped would be The Day. We wanted to squeeze in as many innings as we could, and soon we had enough guys for two teams. Billy and Jake Houle, the two best players, did the choosing up. Jake tossed a bat to Billy, who caught it upside-down on the thick end, and then they went hand-above-hand up the bat until Jake capped the knob with his thumb. First pick. I was a pretty good fielder, so I wasn't worried about getting picked last and exiled to right field. I just hoped Jake would pick me so I could hit against Billy as soon as possible.

"'Allo, les garçons, 'ow you're doing?" said Monsieur Gauthier. He and his chum Monsieur Caron sat at their usual spots along the third-base line. "Hey, I 'ope we're gonna see some better baseball today den we saw at Fenway over de weekend." They were retired from the mill and mostly watched and talked baseball. They'd stop by a few times each day, comment on our games, offer pointers, and move on.

The game was way out of reach, 12–0, so it didn't matter much, but I wasn't going to pass up any chance to swing against Billy. I stepped to the plate and saw that the Phantom Kid had moved closer, eyeballing me as though he knew what an important at-bat this was. He usually leaned over by the far post that supported the elbow-high fence along the first-base grandstands. Now he was up near the home-plate end of the fence. He'd showed up after supper the last couple of weeks, appearing and disappearing without ever talking to anyone. We'd never asked him to play. I wondered how long he'd stay this time before he disappeared.

I focused on Billy again. This could be it. I tugged at my cap, pulled up my pants, tapped the bat on the plate, and spit into the other batter's box. Then — the final touch — I tapped the dirt out of my "spikes" like the pros did. It didn't matter that my spikes were really P.F. Flyers sneakers, so worn that the only dirt I'd tapped loose had been filling the center holes in the soles. I tried to gain that crucial mental edge by giving Billy a look that said, "C'mon, rookie, quit shakin', and fire your best pitch up here to ol' Ted Williams, Jackie Robinson, Yogi Berra, so I can smack it into the next county." It wasn't easy to hold that look, since by then Billy had struck me out 11 times. I was as ready as I could get for Billy's three aspirin tablets.

Then the Phantom Kid shouted, "Hey, can I pinch-hit?"

"You wanna pinch-hit for me?"

"Yeah, if it's okay."

"Well, I dunno, this is my last bat and I . . . "

"But you've been battin' all day," he said.

"Yeah, so what? Hey, what the hell's your name anyway?"

"Charlie. So whaddya think — can I pinch-hit?"

"What de hell, give 'im a try," Monsieur Caron called out. "'E can't do no worse den you guys."

"Damn!" I said under my breath. "Okay, okay. Here ya go." I held the bat out to the Phantom Kid. I figured he'd just strike out. But what if he got a hit with my at-bat? He paused a couple of seconds to reach behind the fence post, pulled a pair of crutches up under his arms, and came swinging out toward home plate.

Everyone watched him now as though he really were a phantom. The sun flashed on the metal braces clamped to his shoes. The kid swung the crutches out and pulled his legs along, but not like those people who get crutches because of a busted leg and usually start getting the hang of it right around the time the cast comes off.

Charlie stood in the lefties' batter's box. He bent down to adjust or maybe lock his leg braces, as I stood there holding the bat. He half-leaned on his crutches and grabbed the bat, and I stepped back toward the bench. Charlie looked out toward the pitcher's mound. He waved the bat in a slow circle like an old pro—or someone who's practiced with a mirror a lot—and waited for the pitch.

We waited. Billy picked up a handful of dirt, squeezed it, and threw it down, then stepped off the mound and back onto it. He took his glove off, wedged it under his arm, and rubbed the ball awhile without ever looking at the batter. No one told Billy to hustle it up. No one spoke at all. Billy's face was filled with a question he couldn't ask, and our eyes ping-ponged between Billy and Charlie. Even Monsieur Gauthier and Monsieur Caron made no comment.

We hadn't seen that look on Billy's face before. Charlie must have seen it someplace, though, because he's the one who finally answered Billy's question. "Hey, pitcher, it's okay. Just fire it in like you always do."

Billy shrugged, grinned at Charlie, eased into a slow windup, and threw a screaming fastball up to the plate—a perfect letter-high strike. It was the kind of pitch that's hard to see, let alone hit. Every batter's dream is to swing perfectly into such a pitch and give it the kind of ride that outfielders must quickly admire before they chase it down. And that's exactly what Charlie did. Pow! The ball sailed over Billy's astonished head and kept climbing. Ritchie Poirier, the center fielder, who had instinctively played Charlie quite shallow, scrambled after the ball as it sliced toward left-center field. "Look at dat, Henri! I be damn. Run, run like hell!" one of the men shouted.

Charlie was swinging, crutches and legs, down the first-base line—crutches and legs, crutches and legs. I couldn't believe it—his first time hitting against Billy. Damn! But soon I was up with the rest of the team, as we followed Charlie down the base path, screaming, "Go, Charlie, go!" and

merging our will with his. The ball took just one bounce, about 15 feet away from a rusty sign that read 410, and settled at the base of the fence under the sign.

Charlie was halfway to first by the time Ritchie picked up the ball and turned to throw. Then Charlie got tangled up and fell forward, somehow managing to hang onto his crutches and fall hand-first. We all froze. You could see guys riffle through the rule books in their minds and then quickly put them aside to help Charlie up. But he waved them away, pushed himself back up, and kept crutching and legging down the line. Ritchie pegged a decent relay to Eugene at shortstop, and Eugene fired a one-hopper to first from shallow left-center field.

The screaming stopped, and the inning ended when the ball smacked into the first-baseman's glove and beat Charlie to the base by eight feet. If he'd been eight inches away, someone would have hollered, "Safe! Tie goes to the runner!" and heard no argument. But we knew that calling Charlie safe would have been the same as Billy's pitching him a slowball he didn't want. Charlie returned to his spot by the post and watched from there. Billy Boudreau walked off the mound, shaking his head. The team behind him came in to bat as though they'd played badly, and we shuffled out to take the field, mouthing infield chatter that quickly faded into infield mumbles. All Monsieur Caron and Monsieur Gauthier could manage was a few whispers to each other. Charlie's turn at bat had filled the game with fiery mystery-juice, and now a hole had been punched into its bottom.

I didn't know what to think. I'd missed my last chance of the day and maybe of the season. The crippled kid who'd pinch-hit for me had practically made history but hadn't even made it to first base. When I finally looked over at Charlie, he was leaning on the fence at his usual spot with a huge smile on his face. What the hell was that about?

When the game ended, nobody said much, especially not to Charlie since no one had any idea what to say. I slipped my glove on the handlebars of my skinny-wheel bike, hopped on the seat, and pointed it toward home. When the other guys left, I turned to Charlie. He was still smiling out to left-center field.

"Hey, Charlie, can I ask you somethin'?"

"Yeah, sure. Hey, what's your name?"

"The guys call me Bidou."

"Hey, thanks for lettin' me pinch-hit."

"Yeah. Listen, I was wonderin' what the heck you're so happy about after what happened."

"I played, man. I played," he said.

The street lights came on as I pedaled down Walnut Street. Rolling past the IGA Food Store, I wondered if Charlie had figured out how to ride a bike. I'd ask him next time. I carried my bike up the steps to our apartment, and I hoped Billy's fastball had even more steam on it when I faced him again, next week or next spring.

Another Shot at Life

Suzanne Chazin

One day in their Memphis, Tennessee, home, six-year-old Justin Helstein asked his father, Warren, what makes some athletes great.

A great athlete has learned to handle fear, the bearded, soft-spoken businessman replied.

"Can you teach me?"

"Here," Warren said, handing Justin a hockey mask. "Put this on and lie on your stomach." Then he grabbed a toy hockey stick and a plastic puck and took a fast, furious slap shot at Justin's face.

Hearing it smack against the mask, Warren bent over and gazed through the mesh protecting the boy's smooth, round features.

It was a sight he'd never forget. Across Justin's face was a wide grin. Warren tousled his boy's dark, wavy hair. "You've sure got an athlete's heart," he said.

Justin's parents divorced when he was nine, and two years later he moved to the suburbs of New York City to live with his father. There his best friend, Chris Saunders, encouraged him to play hockey. Justin was a slow skater, so his father suggested he try out for goalie.

The boy was a natural. He pounced on shots with lightning speed. When there was a knot of commotion near his goal, Justin plunged right in, fiercely elbowing for control. When the coach rocketed a shot off his face mask, Justin flashed an ear-to-ear-grin.

"I've never seen anything like it," the coach said to Warren. "That's one tough kid you've got there."

On a hot June day in 1989, Warren drove to a car dealership with Justin and Chris. The two teen-agers asked to check out a nearby skate-boarding site.

Moments later Warren gazed out the window and saw a crowd gathered by the curb. Suddenly Chris appeared. "There's been a horrible accident," he choked out.

Warren elbowed through the crowd to Justin's body lying face down on the asphalt, a few meters behind a four-door sedan. He saw blood flowing from Justin's ear and knew the boy had sustained a massive head injury.

"He's gone," Warren whispered, cradling his son's cold, curled fingers. "My precious boy is gone." At the hospital, things looked bleak. Every organ began to shut down. As his swollen brain hemorrhaged, Justin lapsed into a coma and was placed in intensive care.

"Touch him. Talk to him," a doctor advised. "We don't know how much coma patients can hear, but let him know you're here."

Warren never left his son's bedside. He wiped Justin's sweat-soaked brow and stroked his hair. He reminded the boy of those magical winter nights at Madison Square Garden when the two of them cheered on Justin's hero, goalie John Vanbiesbrouck.

But after a week had passed, a doctor spoke bluntly to Warren, telling him that Justin was not likely to live. If he did, he'd probably be institutionalized for life.

Warren gazed at the monitor that measured the pressure the boy's delicate swollen brain was exerting on his skull. "You've got to hang in there and fight," Warren pleaded.

Days turned into weeks, and Justin's weight slipped from 48 kg to 32 kg. His body curled into a fetal position.

Alone in a twilight of anxiety, Warren refused to give up. He brought in Justin's hockey sticks and gloves. He put posters of John Vanbiesbrouck on the wall. One night, staring at his son's equipment, he recalled Justin's explaining to him why goalie was the best position of all. "You try not to get hung up over how many goals your opponents score," he told his father. "You concentrate on how many saves you can make."

Warren thought about Justin's words. It would take a miracle to save his son. He'd risk anything for that to happen.

A Hero's Promise. A few kilometers away, in the locker room of a suburban hockey rink, a short, stocky man pulled on his red-white-and-blue New York Rangers jersey. The 38-year-old center, the third-leading scorer in hockey

history, knew this workout would be one of his last. In a few months, Marcel Dionne's 19-year career would be over.

He'd recently bought into a dry-cleaning business, but doubts lingered. He had played hockey full time since he was 15. How could he go from top athlete to suburban store owner?

One morning nearly two months after Justin's accident, Dionne's business partner told him about a 13-year-old hockey fan lying in a coma in a nearby hospital. Dionne called, offering to visit.

"My son is in very bad shape," Warren Helstein told him. "I don't think there's much anyone can do."

Yet a few days later, a fireplug of a man in a golf shirt and jeans approached Warren in the waiting room. "Mr. Helstein? I'm Marcel Dionne." Together they went to Justin's room.

Dionne pulled up a chair and gazed at the boy's sagging bluish-white skin. Justin's right arm lay bent and paralyzed on his chest, the fingers twisted inward like a claw. Dionne closed his eyes as if he could sense the teen-ager's pain. "Do anything you feel would help," Warren encouraged him.

Dionne leaned over the boy for a long, tender moment. Then on impulse, he shook the youth. "Justin," he said in a commanding voice, "this is Marcel Dionne of the Rangers. Wake up."

Justin's face began to twitch. Both men stared in disbelief as the teen-ager's eyes and mouth flashed open, gaping at Dionne for an instant before closing again.

The hockey star, afraid and uncertain of what he'd done, paced the room, taking deep breaths. It was then he noticed the poster of Vanbiesbrouck on the wall. "He's Justin's special hero," Warren said.

Stroking the teen-ager's hair softly, Dionne whispered, "You work on getting better, Justin, and I'll bring Johnny to see you."

Two days later, Dionne returned with two New York Rangers, Pierre Larouche and a sinewy 25-year-old with a cocky hustle in his step, John Vanbiesbrouck.

Warren watched as Larouche cried and kissed Justin's forehead. Vanbiesbrouck was also moved. The thought of ever seeing his own 13-month-old son in this condition shook him deeply.

Vanbiesbrouck talked hockey with the boy, hoping to coax Justin into a response. Nothing happened. Finally he made him a promise: "You get well enough, and you'll be my special guest at a Rangers game."

Justin's Hockey Camp. Over the next few weeks, Justin slowly began to emerge from his coma. His fevers subsided. He gained weight. Sometimes, he'd even open his eyes.

Doctors eventually determined that Justin could see and hear, although he couldn't yet walk or talk, and his right side was still paralyzed. In September, Warren transferred him to a rehabilitation program at Mount Sinai Hospital in New York City. There father and son met Theresa Sullivan, an occupational therapist in her late 20s with long strawberry-blond hair.

Over the next few days, Sullivan began trying to straighten Justin's right arm so that he could relearn to brush his teeth, comb his hair and feed himself. But every time she touched his right side, he screamed and used his left arm to push her away.

Sullivan knew that patients with damage to one side of their brain often feel off-balance. "Are you afraid of falling?" she asked him one day after trying to get him to lean forward in his wheelchair. The teen-ager nodded, eyes wide with fear.

A month into therapy, Justin seemed ready to quit. "I wish there was some way to reach him," Sullivan told Warren. She asked if Justin had any hobbies. Warren told her how his son had responded to Marcel Dionne's visit and how much he loved hockey.

Sullivan smiled. "I grew up in Ontario," she said. "I was raised on hockey."

She drew up a sheet of "hockey drills" and pasted it on Justin's wall. "From now on, this is hockey camp," she told him. "If you want to make the team, you've got to do the drills."

Justin needed to learn to move his right arm, so Sullivan drew the red and blue lines of a hockey rink on a table top, took a quarter and placed it in front

of him. "This is your puck. You've got to move the puck from side to side across the ice and shoot it into my net," she explained, forming a "net" with her thumbs and index fingers.

Slowly, Justin raised his right arm and attempted to lower his wrist on top of the quarter.

Furrowing his brow in concentration, Justin pushed the quarter toward the right side of the table. "Now left," Sullivan said, and again he moved it. "Now shoot," she told him.

Justin took a deep breath and forced his arm rigidly forward. The quarter slid straight through the "net" and onto the floor, where it jingled. "Score," she cried out triumphantly, coming around the table to hug him.

"Sc-oo-re," Justin repeated. It was his first real victory.

Justin resisted learning to dress himself. But now, when his father brought in his hockey jersey, helmet and pads, he helped put them on. He hated straightening his right arm. But when his father brought in his hockey gloves, he yielded to the discomfort. He never wanted to hold a fork to feed himself. So Sullivan substituted a hockey stick, and gradually he began using his right hand.

Soon Sullivan devised other drills. Using a sponge ball instead of a puck, she even challenged him to one-on-one hockey games in his room—an activity that helped him overcome his fear of falling and motivated him to try to get out of his wheelchair.

"Tougher Than Any of Us." Warren blinked back bittersweet tears as he watched his son's progress. The real-estate business he had started with a friend before the accident was failing. With no insurance settlement and his savings running out, he was forced to rent a less expensive home. Doctors told Warren that his son would need special care the rest of his life. These concerns weighed heavily, but he tried to be upbeat whenever he visited Justin.

When John Vanbiesbrouck heard that Justin was recovering, he invited father and son to a game on New Year's Day, 1990. Sitting behind the penalty box, Justin could hear the swoosh of steel blades cutting across the ice and the sharp rap of players' bodies as they smashed against the sides of the rink.

He could see the tense crouch of the goalies and the backslaps of teammates when they made a great save.

As the game ended, Warren wheeled Justin into the locker room. Vanbiesbrouck saw him and turned to his teammates. "You guys may think you're tough, but this kid is a lot tougher than any of us will ever be."

Vanbiesbrouck produced a hockey stick, and players began to autograph it. Then they gave him pucks and asked him questions. Out of nowhere, Vanbiesbrouck began singing "For He's a Jolly Good Fellow." Soon two dozen rough voices were serenading the 14-year-old in the wheelchair. Justin was ecstatic.

When they were ready to leave, Warren urged his son to walk over and shake Vanbiesbrouck's hand. Suddenly Justin's mouth became dry. What if he stumbled in front of all these athletes? Yet hadn't his hero just called him "tough"? How could he let him down?

Justin grasped the arms of his wheelchair, his knuckles clenched on either side. Slowly, painfully, he began to rise, to the stares of the suddenly quiet Rangers. Steadied by his father, he took one small step, then another. His legs wobbled.

Vanbiesbrouck wanted to step forward, but something in Justin's determined gaze stopped him. So Vanbiesbrouck stood still. When he finally felt the boy's trembling hand in his own, Vanbiesbrouck fought for control as the other players cheered. "You've accomplished more in your short life than I ever have," he told Justin.

The teen-ager beamed. "That's because I had in-spi-ration."

Taking the Risk. "I'm gonna skate again, Justin vowed to his father as they drove back to Mount Sinai Hospital. "One day I'm gonna play with the Rangers."

Warren nodded, afraid to say anything that would discourage the boy after he'd come so far. But he shuddered at the thought of a puck racing toward his son's head at 100 km/h.

Justin began to attack his problems with determination. He walked unsteadily into summer-school classes rather than use the wheelchair. He refused a first-floor bedroom in his father's rented duplex, though that meant hoisting himself up the

stairs on his rear end. He began watching team practices. One day at the rink with his friend Chris, Justin fixed his dark brown eyes on his father. "Dad, I want to skate."

Warren started to shake his head no. But then he thought about those days in intensive care when he'd vowed to risk anything to save his son. Hadn't hockey saved Justin? If he loved Justin enough to give him the fullest, most independent life possible, then he had to ignore his fears and let Justin skate.

Warren closed his eyes and took a deep breath. "Okay," he said.

Warren and Chris helped the boy to the ice, bracing him on each side. His legs trembled and his body teetered precariously backward. Often, just skating a few meters took all his strength. Yet weeks passed and the teen-ager never tired of the routine.

One day Vanbiesbrouck showed up at the rink to practice and sign autographs. He was incredulous when he encountered Justin on the ice.

"I'm gonna play hockey again," Justin informed his hero.

"If you're serious, then you need to regain your balance," the goalie said. He disappeared and returned with a plastic chair from the lobby.

"When I was a kid, we learned to skate holding on to one of these," Vanbiesbrouck said, gently guiding the teen-ager's hands across the back of the chair.

Vanbiesbrouck coaxed him forward. Gripping the chair, Justin pushed off with his right skate, then his left. His body leaned forward in a more natural motion as a huge smile broke across his face.

A few days later, Vanbiesbrouck related Justin's progress to Marcel Dionne. The older athlete thought about Justin painstakingly rebuilding his life, putting the past behind him with courage and dignity. Dionne knew that if Justin could start over, so could he. He began to greet his retirement from hockey with newfound optimism.

John Vanbiesbrouck, too, drew strength from Justin. When the Rangers' coach chose rookie goalie Mike Richter over him in the 1991 Stanley Cup playoffs, Vanbiesbrouck became sullen and depressed. But as he reflected on Justin's fighting back without bitterness, he realized he could too.

Vanbiesbrouck began to encourage his teammates from the sidelines, refusing to criticize Richter or the coaching staff. Fans and sportswriters praised his maturity. The following season, he was back on the ice, doing better than ever.

Justin's skating continued to improve. He was now moving up and down the ice with only a hockey stick in his hand. For a youngster with such massive injuries, it was an incredible feat.

One day some talented local players were scrimmaging on the ice. They invited Justin to play goalie. He was delighted.

A week later, little more than two years after the accident, Warren and Justin showed up at the rink and couldn't believe their eyes. There on the ice were several New York Rangers! One of the players explained that Rangers who lived in the area regularly scrimmaged with advanced skaters at the arena to stay in shape during the summer.

Minutes later, Rangers defenseman Mark Hardy skated up to Warren. "I can't believe Justin's skating," he said. "I still remember him in a wheelchair."

Warren smiled. "I can ask him to sit out today," he offered. "He'll slow down your practice."

"If it's okay with you," Hardy said, "the guys would love to play him."

Warren stared at his 15-year-old. Justin would be playing against professional athletes, blocking shots that could reach over 100 km/h. It was the biggest risk he'd ever taken with his son. Yet wasn't this his boy's dream?

"It's okay with me," Warren assured Hardy.

Moment of Terror. That summer, Justin Helstein played once a week. The Rangers took him under their wing, giving him pointers, cheering when he made a great save. "Dad, I'm finally doing it," he said one night after a game. "I'm finally playing with the Rangers."

The Rangers played hard, challenging Justin to block carefully aimed shots. To anyone who didn't know him, Justin's slow reaction and uncoordinated moves made him seem more like an inexperienced player than the victim of a near-fatal accident. One such player who was unaware of Justin's condition was a rookie out to impress his veteran teammates. During a scrimmage, he got the puck, slipped past a defenseman, and charged toward Justin.

In a firecracker burst of sound at less than 18 m from the goal, he rocketed a slap shot that whizzed straight for Justin's face.

"Look out, Justin," somebody yelled. But the boy just stood still, poised and ready. There was a loud, fierce smack as the puck slammed into Justin's face guard.

Every player on the ice froze in terror. That kind of direct hit was enough to stun even a veteran goalie. Several of the Rangers raced toward Justin, while one of his teammates dashed to the lobby to find Warren.

"You'd better come to the ice," he told the father.

Warren's mind was racing as he followed the player to the side of the rink. He had pictured this scene in his head dozens of times. Would he have to go through everything again? Would he lose his son? Would he look back, cursing himself for his stupidity?

Warren took a couple of deep breaths and gazed out on the ice. Justin was back in position, ready for play. Warren peered through the mask that shielded Justin's face and into the boy's eyes, searching for the pain or confusion he'd known so well these past few years. Instead, Justin was flashing one of his famous ear-to ear grins.

Warren stepped back, wiping tears on the sleeve of his sweat shirt. He knew there was nothing Justin couldn't do if he wanted, and nothing Warren wouldn't risk to let him. Father and son had now both learned to handle fear.

Note: Weights and measures have been converted to metric.

Priscilla and the Wimps

Richard Peck

Listen, there was a time when you couldn't even go to the *rest room* around this school without a pass. And I'm not talking about those little pink tickets made out by some teacher. I'm talking about a pass that could cost anywhere up to a buck, sold by Monk Klutter.

Not that Mighty Monk ever touched money, not in public. The gang he ran, which ran the school for him, was his collection agency. They were Klutter's Kobras, a name spelled out in nailheads on six well-known black plastic windbreakers.

Monk's threads were more . . . subtle. A pile-lined suede battle jacket with lizard-skin flaps over tailored Levis and a pair of ostrich-skin boots, brassed-toed and suitable for kicking people around. One of his Kobras did nothing all day but walk a half step behind Monk, carrying a fitted bag with Monk's gym shoes, a roll of rest-room passes, a cashbox, and a switchblade that Monk gave himself manicures with at lunch over at the Kobras' table.

Speaking of lunch, there were a few cases of advanced malnutrition among the newer kids. The ones who were a little slow in handing over a cut of their lunch money and were therefore barred from the cafeteria. Monk ran a tight ship.

I admit it. I'm five foot five, and when the Kobras slithered by, with or without Monk, I shrank. And I admit this, too: I paid up on a regular basis. And I might add: so would you.

This school was old Monk's Garden of Eden. Unfortunately for him, there was a serpent in it. The reason Monk didn't recognize trouble when it was staring him in the face is that the serpent in the Kobras' Eden was a girl.

Practically every guy in school could show you his scars. Fang marks from Kobras, you might say. And they were all highly visible in the shower room: lumps, lacerations, blue bruises, you name it. But girls usually got off with a warning.

Except there was this one girl named Priscilla Roseberry. Picture a girl named Priscilla Roseberry, and you'll be light years off. Priscilla was, hands down, the largest student in our particular institution of learning. I'm not talking fat. I'm talking big. Even beautiful, in a bionic way. Priscilla wasn't inclined toward organized crime. Otherwise, she could have put together a gang that would turn Klutter's Kobras into garter snakes.

Priscilla was basically a loner except she had one friend. A little guy named Melvin Detweiler. You talk about The Odd Couple. Melvin's one of the smallest guys above midget status ever seen. A really nice guy, but, you know—little. They even had lockers next to each other, in the same bank as mine. I don't know what they had going. I'm not saying this was a romance. After all, people deserve their privacy.

Priscilla was sort of above everything, if you'll pardon a pun. And very calm, as only the very big can be. If there was anybody who didn't notice Klutter's Kobras, it was Priscilla.

Until one winter day after school when we were all grabbing our coats out of our lockers. And hurrying, since Klutter's Kobras made sweeps of the halls for after-school shakedowns.

Anyway, up to Melvin's locker swaggers one of the Kobras. Never mind his name. Gang members don't need names. They've got group identity. He reaches down and grabs little Melvin by the neck and slams his head against his locker door. The sound of skull against steel rippled all the way down the locker row, speeding the crowds on their way.

"Okay, let's see your pass," snarls the Kobra.

"A pass for what this time?" Melvin asks, probably still dazed.

"Let's call it a pass for very short people," says the Kobra, "a dwarf tax." He wheezes a little Kobra chuckle at his own wittiness. And already he's reaching for Melvin's wallet with the hand that isn't circling Melvin's windpipe. All this time, of course, Melvin and the Kobra are standing in Priscilla's big shadow.

She's taking her time shoving her books into her locker and pulling on a very large-size coat. Then, quicker than the eye, she brings the side of her enormous hand down in a chop that breaks the Kobra's hold on Melvin's throat. You could hear a pin drop in that hallway. Nobody'd ever laid a finger on a Kobra, let alone a hand the size of Priscilla's.

Then Priscilla, who hardly ever says anything to anybody except to Melvin, says to the Kobra, "Who's your leader, wimp?"

This practically blows the Kobra away. First he's chopped by a girl, and now she's acting like she doesn't know Monk Klutter, the Head Honcho of the World. He's so amazed, he tells her. "Monk Klutter."

"Never heard of him," Priscilla mentions. "Send him to see me." The Kobra just backs away from her like the whole situation is too big for him, which it is.

Pretty soon Monk himself slides up. He jerks his head once, and his Kobras slither off down the hall. He's going to handle this interesting case personally. "Who is it around here doesn't know Monk Klutter?"

He's standing inches from Priscilla, but since he'd have to look up at her, he doesn't. "Never heard of him," says Priscilla.

Monk's not happy with this answer, but by now he's spotted Melvin, who's grown smaller in spite of himself. Monk breaks his own rule by reaching for Melvin with his own hands. "Kid," he says, "you're going to have to educate your girl friend."

His hands never quite make it to Melvin. In a move of pure poetry Priscilla has Monk in a hammerlock. His neck's popping like gunfire, and his head's bowed under the immense weight of her forearm. His suede jacket's peeling back, showing pile.

Priscilla's behind him in another easy motion. And with a single mighty thrust forward, frog-marches Monk into her own locker. It's incredible. His ostrich-skin boots click once in the air. And suddenly he's gone, neatly wedged into the locker, a perfect fit. Priscilla bangs the door shut, twirls the lock, and strolls out of school. Melvin goes with her, of course, trotting along below her shoulder. The last stragglers leave quietly.

Well, this is where fate, an even bigger force than Priscilla, steps in. It snows all that night, a blizzard. The whole town ices up. And school closes for a week.

Remember Me?

Ray Mather

Remember me?
I am the boy who sought friendship;
The boy you turned away.
I the boy who asked you
If I too might play.
I the face at the window
When your party was inside,
I the lonely figure
That walked away and cried.
I the one who hung around
A punchbag for your games.
Someone you could kick and beat,
Someone to call names.
But how strange is the change
After time has hurried by,

Four years have passed since then
Now I'm not so quick to cry.
I'm bigger and I'm stronger,
I've grown a foot in height,
Suddenly I'M popular
And YOU'RE left out the light.
I could, if I wanted,
Be so unkind to you.
I would only have to say
And the other boys would do.
But the memory of my pain
Holds back the revenge I'D planned
And instead, I feel much stronger
By offering you my hand.

The Ugly Duckling

Hans Christian Andersen

The country was lovely just then; it was summer. The wheat was golden and the oats still green; the hay was stacked in the rich low-lying meadows, where the stork was marching about on his long red legs, chattering Egyptian, the language his mother had taught him.

Round about field and meadow lay great woods in the midst of which were deep lakes. Yes, the country certainly was delicious. In the sunniest spot stood an old mansion surrounded by a deep moat, and great dock leaves grew from the walls of the house right down to the water's edge; some of them were so tall that a small child could stand upright under them. In amongst the leaves it was as secluded as in the depths of a forest; and there a duck was sitting on her nest. Her little ducklings were just about to be hatched, but she was nearly tired of sitting, for it had lasted such a long time. Moreover, she had very few visitors, as the other ducks liked swimming about in the moat better than waddling up to sit under the dock leaves and gossip with her.

At last one egg after another began to crack. "Cheep, cheep!" they said. All the chicks had come to life, and were poking their heads out.

"Quack, quack!" said the ducks; and then they all quacked their hardest, and looked about them on all sides among the green leaves; their mother allowed them to look as much as they liked, for green is good for the eyes.

"How big the world is to be sure!" said all the young ones; for they certainly had ever so much more room to move about, than when they were inside in the eggshell.

"Do you imagine this is the whole world?" said the mother. "It stretches a long way on the other side of the garden, right into the parson's field; but I have never been as far as that. I suppose you are all here now?" and she got up. "No! I declare I have not got you all yet. The biggest egg is still there; how long is it going to last?" and then she settled herself on the nest again.

"Well, how are you getting on?" said an old duck who had come to pay her a visit.

"This one egg is taking such a long time," answered the sitting duck, "the shell will not crack; but now you must look at the others; they are the finest ducklings I have ever seen! they are all exactly like their father, the rascal! he never comes to see me."

"Let me look at the egg which won't crack," said the old duck. "You may be sure that it is a turkey's egg! I have been cheated like that once, and I had no end of trouble and worry with the creatures, for I may tell you that they are afraid of the water. I could not get them into it. I quacked and snapped at them, but it was no good. Let me see the egg! Yes, it is a turkey's egg! You just leave it alone and teach the other children to swim."

"I will sit on it a little longer. I have sat so long already, that I may as well go on till the Midsummer Fair comes round."

"Please yourself," said the old duck, and she went away.

At last the big egg cracked. "Cheep, cheep!" said the young one and tumbled out; how big and ugly he was!

The duck looked at him.

"That is a monstrous big duckling," she said; "none of the others looked like that; can he be a turkey chick? Well, we shall soon find that out; into the water he shall go, if I have to kick him in myself."

Next day was gloriously fine, and the sun shone on all the green dock leaves. The mother duck with her whole family went down to the moat.

Splash, into the water she sprang. "Quack, quack!" she said, and one duckling plumped in after the other. The water dashed over their heads, but they came up again and floated beautifully; their legs went of themselves, and they were all there, even the big ugly grey one swam about with them.

"No, that is no turkey," she said; "see how beautifully he uses his legs and how erect he holds himself; he is my own chick! After all, he is not so bad when you come to look at him properly. Quack, quack! Now come with me and I will take you into the world, and introduce you to the duckyard; but keep close to me all the time, so that no one may tread upon you, and beware of the cat!"

Then they went into the duckyard. There was a fearful uproar going on, for two broods were fighting for the head of an eel, and in the end the cat captured it.

"That's how things go in this world," said the mother duck, and she licked her bill for she wanted the eel's head herself.

"Use your legs," said she; "mind you quack properly, and bend your necks to the old duck over there! She is the grandest of them all; she has Spanish blood in her veins and that accounts for her size, and, do you see? she has a red rag round her leg; that is a wonderfully fine thing, and the most extraordinary mark of distinction any duck can have. It shows clearly that she is not to be parted with, and that she is worthy of recognition both by beasts and men! Quack now! don't turn your toes in, a well-brought-up duckling keeps his legs wide apart just like father and mother; that's it, now bend your necks, and say quack."

They did as they were bid, but the other ducks round about looked at them and said, quite loud: "Just look there! now we are to have that tribe! just as if there were not enough of us already, and, oh dear! how ugly that duckling is, we won't stand him!" and a duck flew at him at once and bit him in the neck. "Let him be," said the mother; "he is doing no harm."

"Very likely not, but he is so ungainly and queer," said the biter; "he must be whacked."

"They are handsome children mother has," said the old duck with the rag round her leg; "all good-looking except this one, and he is not a good specimen; it's a pity you can't make him over again."

"That can't be done, your grace," said the mother duck; "he is not handsome, but he is a thorough good creature, and he swims as beautifully as any of the others; nay, I think I might venture even to add that I think he will improve as he goes on, or perhaps in time he may grow smaller! he was too long in the egg, and so he has not come out with a very good figure." And then she patted his neck and stroked him down. "Besides he is a drake," said she; "so it does not matter so much. I believe he will be very strong, and I don't doubt but he will make his way in the world."

"The other ducklings are very pretty," said the old duck. "Now make yourselves quite at home, and if you find the head of an eel you may bring it to me!"

After that they felt quite at home. But the poor duckling which had been the last to come out of the shell, and who was so ugly, was bitten, pushed

about, and made fun of both by the ducks and the hens. "He is too big," they all said; and the turkey-cock, who was born with his spurs on, and therefore thought himself quite an emperor, puffed himself up like a vessel in full sail, made for him, and gobbled and gobbled till he became quite red in the face. The poor duckling was at his wit's end, and did not know which way to turn; he was in despair because he was so ugly, and the butt of the whole duckyard.

So the first day passed, and afterwards matters grew worse and worse. The poor duckling was chased and hustled by all of them; even his brothers and sisters ill-used him; and they were always saying, "If only the cat would get hold of you, you hideous object!"

Even his mother said, "I wish to goodness you were miles away." The ducks bit him, the hens pecked him, and the girl who fed them kicked him aside.

Then he ran off and flew right over the hedge, where the little birds flew up into the air in a fright.

"That is because I am so ugly," thought the poor duckling, shutting his eyes, but he ran on all the same. Then he came to a great marsh where the wild ducks lived; he was so tired and miserable that he stayed there a whole night.

In the morning the wild ducks flew up to inspect their new comrade.

"What sort of creature are you?" they inquired, as the duckling turned from side to side and greeted them as well as he could. "You are frightfully ugly," said the wild ducks; but that does not matter to us, so long as you do not marry into our family!" Poor fellow! he had no thought of marriage; all he wanted was permission to lie among the bushes, and drink a little of the marsh water.

He stayed there two whole days, then two wild geese came, or rather two wild ganders. They were not long out of the shell, and therefore rather pert.

"I say, comrade," they said, "you are so ugly that we have taken quite a fancy to you; will you join us and be a bird of passage? There is another marsh close by, and there are some charming wild geese there, all sweet young ladies, who can say quack! You are ugly enough to make your fortune among them." Just at that moment, bang! bang! was heard up above, and both the wild geese fell dead among the reeds, and the water turned blood red. Bang! bang! went the guns, and whole flocks of wild geese flew up from the rushes and the shot peppered among them again.

There was a grand shooting party, and the sportsmen lay hidden round the marsh, some even sat on the branches of the trees which overhung the water; the blue smoke rose like clouds among the dark trees and swept over the pool.

The water-dogs wandered about in the swamp, splash! splash! The rushes and reeds bent beneath their tread on all sides. It was terribly alarming to the poor duckling. He twisted his head round to get it under his wing and just at that moment a big dog appeared close beside him; his tongue hung right out of his mouth and his eyes glared wickedly. He opened his great chasm of a mouth close to the duckling, showed his sharp teeth—and—splash—went on without touching him.

"Oh, thank Heaven!" sighed the duckling. "I am so ugly that even the dog won't bite me."

Then he lay quite still while the shot whistled among the bushes, and bang after bang rent the air. It only became quiet late in the day, but even then the poor duckling did not dare to get up; he waited several hours more before he looked about and then he hurried away from the marsh as fast as he could. He ran across fields and meadows, and there was such a wind that he had hard work to make his way.

Towards night he reached a poor little cottage; it was such a miserable hovel that it could not make up its mind which way to fall even, and so it remained standing. The wind whistled so fiercely round the duckling that he had to sit on his tail to resist it, and it blew harder and harder; then he saw that the door had fallen off one hinge and hung so crookedly that he could

creep into the house through the crack and by this means he made his way into the room. An old woman lived there with her cat and her hen. The cat, which she called "Sonnie," could arch his back, purr, and give off electric sparks, that is to say if you stroked his fur the wrong way. The hen had quite tiny short legs and so she was called "Chuckie-low-legs." She laid good eggs, and the old woman was as fond of her as if she had been her own child.

In the morning the strange duckling was discovered immediately, and the cat began to purr and the hen to cluck.

"What on earth is that!" said the old woman looking round, but her sight was not good and she thought the duckling was a fat duck which had escaped. "This is a capital find," said she; "now I shall have duck's eggs if only it is not a drake! we must find out about that!"

So she took the duckling on trial for three weeks, but no eggs made their appearance. The cat was the master of the house and the hen the mistress, and they always spoke of "we and the world," for they thought that they represented the half of the world, and that quite the better half.

The duckling thought there might be two opinions on the subject, but the hen would not hear of it.

"Can you lay eggs?" she asked.

"No!"

"Will you have the goodness to hold your tongue then!"

And the cat said:

"Can you arch your back, purr, or give off sparks!"

"No."

"Then you had better keep your opinions to yourself when people of sense are speaking!"

The duckling sat in the corner nursing his ill-humour; then he began to think of the fresh air and the sunshine, an uncontrollable longing seized him to float on the water, and at last he could not help telling the hen about it.

"What on earth possesses you?" she asked; "You have nothing to do, that is why you get these freaks into your head. Lay some eggs or take to purring, and you will get over it."

"But it is so delicious to float on the water," said the duckling; "so delicious to feel it rushing over your head when you dive to the bottom."

"That would be a fine amusement," said the hen. "I think you have gone mad. Ask the cat about it, he is the wisest creature I know; ask him if he is fond of floating on the water or diving under it. I say nothing about myself. Ask our mistress yourself, the old woman, there is no one in the world cleverer than she is. Do you suppose she has any desire to float on the water, or to duck underneath it?"

"You do not understand me," said the duckling.

"Well, if we don't understand you, who should? I suppose you don't consider yourself cleverer than the cat or the old woman, not to mention me. Don't make a fool of yourself, child, and thank your stars for all the good we have done you! Have you not lived in this warm room, and in such society that you might have learnt something? But you are an idiot, and there is no pleasure in associating with you. You may believe me I mean you well, I tell you home truths, and there is no surer way than that, of knowing who are one's friends. You just see about laying some eggs, or learn to purr, or to emit sparks."

"I think I will go out into the wide world," said the duckling.

"Oh, do so by all means," said the hen.

So away went the duckling. He floated on the water and ducked underneath it, but he was looked askance at by every living creature for his ugliness. Now the autumn came on, the leaves in the woods turned yellow and brown; the wind took hold of them, and they danced about. The sky looked very cold, and the clouds hung heavy with snow and hail. A raven stood on the fence and croaked Caw! Caw! from sheer cold; it made one shiver only to think of it. The poor duckling certainly was in a bad case.

One evening, the sun was just setting in wintry splendour, when a flock of beautiful large birds appeared out of the bushes; the duckling had never seen anything so beautiful. They were dazzlingly white with long waving necks; they were swans, and uttering a peculiar cry they spread out their magnificent broad wings and flew away from the cold regions to warmer lands and open seas. They mounted so high, so very high, and the ugly

duckling became strangely uneasy, he circled round and round in the water like a wheel, craning his neck up into the air after them. Then he uttered a shriek so piercing and so strange, that he was quite frightened by it himself. Oh, he could not forget those beautiful birds, those happy birds, and as soon as they were out of sight he ducked right down to the bottom, and when he came up again he was quite beside himself. He did not know what the birds were, or whither they flew, but all the same he was more drawn towards them than he had ever been by any creatures before. He did not envy them in the least, how could it occur to him even to wish to be such a marvel of beauty; he would have been thankful if only the ducks would have tolerated him among them—the poor ugly creature!

The winter was so bitterly cold that the duckling was obliged to swim about in the water to keep it from freezing, but every night the hole in which he swam got smaller and smaller. Then it froze so hard that the surface ice cracked, and the duckling had to use his legs all the time, so that the ice should not close in round him: at last he was so weary that he could move no more, and he was frozen fast into the ice.

Early in the morning a peasant came along and saw him; he went out on to the ice and hammered a hole in it with his heavy wooden shoe, and carried the duckling home to his wife. There he soon revived. The children wanted to play with him, but the duckling thought they were going to ill-use him, and rushed in his fright into the milk pan, and the milk spurted out all over the room. The woman shrieked and threw up her hands, then he flew into the butter cask, and down into the meal tub and out again. Just imagine what he looked like by this time! The woman screamed and tried to hit him with the tongs, and the children tumbled over one another in trying to catch him, and they screamed with laughter—by good luck the door stood open, and the duckling flew out among the bushes and the new fallen snow—and he lay there thoroughly exhausted.

But it would be too sad to mention all the privation and misery he had to go through during that hard winter. When the sun began to shine warmly again, the duckling was in the marsh, lying among the rushes, the larks were singing and the beautiful spring had come.

Then all at once he raised his wings and they flapped with much greater strength than before, and bore him off vigorously. Before he knew where he was, he found himself in a large garden where the apple trees were in full blossom, and the air was scented with lilacs, the long branches of which overhung the indented shores of the lake! Oh! the spring freshness was so delicious!

Just in front of him he saw three beautiful white swans advancing towards him from a thicket; with rustling feathers they swam lightly over the water. The duckling recognized the majestic birds, and he was overcome by a strange melancholy.

"I will fly to them, the royal birds, and they will hack me to pieces, because I, who am so ugly, venture to approach them! But it won't matter; better be killed by them than be snapped at by the ducks, pecked by the hens, or spurned by the henwife, or suffer so much misery in the winter."

So he flew into the water and swam towards the stately swans; they saw him and darted towards him with ruffled feathers.

"Kill me, oh, kill me!" said the poor creature, and bowing his head towards the water he awaited his death. But what did he see reflected in the transparent water?

He saw below him his own image, but he was no longer a clumsy dark grey bird, ugly and ungainly, he was himself a swan! It does not matter in the least having been born in a duckyard, if only you come out of a swan's egg!

He felt quite glad of all the misery and tribulation he had gone through; he was the better able to appreciate his good fortune now, and all the beauty which greeted him. The big swans swam round and round him, and stroked him with their bills.

Some little children came into the garden with corn and pieces of bread, which they threw into the water; and the smallest one cried out: "There is a new one!" The other children shouted with joy. "Yes, a new one has come!" And they clapped their hands and danced about, running after their father and mother. They threw the bread into the water, and one and all said that the new one was the prettiest; he was so young and handsome. And the old swans bent their heads and did homage before him.

He felt quite shy, and hid his head under his wing; he did not know what to think; he was so very happy, but not at all proud; a good heart never becomes proud. He thought of how he had been pursued and scorned, and now he heard them all say that he was the most beautiful of all beautiful birds. The lilacs bent their boughs right down into the water before him, and the bright sun was warm and cheering, and he rustled his feathers and raised his slender neck aloft, saying with exultation in his heart: "I never dreamt of so much happiness when I was the Ugly Duckling!"

On The Inside

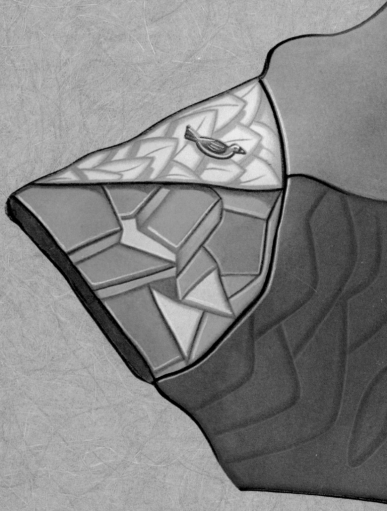

25 Good Reasons for Hating My Brother Todd

Peter D. Sieruta

Give me a pencil and a piece of paper and I'll start to make a list. That's just the way I am. My brother thinks it's dumb.

1. My brother thinks most of the things I do are dumb.

But I don't care. Lists are the only way to get life into order. Can I help it if I like being organized?

2. My brother thinks I'm too organized.

"You're too uptight, kid," Todd told me tonight at dinner. "You gotta loosen up, mellow out, go with the flow."

I chewed my pork chop slowly, trying to think of the ultimate putdown that would make him clutch his heart and gasp for air. But by the time I swallowed, I still hadn't thought of it. So I just said, "Do you have any suggestions?"

"The briefcase has *got* to go," he said. "*Nobody* at school carries a briefcase."

"Mr. Samuels does."

"He's the principal! The principal can get away with it! A tenth grader can't."

"I like to keep my papers in order."

"And those glasses, they're ancient history! Nobody wears that kind anymore. Not to mention your clothes."

"What's wrong with my clothes?" I asked.

"What's *right* with them?"

"I think your brother dresses very nicely," said my mother. "He dresses like he takes school seriously. You don't see him in jeans and a T-shirt."

"That's what I mean," said Todd. "Of *course* you like how he dresses. He dresses like *Dad*."

"What's wrong with the way I dress?" my father asked.

"Nothing, but you're old. Emery shouldn't dress like a *forty-year-old*, for God's sake!"

"Please don't take the Lord's name in vain," said my mother.

"Forget it then! Forget it! Let him act like he's forty years old!" Todd shouted, gesturing wildly. "I thought I was doing him a favor. At school they're calling him *nerd*, Mom! And everyone knows he's my brother!" He stormed out of the room.

3. My brother is ashamed of me.

I folded my napkin and placed it beside my plate. "I've never heard anyone at school call me a nerd," I said. This wasn't quite true, but I thought it made me look a little better in their eyes. Who wants a son that people call nerd?

"Of course they don't," said my mother.

"And nobody says anything about my clothes, or my glasses or my briefcase either."

"Of course they don't," said my father.

"May I be excused?" I asked.

I didn't hear the answer because right then Todd's stereo broke the sound barrier. He always sets the volume at 10+, and his favorite music is punk rock.

4. He has no consideration for others.

5. He has rotten taste in music.

My mother cupped her hands to her mouth and yelled, "Don't worry, he'll be leaving soon. He's supposed to pick up his date at seven thirty."

I had to go to the bathroom, but when I got to the top of the stairs I saw the bathroom door was closed and heard the shower running.

6. He always hogs the bathroom.

I pounded on the door. "Hurry up. I have to go to the bathroom."

"What?"

"Hurry up, I have to go to the bathroom."

"*What?*"

Then he suddenly turned the shower off while I continued yelling, and the whole neighborhood probably heard me shout, "I have to go to the bathroom!"

7. Often, he deliberately embarrasses me.

He said, "Well come on in and use it then, you idiot."

"With you in there?" I said. "Forget it."

The shower started up again. "It's your bladder," he yelled.

8. He is disgusting!

I went into my room, shut the door, and started making a list of twenty-five ways to kill my brother. Wire his bed with dynamite? Put a rattlesnake in his closet? A couple seconds later he came in without knocking.

9. He has no respect for my privacy.

He padded across the room in his underwear. "I need socks," he said, pulling open my drawer.

10. He has no respect for my property.

"Leave my socks alone," I said.

"Oh come on, little bro," he said, trying on my only-worn-once brown argyles. "I need 'em for my date." He danced around my room. "Now I've got socks appeal!"

11. My brother has a very, very bad sense of humor.

"Just get the hell out of my room," I said. I could feel my face getting red— and all because he'd mentioned the date out loud.

He put on his mock shocked look and clapped his hands to the sides of his face. "Oh, Mom," he yelled. "Emery said the *h* word!"

12. *He's always trying to get me in trouble.*

"I mean it, Todd, leave me alone. Go on your stupid date and leave me alone!"

"All right, all right, I'm going," he said. Then he mooned me.

"You're sick," I said, throwing a notebook at him.

He ran out of my room laughing, and I returned to my list of ways to kill him. Put insect repellent in his milk? Disconnect the brakes on his ten-speed? But none of my ideas seemed cruel enough. I crumpled the paper and tossed it toward the wastepaper basket. Of course it landed on the floor.

13. *My brother has never missed a shot in wastepaper basketball.*

Why did he have to mention the stupid date, anyway? Was he just trying to see my reaction? Well, forget it! I wasn't about to give him the satisfaction. I pulled out another notebook and started working on my science project, but I couldn't stop myself from going over the last couple days in my mind. Because it was the science project that had started the whole thing.

Let me make one thing perfectly clear: I hate group projects, team projects, class projects, et cetera. In other words, anything that means I can't work alone. Frankly, there's nobody in my classes that I care to work with. Even more frankly: There's nobody that cares to work with me. So when Mr. Jamison said we'd have to pair off for our final science project, I didn't exactly jump for joy. Usually everyone teamed with their friends and I was one of the leftovers, destined to be paired off with some other loser by the teacher—a situation that had, in the past, made me partners with an illiterate girl, our class dope pusher, and a Swedish exchange student who could only say "yah." But this time Mr. Jamison said that partners were going to be assigned.

As he read through the list, accompanied by cheers and groans from the class, I read the next chapter in the textbook. It really didn't matter whom I was paired with—I'd probably end up doing all the work. Just then I heard my name. "Emery, you and Jodi Meriwether will be working together."

Everyone started laughing, and I turned to look at Jodi just in time to see her making barfing faces at the girl sitting next to her. I had to turn away, because Jodi was just too lovely to look at for more than a second. Ever since fourth grade I've wanted to marry Jodi Meriwether. She is, without a single doubt, the most beautiful, popular, poised teenage person ever to attend Truman High. I knew she wasn't too crazy about me, but then, we'd never really gotten to know each other very well.

For the rest of the class period I calmly copied lecture notes, while in a corner of my mind I had visions of Jodi and myself accepting our Nobel Prize in Chemistry. I also had other visions of us, but they were X rated.

The bell rang and I jumped out of my seat. Usually it takes Jodi a long time to leave the classroom. She always stops to talk to at least three or four people (never me) and sometimes even the teacher. I know, because sometimes I have trouble with the lock on my briefcase and it takes me a long time to leave too. But that day the bell hadn't even finished ringing before Jodi was out of her seat and running toward the door. She was fumbling with her books, trying to shove her papers into a binder. I got to the doorway just in time to see her books crash to the floor.

I knelt down to help her, saying, "When should we start working on the project?"

"Don't mention that project!" she snapped.

"How about today—this afternoon?"

"No. Would you get away from me!"

"We're going to have to start someday," I said, then swallowed the heartbeat in my throat and added, "Jodi."

"What?"

"What what?" I said.

"You said my name."

"I said that we're going to have to start someday . . . Jodi."

People were coming out of the room, making sarcastic remarks about Jodi and me on the floor together. Jodi looked like she wanted to bite someone.

"Can't we start today?" I asked. "At my house?"

She looked past me at all the other people streaming into the hallway and hissed, "Yesss, okay, all right, now just *get out of here!*"

I didn't think that was a very gracious thing to say, but I handed her my address and went on to my next class.

On the way home from school I ran into the corner store for a snack to serve when Jodi came over, though I wasn't sure what to buy. Todd would probably pick up a bag of Doritos, but I rejected that as too common. I also rejected pizza rolls (too messy) and cupcakes (too sticky). So I ended up buying Doritos anyway, though they turned out to be a complete waste because when I got home I accidentally dropped my briefcase on top of them and smashed the whole bag.

I was right back where I started from, and the only things in the refrigerator were a pot roast and some vegetables. I raced back and forth, finding a pot and cutting up potatoes, and almost had the roast in the oven when I realized something: Pot roast is not your typical after-school snack. Okay, Emery, *calm down*, I told myself. Everything's going to be all right. I sat down and began making a list of all the things we could talk about (the weather, classes, the science project). Then I began pacing, running to the window every five seconds and not acting like myself at all.

When the doorbell rang, I tripped over a throw rug and hit the door with my head. "What was that thud?" was the first thing Jodi said after I opened the door.

"What thud?" I said, pressing my hand against my forehead and praying there wouldn't be a lump.

I had planned to say "Jodi, Jodi, Jodi" when I opened the door, because that's the kind of thing Todd's always saying to girls, but the thud had destroyed the moment.

It was almost like a dream come true to see Jodi standing in the middle of

our living room, slowly unwinding her long orange scarf. "Isn't your mother or somebody here?" she asked, looking around.

"Are you afraid to be alone with me?" I asked.

"You've *got* to be kidding," she snorted.

"I was thinking, maybe, the kitchen . . . we could study there." My words were coming out all mixed up, and it was all Jodi's fault for looking the way she did. Nobody should look that good, except maybe Miss America or a TV star. Jodi was wearing a purple sweater and jeans. They were both very tight.

She followed me into the kitchen, and I turned on the light over the table. "I had some Doritos, but I dropped my briefcase on them." I hadn't meant to say that, but I was really stumped for a conversation opener.

Jodi snorted.

"How do you feel about pot roast?"

"I'm on a diet. Now, about this science project—"

"A diet? Jodi, no. You don't need to diet. You're perfect. Your figure, I mean." I could feel my face turning hot, so finished up with a lame: "I mean, you're not fat."

She said, "About this science project. I know you're supposed to be this big brain and everything, but really, science just isn't my thing. So I was thinking, my older brother's got this solar-system thing he made about five years ago out of coat hangers and spray-painted Styrofoam balls. What if I just brought that over as *my* contribution and then *you* could write up some kind of really complicated paper about it and we could turn it in? I'm not into science."

"A brain?" I said. "You think I'm a brain?" That clinched it. I was in love.

"So what do you think?" she asked, getting up from her chair as if the whole discussion were over. The light glowed on her long blond hair.

"About what?"

"The Styrofoam solar system! Aren't you listening to me?"

"Of course I'm listening." I paused for a second, thinking: *A Styrofoam solar system?* How do you tell the girl you love that her suggestion is the pits?

I straightened my glasses and cleared my throat.

"Sit down, Jodi," I said in a calm voice. She looked a little bewildered, but she did sit down. "Solar systems are good—very good—for science projects, but you have to remember this is *tenth* grade. I think maybe we should try for something a little more challenging."

"My cousin's got a plaster-of-paris volcano I could probably borrow," she said.

"Maybe something even more challenging than that," I said.

"It really erupts, too."

"What would you say if I told you we might be capable—you and I—of turning in the best science project ever at that school? I think we could do it."

"The best?" she asked, her eyes widening. Because if there was one thing Jodi was interested in, it was being the best.

I leaned in closer and looked her right in the eyes. "The best *ever*," I said, opening my notebook. "I made a list of some concepts in study hall." And there they were—twenty-five individual suggestions—not just ideas, but real concepts with pros and cons and costs and conclusions and everything. Jodi pulled the notebook toward her and began reading through the list. I loved the way her lips moved slightly as she read but pushed that thought from my mind; now wasn't the time to think about love. First I should win her respect and admiration. Love was sure to follow.

Just then I heard the front door open. "Anybody home?" yelled Todd. "Mama Bear? Papa Bear? Emery Bear?"

14. He can't even walk in the front door without making a big deal out of it.

"Who's that?" asked Jodi, looking up from the notebook.

I said, "Keep reading."

Todd appeared in the kitchen doorway wearing his soccer uniform and bouncing a soccer ball off his biceps.

15. He has biceps. Big ones.

"Hi," he said.

Jodi looked up, and a slow smile spread across her face. "Hi!" she said.

"We're working," I told Todd sternly.

"Okay. See you later. I've got to shower." He turned and walked down the hall. Jodi and I were both watching him. When he got out of sight, he said, "By the way, who's the beautiful girl sitting at our kitchen table?"

Jodi burst out laughing as if that were the wittiest remark she had ever heard. "I'm Jodi Meriwether," she called.

We could hear his footsteps going up the stairs. "Glad to know you, Jodi."

Jodi turned back to look at me with a stunned smile on her face. "Wow," was all she said.

"Back to these concepts—" I said.

"Was that your *brother*?" she gasped.

"Him? Oh, yeah, I guess it was."

"Your brother? How can it be?"

"Well, let's see, project thirteen right here is all about genetics. Maybe if we work on that you'll get a better understa—"

"Is he *adopted* or something?" she asked. She was looking at me more intensely than she had all afternoon.

"No. And neither am I."

"But he's so . . . so . . . blond!"

"So what?" I said. My mother has blond hair, my father has blond hair, all my grandparents have or had blond hair. My hair is dark. Very dark. People are always asking us what color hair our milkman has. I don't find this funny. Neither do my parents. My brother finds it hilarious.

"He's like . . . like . . . a Norse god!"

"Jodi, have you ever actually *seen* a Norse god?"

16. *He's six feet tall.*

17. *He has green eyes.*

18. *He has teeth like Chiclets.*

19. *He looks great in a soccer uniform.*

"Does your brother go to another school or something, Emery?" It was the first time she ever said my name out loud.

"No, he goes to Truman too."

"What! I've never seen him around!"

"Well, you know how it is. He's a senior, and—"

Jodi grabbed onto the edge of the kitchen table. "A senior?" she shrieked.

"We won't get to be *juniors* if we don't pass this science class," I said, trying to turn the conversation back to where I could handle it.

She looked down at the notebook in front of her as if she'd forgotten its existence. "Oh, that's right," she said.

"Look, maybe a Styrofoam solar system is the way to go," I said.

"Oh, no. No, Emery. I think we should do the *greatest* project ever in the history of the school."

"Really?"

"Absolutely. We could work on it every afternoon, over here."

"Which concept are you interested in?" I asked.

"Um . . . eight," she said, pointing at the notebook.

The shower stopped running. Todd yelled down the stairs, "Hey, who wants to help dry my back?"

Jodi actually jumped up!

I grabbed her wrist. She looked embarrassed. I pretended not to notice. She said, "Not too cool." I could feel little sparks of electricity dancing up and down my arm. My hand was still around her wrist as she sat down again. The electric sparks had turned to jolts. I looked at her face, but all I could see was her embarrassment for jumping up like that. I let go.

She looked down at the Formica tabletop. After a second she said, "God. Embarrassment. I'm not usually like this."

"It's all right, Jodi," I said.

She looked at me then. Her eyes were partly hidden by her hair, but a slow smile began to appear. I wanted to hug her. "You know, I've misjudged you. I used to think you were a nerd, like everyone says, but really, you're not."

"Thanks."

"I mean that. You're different than I thought. You're okay, Emery."

"Thanks." What did this mean? I didn't want to get my hopes up.

Jodi continued: "And I'm really looking forward to this project. I know we'll do a good job, with you being such a brain and everything. I really mean it. I'm not saying that because of . . . him."

"What's up, guys?" Todd was standing in the doorway. He had changed clothes, and his hair was still wet.

"We're working on a science project together," said Jodi. She was still blushing, but it just made her look even prettier.

"Oh," he said, pouring some orange juice. "Then you've got yourself a great partner, Jodi. This kid's a brain."

"I know!" she said.

"Oh, cut it out," I said modestly.

"And he's so *organized*," said Jodi. "You should see this list."

"Oh, I've *seen* his lists." Todd sat down at the table and said, "Emer—ee—ee—ee—ee—ee—ee—ee," giving the back of my hair a tug with each "ee." He does that all the time and he knows it drives me crazy.

"Stop it," I said.

Jodi was laughing. So was Todd.

He tilted his chair back until the front legs rose off the floor. Just one little push backward, I thought. . . . But instead I held my hands very tightly together and watched while Todd hung perfectly balanced in the air, taking a long, long swallow of juice.

20. He's a show-off.

Then he brought the chair back down and said, "Science projects, huh?" I remember them well. I had Jamison for tenth-grade science."

"Me too!" shrieked Jodi. "He's our teacher! What a coincidence!"

"Old Blue Hands," said Todd, then started to laugh.

"Blue hands? *What!*" said Jodi, laughing too. She was leaning halfway across the table.

"Jamison used to have blue hands—no joke! We were doing this experiment, making crystals on charcoal briquets, and he accidentally spilled the solution all over the lab table and tried to clean it up with some Kleenex, and he ended up with bright blue hands. And it wouldn't come off. He had blue hands for the whole semester!"

Jodi was laughing hysterically.

Todd was laughing so hard at his own story that he was pounding his fist on the table.

21. He always laughs at his own jokes.

"Well, he *deserved* the blue hands, for God's sake," said Todd, wiping at his eyes. "That's what he gets for doing those dumb first-grade type of experiments. I mean, we used to make crystals on charcoal in *grade* school, right, Em?"

"I don't recall."

"Well, what kind of experiments would *you* suggest for a tenth-grade class?" said Jodi.

"*Transplants!*" shouted Todd, pounding the table again. "And test-tube babies!"

"Oh, for goodness' sakes, Todd. We're trying to study."

"Can't you just see it, Todd?" said Jodi. "Hey, Mr. Jamison, come look in my test tube. I think it's *breathing!*"

"My test tube's having twins!" said Todd, then "Where are you going?"

"To get my briefcase, if that's okay with you two!" I stomped into the living room, grabbed the case, then stomped back into the kitchen. "Since I don't think we'll be doing much more work on this today, I'm going to put away all these notes," I said to Jodi.

"Oh, Emery, don't be so . . . so . . ." she said. "Come on, sit down, we can work on it in a while."

I sat down because I wanted to please Jodi. But as I listened to them talk and laugh, I knew I was watching my beloved, my sweetness, my life, slowly ebb away.

And I knew damn well whose fault it was.

Later, after Jodi left, Todd came into my room and sat on my bed, messing up the fresh sheets as he bounced around. "So how goes it, little bro?" he asked.

"I'm trying to study."

"It kills me," he said. "Here you are, straight-A brain, you don't even *need* to study, but you do it all the time. Then there's me, dummo jock who *should* study all the time, and I *never* do."

"You do okay."

"*Okay*, yeah, but not all A's like you."

He was trying to get on my good side.

"What do you want from me?"

"Can't you trust me, for God's sake? Can't I even give you a compliment? Do you always think I've got an ulterior motive?"

I turned and stared at him. Finally I nodded. He laughed, then looked up at me sheepishly. "Okay, you're right. There *is* an ulterior motive. Would it be okay with you if I asked Jodi for a date?"

I knew it! But still . . . hearing it out loud was something else. It hurt.

I looked at the wall in front of my desk. It was very white. "Sure," I said. "Why are you asking *me*, anyway? We don't have anything going."

"I know. But she is your friend and all, so I wouldn't feel right about it if you had objections."

"No objections," I said.

"She's pretty neat, huh?"

"I guess."

"Pretty neat looking. And I like the way she laughs."

"She laughs okay, if you like laughing."

"*Like* laughing? I *love* laughing!" He bounced up and down on my bed a few more times.

Suddenly I jumped up and shouted, "Would you stop doing that, please? Would you stop bouncing on my bed?"

He stopped. He just sat there in the middle of the bed, staring at me in surprise.

I gripped the back of my chair as hard as I could. "Maybe you should have a little consideration for other people once in a while instead of jumping on their beds all the time!" I shouted. "I wish you'd grow up. You're supposed to be the older brother, after all. But no! You're always running all over the place, waving your arms around, talking in italics. You make me mad, Todd!"

"Talking in *italics*?" he said. "What are you talking about?"

"There! You just did it there. You said, 'Talking in *italics*?' If you were in a book, half the things you'd say would be in italics!"

"I don't get it, Emery."

"Of course you don't. You don't get *anything*!" That's how far he'd driven me. Now even *I* was talking in italics.

"Does this have anything to do with Jodi?"

Suddenly I was tired. I sat down at my desk and laid my head in my arms. When I spoke, my voice sounded weak. "Of course it doesn't have anything to do with Jodi. Go ahead, take her out, she's nice."

"You feeling okay, Em?" He sounded concerned.

I hate being pitied.

I tried to turn it into a joke and said, "I'm just tired. It's not easy being a ner—" The word broke in half as it came out of my mouth. "—erd."

"You're not . . . crying, are you?"

"No! Why would I be?" I lifted my head and took off my glasses to prove my eyes were completely dry.

Then I dropped my head back on the desk and shut my eyes. I could still feel Todd standing right behind the chair. He lightly punched me in the shoulder a couple of times. Then he took his fist and rubbed it up and down my back for a second. I really did start to cry at this point, but very quietly, so he couldn't tell. In fact, he probably thought I'd fallen asleep, because shortly after that he tiptoed from the room.

That was last night, and tonight was The Date. Of course she said yes when he called her.

22. *Girls always say yes to Todd.*

As I sat in my room, I could hear him downstairs, talking to my parents.

"Emery! Emery!" my mother called. "Bring your camera down and take a picture of Todd."

"Mother, for goodness' sakes, why?" I asked, but brought the camera downstairs anyway. "It's not as if he's going to his senior prom or anything. He's just going to see another horror movie with some girl."

"Yes, but I'd like to have a reminder that at some point in his adolescence, Todd got dressed up in something other than jeans or a soccer uniform."

I said, "Don't you usually wear jeans and a T-shirt on a date anyway?"

"Yeah, but this isn't just any date. *You* know. Jodi's pretty special. She doesn't seem like the jeans type." I wondered what Jodi would wear.

"Should I take the picture or shouldn't I?" I asked. "I've got more important things to do."

"Take the picture," my mother said firmly.

Todd stood in front of the curtains and raised his eyebrows and smiled at me, as if he hated getting his picture taken but was just humoring our mother.

23. *He loves getting his picture taken.*

I snapped the picture, making sure that my thumb was in front of the lens.

"Let's take another one, just in case the first one doesn't come out or something," he said.

"Sure," I said, taking another picture of my thumb.

He grabbed his car keys and said, "Who knows what the night holds? Movies, dinner, dancing?" He grabbed my mother and twirled her through a few dance steps.

"You're just going to some dumb horror movie. You've already eaten, so you're not going to dinner. And you're not going dancing . . . are you?" The thought of Todd holding Jodi in his arms was too much to take.

"Don't know, can't say, not sure," said Todd.

"Just be careful with the car," said my father, "and be back by midnight."

"Sure thing. I'll be back by midnight. Twelve thirty at the latest, Dad. . . . Maybe one o'clock if traffic's heavy." He ran out the door and vaulted over the hedge next to the driveway.

My father shook his head, smiled, and said, "Son of a gun."

24. Todd always, always *gets whatever he wants.*

The car radio suddenly began to scream at its maximum volume, and our old Pontiac went roaring down into the street.

I don't know what kept me standing at the doorway, watching the car until it went out of sight. By all rights, I should have been the one driving off to Jodi's house at that very moment . . . even if I don't know how to drive yet. I sighed and sat down in a living-room chair.

"What's the matter?" said my mother.

"Nothing."

I took out my ballpoint and wrote on the first page of this notebook, "25 Good Reasons for Hating My Brother Todd." The first thing I thought of was that my brother thinks it's dumb that I like lists. "What are you doing?" my mother asked, snooping over my shoulder.

"Making a list of all the reasons I hate Todd."

"Oh, stop that nonsense. You don't hate Todd. What's wrong? Are you angry because he's taking out that girl from your class?"

"Angry?" I said. "Why should I care? I hate Jodi Meriwether. I never have liked her. You might say I despise her."

"Okay, okay, I'm sorry I asked."

"You should be," I muttered under my breath.

She said, "I just don't see why you have to behave so poorly toward your brother."

25. My mother always did like him best.

What Cool Is

Christopher Shulgan

Characters

Author	Girl 2	Vice-Principal	Craig
Girl 1	Girl 3	Red Smith	Bob

The stage is set up to mimic a high school. To the left (if one is facing the stage) is a cafeteria table. The centre of the stage is dominated by two sets of stairs, leading up to the same landing. Underneath this landing is a card table, with a pack of cards on it. To the right is an office, with a desk and two chairs. Throughout the play, students walk by the actual characters, but these wanderers mind their own business and do not take part in the scenes. These wanderers can show up at any time in the play. Every student in the play except the AUTHOR and the VICE-PRINCIPAL is dressed mainly in a single colour, with the majority of students in blue. Just after the curtain opens a bell rings, to signal beginning of class. A number of stragglers run across the stage, late getting to class, but this quickly stops, until the only people on the stage are three girls sitting at the cafeteria table. These girls are obviously in style; however, all their clothing and accessories are blue. They whisper quietly to themselves. A teenager, just on the edge of adulthood, emerges from the right, conspicuous in that he does not wear mainly one colour, but is dressed normally. He walks to the centre of the stage, and once he reaches the centre all noise hushes, for this is the true beginning of the play. Whenever a wanderer walks by the AUTHOR, he falls silent. The girls at the cafeteria table take no notice of the AUTHOR.

AUTHOR: (*spoken reflectively, slowly*) You know, I have trouble writing these things . . . plays, I mean. I just finished reading a biography of Orwell, and they said that he wrote for hours at a time, all the time that he could. That that was all he did. He was a writing madman. Me, I like to think sometimes that I can write, but when I read something like that, I realize how lame I am compared to him. I mean, I write for two hours, and I think I'm a big shot. (*Pause.*) The thing is, I never finish anything that I write. (*Absently takes a ball from his pocket, occasionally bouncing it.*) I get plenty of ideas, tonnes of them, in fact, but . . . I don't know. Movies, they always give me ideas. By the end of a movie, I can have a whole novel planned out. Characters, setting, plot . . . The other day . . . (*Takes another two balls out of pocket, starts to juggle.*) I was watching some movie — New York Stories, I think — and I got this idea about high school. All it would be is a conversation between three girls, but . . . it would satirize them, through their own conversation. Like, it would summarize their whole clique system, how they're so nasty to each other . . . (*Juggling up a storm.*) . . . and all this would just be their own conversation. But the questions I was presenting, like why were the girls so mean to each other, or what makes one girl hated and another admired, and all that stuff . . . (*Drops a ball, then all balls, and lets them roll away.*) I didn't have any answers for them. I couldn't figure out, like I had no idea why they stuck in their cliques, or were so nasty to each other. I couldn't figure it out, and if you can't answer the questions that pop up in your own play, then you're not worth anything as a writer. Because that's all a play is, an answer to the questions you present through it. So I couldn't finish that one play. But it's not just that one . . . whenever I write about high school, my plays fall apart . . . I can't figure out why. (*Fading out.*) I always miss something . . . something crucial.

(*The conversation the three girls at the cafeteria table are having gradually rises in volume. They speak as if what they have to say is of the utmost importance, to be kept secret at all costs. As a result they also speak quickly. AUTHOR plays absently with his three juggling balls, as if bored.*)

GIRL 1: It can't be described, that's what it is. I can't put my finger on it. But . . .
GIRL 2: . . . it's definitely something. She's not one of us. And she wears . . .

G1: . . . purple, for heaven's sake, purple. That was out how long ago? Like, we wore that long before the colour was red, and red is even out of style, none of . . .

G2: . . . us would even be caught dead in red, and she is wearing purple? And she talks to us? I mean, didn't the . . .

G1: . . . disco queens . . .

G2: . . . wear red?

G1: To tell you the truth, it all makes . . .

G2: . . . me want to yak. (*Both girls shudder.*)

GIRL 3: So that's fine. She doesn't hang out with us. (*Sarcastic.*) I'm sure, besides, that we would hang out with someone who's stupid enough to wear purple, and that's final.

G1: But what do we . . .

G2: . . . tell her?

G1: We can't just . . .

G2: . . . say . . .

G3: (*interrupting*) Why not? You guys already said she wore purple. That's enough, and she should know that. Why . . . (*Trails off.*)

G2: She probably doesn't even own . . .

G1: . . . a pair of Tretorns.

G2: Get serious.

G3: Melissa Mathews was in my last class. She was wearing mauve.

G2: (*both almost awed*) Really?

G1: (*hushed*) Holy . . .

G2: I heard that's the latest colour. That was in *Vogue* and . . .

G1: . . . *Elle* too. I wonder where she got it?

G3: Her father probably bought it for her, that's where. She's so spoiled all she probably had to do was ask dear old daddy, and she got it. (*Mimicking.*) Mauve, honey? Coming right up. Would you like fries with that?

(*GIRL 1 and GIRL 2 both giggle.*)

G1: Would you like . . .

G2: . . . fries with that! (*They laugh again.*)

G3: Plus, she thinks she's so chic, too. Like, just because she wears her cutting-edge-of-fashion mauve that she's too good for us. Snobby little . . .

G1: That's true. (*GIRL 1 and GIRL 2 both nod.*)

(*AUTHOR takes his three juggling balls and begins, once again, to juggle.*)

G3: She probably doesn't even like mauve. She just wears it because she thinks she's so fashionable.

G2 and G1: Yeah, you're probably right.

(*Two girls enter, one in mauve, the other in purple. They both wave to the girls at the table, smile, and walk by. The girls at the table also smile and wave. Nothing on the part of either the mauve or purple girl gives the impression of malice.*)

G1: Melissa and her? What are those two doing together? Melissa's so popular and she's so . . . (*Shudders.*)

G2: . . . unpopular. I mean, really . . .

G3: Yeah, really. Melissa's probably just slumming or something. They couldn't really be hanging around together. (*Pause.*) And did you see the way they looked at us? You could tell they had been talking about us. Backstabbing fakes, that's what they are, all right.

G1: Oh . . .

G2: . . . totally. Personally, I . . .

G1: . . . heard that Melissa thinks we're out of style, that . . .

G2: . . . we're hokey.

G3: Do you see how two-faced she is? How snobby she is? How she sees everything materially? She probably wouldn't even care to know us for who we are.

G1: Yeah.

G2: Right.

G1: I always knew . . .

G2: . . . that she was a backstabber.

(*Long pause, during which the three girls get increasingly panicky. They do this silently, looking at each other wildly, each one expecting the other to say something. While this happens, the* AUTHOR *begins to bobble his balls, losing control, regaining it, and finally, though he is trying desperately to keep juggling, he drops all three balls.*)

AUTHOR: (*resignedly*) Just great.

G3: (*finally*) . . . ummmm. (*Whispering.*) Who's got . . . (*Clears throat and coughs, then louder.*) Who's got the next line?

G2: I thought . . .

G1: . . . you did.

G3: I don't.

G2: I don't. (*Both look at* GIRL 1.)

G1: Hey, neither do I.

G3: (*thoughtfully*) You know . . . I can't even remember what the point of this part is.

G1: Aren't we supposed to figure out that in actuality . . .

G2: . . . we're really nasty, and finally reveal . . .

G1: . . . why we're so mean to everybody?

G3: I thought so, but if none of us knows the next line, how can we?

G2: (*indignantly*) This is . . .

G1: . . . a real pain in the neck.

G3: (*uncertain*) Well, just a second. (*She twists around in her seat, to look back at the* AUTHOR, *who is picking up his juggling balls.*) Hey! Mr. Author Man? What's the deal?

(AUTHOR *looks up, surprised.*)

AUTHOR: Me?!

G3: Yeah, you. What's the deal? What's at the base of this awful clique system we're portraying here?

G2: What makes us so . . .

G1: . . . incredibly nasty to everybody not in our own clique?

G3: Why can't we be nice to each other? Mr. Author Man, what's our next line?

AUTHOR: Oh, well . . . (*Readjusts glasses.*) There is a small problem that way, see. I, umm, I'm not quite sure. I don't know why you are so nasty to each other.

G1: What?

G2: Pardon me?

G3: You don't know? How? I mean, what? How can you not know? You're the author of this play. The man who wrote it. . . . Why bother to write it if you can't finish it? Mr. Author Man, what were you thinking?

AUTHOR: (*throws up hands*) I thought I'd figure out all this stuff while we were rehearsing . . .

G3: (*accusingly*) You're an idiot! (*Turns around to look at other girls.*) This guy's an idiot! I don't believe this!

AUTHOR: I'm sorry that I wasted your time . . .

G3: You're sorry you wasted our time. Right. (*The bell rings.*) Let's go to class, girls, and leave this loser be.

G2: (*as leaving*) Man, you are . . .

G1: . . . some writer.

(*They exit, as the stage fills up with people getting to class. All are dressed in one colour, with most people choosing blue. The* VICE-PRINCIPAL, *in a grey suit, walks onto the stage, sees a kid push another kid, and grabs him, taking him into his office at left. During this, someone bumps into the* AUTHOR, *and drops an armload of books. The* AUTHOR *helps pick up the kid's books, and when he's done, the stage is mostly empty, except for the occasional wanderer and the* VICE-PRINCIPAL *and a hat-wearer in the office.* AUTHOR *sits on edge of cafeteria table.*)

AUTHOR: Man. (*He shakes his head. Stage becomes quiet.*) They're right though. I have no idea what fuels all their nastiness, and their cliques and stuff. I sit at their cafeteria tables with them, and at parties and all that, because, really, they're pretty nice to me. And, I guess, because I like the way they flirt with me. It's. . . . But when they start talking about other girls . . . it's like they all of a sudden turned on a blast furnace, and all this bitterness and hatred and jealousy just shoots out from their mouths. But what are they so jealous about? They hate the people that are more popular than them, but they hate the ones that are way less popular than them, too. They rip apart people who wear the clothes they wore two months ago, and then rip apart the people who are wearing the clothes now that they'll be wearing in two months. They talk about people bitterly and meanly, and crucify anyone who does the same to them. They don't make sense. Not to me, anyway. And the thing is, these girls only do this to each other. They don't seem to condemn or hate any guys. It seems like they reserve all that for each other. (*Shrugs.*) I don't know. I can't figure it out. What is it that makes them so jealous of each other? (*Sits at card table below stairway landing. Begins to play with the pack of cards on the table.*) We just finished doing this thing in Chemistry. It's called a dynamic equilibrium. What happens is that you get a bunch of chemicals and stick them together, and they react. And the solution bubbles and fizzes and just generally messes about, and when the solution is done fizzing, everybody thinks it's done reacting. Of course they do, because, on the surface, it's not fizzing, its colour isn't changing, it's fine. But it's not. All these atoms are still whizzing about, reacting with each other, colliding and making bigger atoms. Only these bigger atoms are also whizzing around, decomposing back into the smaller atoms. The two processes balance out. On the bigger scale you can't tell that anything's going on, because nothing in the solution is changing. That's what high school is like. It never changes, not on the surface. You always have cliques and classes, and bells and hall passes. There is always the principal. And the cliques pretty well always play the same roles, like the greasers of the fifties are like the headbangers of the nineties. It never really changes. But on the molecular, on the person-to-person scale, if you are actually in the reaction, then everything is changing, all the time. The atoms, I mean the people's lives, collide with each other, and they react, or I mean change, somehow, according to what they collided with. It could be a fight, or a date. Or a friend is made. It's whatever. And all this stuff balances out. But what makes all this stuff happen? What's the cause of the reaction? I can't figure it out. (*Three guys, all about eighteen, appear on the landing. Two are dressed in blue, the other in red. They talk quietly among themselves.*) Why is everyone so mean to everyone else? And what makes them hate some-body? What is it that makes one person admired, and one hated? I don't know.

(*As before, the voices of the boys on the landing gradually rise in volume. RED is the boy dressed in red. All three hang over the railing of the landing, but do not seem to notice AUTHOR. AUTHOR starts to build a card house, and does so throughout this scene.*)

RED: You know, Craig, you still owe me ten bucks.

CRAIG: Ten bucks . . . for what?

BOB: Yeah, for what?

RED: Remember at the mall? You bet me that I wouldn't go meet those two hot girls? That's what.

CRAIG: Yeah, but that was ages ago, man. Too long ago.

BOB: That was pretty long ago, Red.

RED: (*indignant*) Give me a break! That was last week, for crying out loud! I did the deed; now you owe me! I knew I shouldn't have bet you. You always do that.

CRAIG: Hey, buddy, calm down! You're getting all worked up over a matter of ten little loonies . . . I'll pay you, man; don't worry about it.

BOB: Holy . . .

(*Reflective pause, on everyone's part. AUTHOR still builds house of cards.*)

CRAIG: But, man, those girls were hot, eh, dude?

BOB: Were they ever. . . . But there were only two of them. Somebody would have been left out in the cold.

RED: (*sarcastic*) Somebody . . . yeah, right. You, more like.

CRAIG: They were kind of snobby, though. Too concerned about status or something.

BOB: True. Totally uncool. And there were only two of them.

RED: They were all right, I thought.

CRAIG: We all know what you wanted, man-o. But Bob does have a point, you know. (*Speaking mostly to RED.*) You never see girls in groups of threes. You notice that?

BOB: Yeah . . . (*As if that just occurred to him.*)

RED: You never see anyone in groups of threes.

CRAIG: I know. Except us. And you know why that is? Because three is the oddest number around.

BOB: Yeah . . .

RED: Bad things come in threes.

CRAIG: And that's a known fact. The thing is, three friends is an unstable triad. Two of the friends invariably, and slowly, almost against everyone's will . . . two of the friends start hanging around with each other more than with the other guy. And then, wham, bam, thank you ma'am, that unstable triad has turned into a stable pair and a loner. But with us, that hasn't happened, and you know why?

BOB: How come, Craig?

CRAIG: Because we are three caring, kind-hearted and cool guys, and there isn't a leader (RED *coughs.*) among us. No leaders, no losers, just the three of us and that's it. We always include each other in everything that we do, and that's a fact. We're . . . we're the Three Musketeers, man; that's what we are.

BOB: Hey, all right!

RED: The Three Stooges. (*Laughs to himself.*)

CRAIG: What? (*No one says anything.*) Anyway . . . hey! How long have we been friends?

BOB: Eight, maybe nine years.

RED: That's about right.

CRAIG: And here it is, the end of high school, and we're all still best friends. (RED *coughs, worse this time.*) Hey, Red, are you okay?

(RED *nods, almost done coughing. When he's done . . .*)

CRAIG: I think that's pretty cool.

BOB: Me too.

RED: (*sarcastically*) The Three Musketeers . . .

CRAIG: (*oblivious to the sarcasm*) Yeah, right. Hey! Bobby, what'd they always say?

BOB: All for one . . .

RED: And one for all.

CRAIG: Yeah, that's it.

BOB: (*yelling*) All for one!

(*Silence.*)

BOB: (*coughs*) Ummm . . . you guys are supposed to say "one for all" after that.

RED: (*half-giggling*) Oh, are we?

CRAIG: Sorry, Bobby. Say, do it again, and we'll do it this time.

BOB: 'kay. (*Takes a deep breath, and then yells.*) All for one!

(*Silence, except for* CRAIG'S *muffled laughter.* RED *just smiles.*)

RED: Hey, Craig, I think we forgot something.

(BOB *sulks a little bit.*)

CRAIG: (*sounding sympathetic*) Awwww, old man, did we forget something? (*In* BOBBY'S *face, then pinches his cheek and ruffles his hair.*) We're very very sorry, aren't we? (*Cooing, as if to a baby.*)

BOB: (*recoiling*) Hey—don't! I'm not your dog or something. (*Trying to get away from* CRAIG, *who is tickling and just generally bothering* BOB. *They play-fight, narrating the moves they do to each other, until finally,* CRAIG *ends up on* BOB's *chest. During all this,* RED *moves off to the side, away from the play-fight, and studies the stair railing as if he is interested in it.*)

CRAIG: The winner! (*Holding up his hands.*) Yes!

BOB: Awwww, I just wasn't tryin', that's all. Hey! (*Noticing* RED) How come you don't want to play, Red?

RED: I just don't want to, that's all.

CRAIG: (*getting off* BOB, *faking sounding hurt*) How come you don't want to play with us, huh, RED? You too old?

BOB: (*catching* CRAIG's *mischievous mood, and both boys move to get into* RED's *face*) Yeah, Red, you don't want to wrestle?

RED: Naw, you know guys, I just don't like to play that stuff, you know?

(*Smiling,* CRAIG *and* BOB *push* RED *a little bit.* RED *pushes them back and walks to the other side of the landing, away from the other two.* RED *is also smiling, but his is forced and uneasy.*) There's no particular reason, I just . . . (CRAIG *tackles* RED's *leg, and* RED *falls down, to the landing.* BOB *also jumps in, and with* BOB *and* CRAIG *giggling, once again the tussle starts, with both* BOB *and* CRAIG *narrating their moves while* RED *just tries to get away. All three are on the ground.*)

RED: Ow! Stop, you jerks! I said stop! (RED *punches both in the head, and they stop and stand up. When* RED *stands up, his nose is bleeding, and he holds it, while the other two just hold their heads. All three are panting.*)

BOB: What'd you punch us in the head for?

RED: Because somebody punched me, you stupid oaf. I think you guys broke my nose. (*Awkward silence.*) Man. . . . I told you guys that I didn't

want to play-fight. . . . Something like this always happens to me. Always
. . . man . . .

CRAIG: I didn't mean to break your nose, old man.

RED: Hmmmph . . . what am I supposed to say? No problem? I wanted it
crooked? (*Accusingly.*) Loser.

BOB: He didn't mean it.

RED: (*almost yelling*) Shut up!

BOB: You're not the boss of me.

RED: *I'm* not.

BOB: What does that mean?

RED: Nothing . . . forget I said it . . . (*Waves them gone.*) Get lost.

CRAIG: I have to split, anyway. (*Walks halfway down the stairs; then turns
around.*) Let's go, Bobby. (BOB *hesitates, torn, then hurries down the stairs, and
they both exit. By this time, the card house the* AUTHOR *has been building has
become quite extensive.*)

RED: (*Watches them leave.*) (*Wipes nose off with T-shirt.*) I bet it is broken, too.
Jerks. Stupid moronic jerks. (*Hits railing of stairway and walks down the
stairway opposite the one that the other two went down; then sits on bottom
step, picking up one of the juggling balls still left on the ground. He doesn't take
any notice of* AUTHOR.)

RED: Musketeers, my butt. Two friends and a loner would exactly describe my
situation. Just look at them. Bob follows Craig around like a puppy. Disgusting. Craig says jump, and what does Bobby do but jump. Man . . . (*Hits
stair railing again.*) That's what always happens with us. Everytime we meet
girls, Craig gets them. He's not even the nicer guy! He's bossy, he can be
mean, like with me, and still every girl we meet likes him better. And Bobby
follows him around so much . . . And my nose is broken! (*Rising in volume.*) I can't believe this. (RED *whips the ball, and the ball takes down the card
house* AUTHOR *has been building.*)

AUTHOR: (*staring at cards with quiet resignation*) Man!

RED: What? (*Sees* AUTHOR.) Oh, hey . . . I've been looking for you.

AUTHOR: You have?

RED: Yeah, I've got some questions for you.

AUTHOR: (*sarcastic*) Great. Shoot. (RED *groans.*) What's the matter?

RED: I think CRAIG broke my nose . . .

AUTHOR: Why'd he break your nose?

RED: You mean, you don't know?

AUTHOR: No . . .

RED: But you wrote this play. I was going to ask you that.

AUTHOR: I know. Look, man, I've already been through this.

RED: You don't know. (*Giggles to himself.*) Well that messes up the whole play, then. Holy Cow. . . . See, the thing is, this always happens with us. It seems to me that those two, Craig and Bob, always gang up on me. When we're wrestling, or arguing, whatever, it always ends up that I'm the loner, that it's them against me. Craig isn't the one that does it though. It's Bob. For some reason he feels this need to hurt me.

AUTHOR: But it was Craig that punched you.

RED: Yeah, but that was an accident. At least, I think it was. Bob is the guy that was really punching me. It's like he wants to impress Craig, or something.

AUTHOR: Why impress Craig? Why want to?

RED: See, I think that that's the question of the hour. Why does Bob want to impress Craig, and why does he follow Craig so much? If Bob didn't feel it so necessary to suck up to Craig, to like him so much better than me, then we actually could be the Three Musketeers. Bob probably can't help it, and Craig can't prevent Bob from liking him better, but I'd still like to know. What does Craig have that makes Bob like him so much more than me? (*Pause.*) I sound jealous, eh? I'm not though, not really. Just curious. (*Pause.*) You know, it used to be that we all wore red. Everybody did. I loved it, red, I mean, and everything was great. But then Craig started to wear blue. Just out of the blue. And then other people did, and now most of the school does, just because Craig started it.

AUTHOR: So your question is, what does he have that gives him the ability to start trends and stuff, eh?

(*The* VICE-PRINCIPAL, *done with the guy he was yelling at before, walks across the stage and stops at the two boys.*)

RED: Yeah, that's . . .

VP: (*barks*) Ho! What's going on here? Why aren't you in class?

AUTHOR: We were just discussing the play, buddy. Do you mind? (*RED, taken aback, gapes at* AUTHOR.)

VP: Look, buddy. No little worm of a student calls me buddy. I think maybe you two class-skipping Suzies should come with me to my office. Come on. (*Snaps fingers as he turns to go to his office.*) Move it.

(VICE-PRINCIPAL *leads the way, while* RED *follows, with* AUTHOR *following* RED.)

AUTHOR: (*to VICE-PRINCIPAL's back*) Look, man, I don't know who you think you are, but I'm the one who wrote this play and you can just get lost with your power-hungry tactics. So I wrote a play that I don't know the ending to. Big deal. You can't boss me around on my own set! Does the director know what . . .

RED: (*has been trying to silence AUTHOR, now yells*) Shut up!

AUTHOR: . . . you're doing?

(*VICE-PRINCIPAL ignores them, and sits at his desk. RED sits down in one of the chairs provided. AUTHOR stands and waits for an answer.*)

VP: (*looking up*) Do you boys know that I could give you a little three-day holiday for skipping class?

AUTHOR: A what?

VP: That I could suspend you guys? (*Irritably.*) And sit down.

RED: Yes, sir. (AUTHOR *scratches head and then sits down, bewildered.*)

VP: Now. . . . Names.

RED: Uhhh . . . Red. Red Smith.

VP: And you are? . . .

AUTHOR: I am the author of this play.

VP: Arthur . . . Arthur what?

AUTHOR: No, you see, I wrote this play.

VP: Arthur Wrote. (*Exhaling.*) Okay. Now what seems to be the problem here? What . . . what was so important that you two deemed it important enough to skip classes for?

AUTHOR: (*clears throat*) Yeah, well, we were just discussing the nature of high school, I guess.

RED: What makes the styles change and stuff.

VP: (*to himself*) The nature of high school . . . (*To them.*) Well, what about it?

RED: Neither one of us knows what it is.

AUTHOR: See, it all started this morning, when I couldn't figure out why girls are so mean to each other. Why they treat everyone else so badly.

RED: And then we tried to figure out what makes one guy so admired and another so ignored. What does the one guy have that the others don't?

VP: And you don't know the answers to either of these questions? (*Both shake their heads.*)

VP: Well, really, you are asking the same question. (*He pauses and twiddles his thumbs.*)

AUTHOR: (*not understanding*) What?

VP: It's coolness, through and through. Coolness permeates every level of high school, and, to some extent, that's all high school is. It's what drives the machine, boys. What fuels the reaction. You know (*Pausing to look at both guys.*) it is a tragedy that no one ever figures that out while still in high school, because it would make school life a lot easier for most students. Anyway . . . (*Sighs, stretches, and yawns.*) We'll send your student records to whatever school you guys choose to go to.

AUTHOR: What?

VP: I won't even tell them about your expulsion. That looks very bad on university applications, you know.

RED: What? What are you talking about?

VP: Don't you see? You guys *know*. (*AUTHOR crosses arms, deep in thought.*) Two students in one school that know what makes high school cliques, and indeed, student life itself, tick, could have catastrophic implications for the very fabric of high school life itself. Utter catastrophe. And let me tell you that I didn't work my butt off to become the discipline-wielding arm of this administration to have my school torn apart by a couple of punks such as yourselves. Do it somewhere else.

RED: But where will I go to school?

VP: Young man, that is not my problem.

AUTHOR: Don't worry about it Red. Be quiet for a sec. Mr. VP, what exactly do you mean by coolness?

VP: It's simple, boy. Certain people are more cool than others, just like certain people are better looking than others. High school revolves around them. Look, if school were a solar system, the cool people would be the sun. People who follow the cool people, they're planets, like your friend Bob. Some suns are bigger, some are smaller, but it's these people who accidentally create all the nastiness in the universe. Just like sometimes planets collide and cause asteroids, sometimes when the planets are jockeying, I mean the followers, are jockeying for their places in the big race to gain favour with the cool people, others get hurt.

AUTHOR: (*interrupting RED, and then silencing him with an arm*) So what about all the girls? Why do they hate the cool people and the nothings alike?

VP: Oh . . . this applies to everybody, it's just more obvious with the girls. They see the nothings, the people who are neither planets or suns, as beneath them. They want to distance themselves from the nothings as much as possible, so they cut them down. The girls who are cool, they're jealous of anyone else with any coolness, and so they cut the other cool people down, because the others threaten their own coolness. It's a vicious cycle, really, but that's the way it always has been. That's high school, and it's nasty.

(*RED stares angrily off into space for all this time.*)

AUTHOR: (*thoughtfully*) So what is it that makes a person cool?

VP: Nothing. They're born with it, just like they're born with their intelligence. It's genetic.

RED: So what am I?

VP: You haven't been listening, Mr. Smith. You are nothing. Not a planet, not a sun; you are destined to drift through high school friendless, and unhappy.

AUTHOR: (*hastily, before RED tells him off*) Well, thank you for clearing that up, Mr. VP, and . . . (*Shaking his hand.*) I must say that what little time I spent at your school was a learning experience. You want to split, Red? (*Before RED responds, AUTHOR grabs his hand, and he drags RED out of the office.*)

VP: (*as they're leaving*) Sorry about all this.

(*The farther RED and AUTHOR get from the office, the happier AUTHOR acts, until when the two guys sit at the cafeteria table, he's exuberant.*)

RED: (*sulking*) What are you so happy about?

AUTHOR: I could just as easily ask you what's wrong with you.

RED: (*indignant*) What's wrong with me? I get kicked out of school by the

Vice-Principal of my school, who also tells me that I'm doomed to be friendless forever, and you ask me what it is that's bothering me?

AUTHOR: Don't worry about the school, man. I'll just write up another, better one for you. And, listen, don't listen to what that guy said about you. He doesn't know what he's talking about. He was an idiot. (*To himself.*) But he gave me a couple of good ideas . . .

RED: That guy wasn't right about me?

AUTHOR: No, not really. See, he was wrong when he said that people are born with coolness, just like he was wrong about you. Coolness is self-confidence. Period. You have that, and you do what you want because you're strong enough to know that somebody else's opinions are not necessarily better than your own. Other people see your strength, and they're either jealous or awed by it. So those of you with enough self-confidence go your own way, and the others orbit you, following those that are cool.

RED: So where do I fit?

AUTHOR: Coolness is a two-bladed sword. The admired guys, the ones that are all so popular, they get the good end of the deal. But then, the other cool people, whose ideas and tastes aren't in style at that time, they're ignored and abused by the followers who mistake them for losers, and try to distance themselves from you guys.

RED: So I'm cool, too?

AUTHOR: Yeah. The thing about being cool, about being a sun, is that you're really visible. You shine all over the place. For the people whose brand of coolness is in, that's good, but for the others, that just means that they stick out from the followers like sore thumbs.

RED: (*after a pause*) I still don't have any real friends.

AUTHOR: But you will. With this knowledge you will. (*Period bell rings, and the halls begin to get much more crowded.*) And don't forget that you're going to another school, and that you'll meet friends there. Hey, people mistake cool for attitude, but they're wrong. Cool is a lot harder than attitude. You have to believe in your own way of doing things, and risk being ostracized for it. That's what cool is. Always remember that the losers, the people everyone else sees as total nerds, are cooler than any follower there ever was. (*Pause.*)

RED: So what do you do now? You've done your play. Finally.

AUTHOR: Yessir. (*Pause.*)

RED: Well, are you going to go back to your own school?

AUTHOR: Naw, man. That's over for me. I just graduated.

(*Curtain*)

Being Comfortable
with Being 'Weird'

Naomi C. Powell

When you're 12, the last thing you want to be is different. In preteen dialect, "different" is a direct synonym for "weird," and to be weird is to be an outcast. In my elementary school, the weird kids were usually the ones who couldn't afford designer jeans and who failed miserably at sports, often being laughed off the soccer field for their clumsiness.

They usually sat by themselves or with other outcasts, playing quietly or eating their lunches while watching enviously as the "cool" kids scored touchdowns and gave each other high fives. But even for the weird kids, the doors to "coolness" and social acceptance were relatively open: All they had to do was squeeze a new pair of jeans out of their mother and learn how to throw a spiral.

On the other hand, for people like myself, the ultraweird, the doors were not only shut; they were locked so tightly that no amount of Levi's or athletic ability could get them open.

Unlike a lot of other youngsters, I wasn't burdened with a weight problem or unattractive appearance. In fact, I was a rather good-looking kid; I just wasn't interested in being popular. When I hit Grade 7, I was still wearing my older brother's hand-me-down overalls and tennis shoes and had no idea that any world existed outside the one my best friend Lynn and I had created for ourselves. We didn't really have any friends besides each other, but I can't remember ever being lonely or wanting another pal. When I wasn't with Lynn I was perfectly content with my own company, reading, swimming or riding my bike.

In fact, it wasn't until Lynn moved away that I even realized such a treacherous social ladder existed at my school and that, even worse, I was on the bottom rung. All of a sudden I had no one to eat lunch with, to play with or to walk home from school with. I made a few futile attempts to find new friends, but none of the girls were interested in spending time with someone who couldn't care less about shopping or boys or any of the other activities that were of prime importance in Grade 7.

I began to feel like Dorothy in *The Wizard of Oz*, lost in a colourful, complicated world of "cool" kids and "geeks." Unlike Dorothy, I didn't have three good friends to guide me through this social maze; I didn't even have a yellow brick road to tell me if I was going in the right direction.

I spent the next few months in utter misery, begging my mother to let Lynn move in with us or at least to buy me a pair of jeans like the other kids wore. Mom flat out refused to adopt Lynn but did consent to get a few new clothes for me if I would just keep quiet.

With the new jeans I was boosted from ultraweird to just plain weird and was invited to my first Grade 7 party. I dressed with more caution than a bride before her wedding and flounced down the stairs in my new frilly lace skirt and white sweater, determined to find a new best friend.

I had adopted all the cool sayings into my vocabulary, had begun watching TV (something I never had time for in the past), and had started making beaded necklaces—which I found excruciatingly boring, but everyone else thought it was "rad." While I didn't know the names of more than two kids at school when Lynn was around, I knew everyone now, as well as the kids they hung around with and the ones they hated. My parents had had it up to their eyeballs with this makeup-coated, gum-cracking stranger who kept saying "like" and "bitchin'" and talked on the phone for hours. I was a walking, talking, teen magazine, and I may have been popular, but I wasn't happy.

The party turned out to be a failure; I spent the entire evening playing basketball in the host's driveway with the boys while the girls looked on with disgust. When I took a break for some punch, I heard one of the "cool" girls whisper to her friend;

"Like, oh my God, she is so weird."

All at once it occurred to me this superficial little wench was right: I was weird. I had tried to be someone I wasn't but couldn't pull it off. I hated "normal" things like makeup, TV and clothes. I wasn't like these girls; I didn't giggle like a three-year-old when a boy spoke to me and I didn't enjoy slathering cosmetics on my face, and I didn't belong at that party.

I left without saying good night, went straight home and scrubbed my face, fighting desperately with the thick globs of mascara and eye liner that had been eating into my eyes all evening. I ripped the uncomfortable, skin-irritating party clothes from my body and donned my overalls, revelling in their soft denim, so worn it fit every curve of my body like a loose glove. I slipped my feet into my tattered tennis shoes, pulled the laces tight and ran down the stairs to go for a ride on my old 10-speed. I felt a wave of relief roll through my body and decided that even if "weirdness" meant having no friends at all, I was never going to be that person again. I had to be myself, and for the most part, it was a hell of a lot more fun.

Fortunately, I did make a few friends who were just as weird as I was, and I finished Grade 8 with a smile on my face. But I learned something I've never forgotten and that is to be true to myself. So if there are any parents out there wondering if they're living with their 12-year-old daughter or an explosive pre-teen nightmare, relax, and have her read this article.

Ending the Blame Game

Roberta Beecroft

"Hey! I'm not happy and it's your fault! So, change!" We do some crazy things when we don't like the way our life is going. Too often we blame someone else.

"If only you treated me as nicely as Jason treats Allison."

"I wish my parents were more generous and understanding."

"I have such a lousy Chemistry teacher!"

"My friends are so boring and self-centred. They make my life miserable."

Blame! Blame! Blame!

It's tempting to sing this self-pitying song, but the truth is, if you don't like your life, you are responsible for doing something about it. No one else is responsible for your happiness. No one else knows exactly how you feel or what you need. No one can read your mind magically and grant your every wish. You are the only one with the right and the opportunity to examine your life, and if you want it to be different, you can change what you're doing. You can take clear, definite steps to act on your own behalf. You can choose an active approach to situations instead of simply reacting to someone else's behaviour.

This means asking . . . *"what do I need? what do I want to do? what am I willing to do?"* instead of focussing only on others' demands. For example, it means deciding how you want to spend your evening instead of groaning, *"oh no! Lisa's so depressed she'll expect me to spend the whole night listening to her on the phone!"* We teach other people how we're willing to be treated. If we don't respect our own needs and limits, no one else will either.

Right about now I can hear you working up your "yeah, but" argument . . . *"yeah, but you don't know my principal!"* . . . *"yeah, but you don't have to live with my brother! . . . "yeah, but you don't have to watch your ex-sweetheart making out with her latest, two lockers away; you wouldn't like it either and you'd feel bad and put-down, too."*

In difficult situations, don't give away your power to decide how you feel about yourself. Choose—thoughtfully, consciously choose—your response to the situations in your life. Choose how you want to think and act. Other people can't **make** you unhappy or angry. Other people behave as they do and then it's up to you to decide how you will respond. For example: your friends went out to lunch without you. You feel angry, left out, insecure. How are you going to act in this situation? You could blame your friends . . . *"they're so thoughtless and inconsiderate; who needs them anyway?"* or you could tell your friends how you feel, listen to their explanation, and let them know you'd like to be included next time.

When you take responsibility for your actions, when you act purposefully, you're grasping hold of your own life, shaping it according to your beliefs, your values and feelings. Make choices instead of waiting for others to have an impact on you. It's up to you. You can choose to be happy, to make friends, to build an interesting life. When you blame others for what is or isn't happening in your life, you get stuck and stop growing and learning.

One of the most important "laws of human nature" is that you can never, ever change another person by your direct action. The **only** person you have the right and power to change is yourself. Once you change, the other person then has something different to respond to and change is possible. If you want change in your life, begin with yourself . . . add love, respect, gentleness and a relentless belief in your power to take action.

Goodbye blame! Hello, self-esteem!

Reprinted with permission by TG Magazine, 202 Cleveland St., Toronto, ON, M4S 2W6, 416-487-3204.

A Look of Pity

Christy Brown

Thirteen—and still very much the boy artist who hadn't yet discovered himself or come to know his own abilities sufficiently to make use of them. Painting became everything to me. By it I learnt to express myself in many subtle ways. Through it I made articulate all that I saw and felt, all that went on inside the mind that was housed within my useless body like a prisoner in a cell looking out on a world that hadn't yet become a reality to me.

I saw more with my mind than with my eyes. I'd sit for hours sometimes, alone in my bedroom, not painting or doing anything else, but just sitting and staring into a world of my own, away and beyond everything that made up my ordinary life. When I went into one of those day-dreams I forgot everything else: the loud voices in the stuffy little kitchen below. . . . Peter trying to play the mouth organ on the doorstep. . . . The sound of jazz music coming from the wireless downstairs. . . . The high shrill voice of the ragman in the street outside. . . . They all melted and faded into one confused blurring noise, and then gradually I'd hear nothing more or see nothing more. I'd just sit there, thinking. . . .

I didn't go out at all now. I had stopped going out a long time ago. I didn't even play in the house with my brothers any more. This puzzled them at first, but they slowly began to accept the new kind of relationship that had come between us. I didn't become a stranger to the rest of the family, of course, because with so many of us all living together in the same house that was impossible; we all formed part of one another, so to speak. But I had come to live more within myself. I lived *with* the others, but at the same time I lived *apart* from them, apart from all the things that meant most to them. I was happy by myself, but I didn't know then how far I really was from being self-sufficient.

And yet, withdrawn as I was from the ordinary life of a boy, the life of the streets and back alleys, I found that my heart was still miles ahead of my body in growth and development. I lost it again, good and truly this time. Another 'dream-girl' had come into my vision, not as tall and beautiful as my old one, but more my own age. She was called Jenny. She lived a few doors away from my house. She was small, energetic, gay, with a mass of brown curls framing her pretty elfin face with its lively green eyes and pouting lips. Unfortunately Jenny was a coquette; she could start a riot among all the boys on our street by just using those lovely eyes of hers in the right way. They were all crazy about her and there were many fights when they started arguing about who would marry her when they grew up into men.

I didn't go out any more, but that didn't stop me from seeing Jenny. I worshipped her from afar, that is from my bedroom window. It made me lazy in my painting, for whenever I heard Jenny's voice in the street below I'd crawl over to the window and sit on the bed, gazing out at her as she ran and skipped about with the other girls, whom I didn't notice at all. One day she looked up at me as I sat gazing down on her. I felt my face grow hot and made to draw back, but at that moment she smiled. I managed to smile back, and then she threw me a kiss. I could hardly believe my eyes when she did this, but she did it again before running away down the street, her dark curls flying and her white dress blowing in the wind.

That night I tore a page from an old jotter and, holding the pencil in my shaking toes, I wrote a passionate little note to Jenny, which I got one of my younger brothers to deliver, threatening him with my foot if he didn't give it to Jenny herself. I told her in the note that I thought she was the prettiest kid on our street and that I'd paint her lots of pictures if she'd let me. Then, in a hurried postscript, I told her that I loved her 'lots and lots of times'.

I waited for my brother to come back in excitement and fear, not daring to hope that Jenny would reply. In a half an hour's time he returned—with a note from her tucked up his jersey!

I took the note and read it eagerly, quite forgetful of my brother, who stood by staring at me in a funny way as if he thought I'd gone mad or something. I read Jenny's little letter over and over again, especially the part where she said she'd come and see me in my back yard the next day if I wanted her to. There was a queer fluttering inside me and a lightness in my head. I felt

myself go hot and cold in turn. After a while I looked up. My brother was still standing with his hands behind his back and his mouth open, a look of bewilderment in his big blue eyes as he fixed them on my face. I yelled at him to 'scram', and he scuttled from the room like a startled rabbit. Then I threw myself back on the pillow and sighed, my heart jumping crazily.

I kept the appointment next day, all spruce and 'done up' with Tony's de luxe hair grease actually dripping down my forehead. Little Jenny was very sweet. We sat and looked over some of my paintings, and she gave a little gasp of admiration at each one I showed her. I was shy and awkward at first because of my slurred speech and the way I used my foot instead of my hands. But Jenny was either a very innocent person or a very tactful one, for she didn't seem to notice anything queer about me, but talked on gaily to me about games and parties and the boy next door the same as if I had been Peter of Paddy. I liked her for that.

We became great pals, Jenny and I. We never said a great deal to each other, but we exchanged innumerable little notes each week and she'd steal over to see me every Saturday night, bringing me little books and magazines which I never read but which I treasured very much, storing them all away in the old worm-eaten cupboard in my bedroom.

I was secretly proud that I, a cripple, had made friends with the prettiest and most sought-after girl in our neighbourhood. I often heard Peter saying fervently that Jenny was a 'peach' and that he'd do anything to be her favourite 'beau'. Every time I heard this I felt very proud of myself and enormously vain, thinking myself quite a conqueror, because it was not I who went to Jenny, but Jenny who came to me!

Peter became suspicious and one Saturday he came upon Jenny and me as we sat together in the back yard, our heads very close to one another, although we were only looking at some old story book that Jenny had brought along. I got red in the face, but Jenny didn't move. She just lifted her head, smiled at my brother briefly, and bent over the book again. Peter gave me a murderous look and went into the house, banging the door after him.

That evening, before she left, Jenny sat very quietly, toying idly with the book, a little frown creasing her forehead and her lower lip pushed out, as she always looked when she wanted to say something difficult. After a little while she got up, hesitated, then suddenly knelt down on the grass beside me and kissed me very tenderly on the forehead. I drew back, surprised, bewildered, for she had never kissed me before.

I opened my mouth to try and say something, but at that moment Jenny sprang to her feet, her face flushed and her eyes wet with tears, and rushed from the garden, her small black shoes clattering noisily as she ran down the stone path and disappeared into the street.

She didn't come for weeks after this, and I didn't hear from her although I fairly bombarded her with notes. In the meantime Peter tried to discourage me by telling me many wicked tales about poor little Jenny, but I didn't believe him a bit, not even when he told me that she made every one of the boys pay her a penny for every kiss she gave them.

'That's why I'm always broke!' he said mournfully, his hands stuck in his empty pockets.

I often sat up in my bed at night, thinking of Jenny and the way she kissed me that day in the back garden. I felt very melancholy and alone. Why doesn't she come, I asked myself, as I tossed restlessly in the dark, hearing Peter snoring comfortably at my side.

My fourteenth birthday came along, and among the other birthday cards I got that morning there was one written in a small childish hand which was Jenny's: but still she never came to see me. I often saw her from my bedroom window playing in the streets below, but she kept her eyes away from my house and never looked up once. I'd sit at the window for hours, hoping she'd glance up at me, until the twilight came and everything grew dark and I could see nothing more save the dim whiteness of her frock as she ran along the street with the other girls, while a laughing crowd of boys chased after them.

To hide my disappointment I painted furiously for the whole of every day, painting crazy little pictures that had neither pattern or theme. They were just haphazard slices of my boiling mind dashed on to the paper wildly and recklessly.

Then one day as I sat disconsolately in the back yard with my back against a soapbox I heard a step close by. I looked up wearily. . . . It was *Jenny*! She stood a few feet away, at the entrance to the yard, her slim, childish figure outlined against the white wall behind her, vividly bright in the June sunshine, her shadow falling crookedly on the warm concrete ground. She was looking across at me, but—it was with a *look of pity*.

I knew then, as I came to know many times later, how bitter and crushing a simple look of pity can be to someone like myself who needs something other than sympathy—the strength that only genuine human affection can give to the weakest heart.

I lowered by head under her pitying gaze and without a word being said on either side Jenny turned slowly and left me to myself in the yard.

The Piano

Frank Davey

I sit on the edge
of the dining room, almost
in the living room where my parents,
my grandmother, & the visitors
sit knee to knee along the chesterfield & in
the easy chairs. The room is full, & my feet
do not touch the floor, barely
reach the rail across the front
of my seat. 'Of course
you will want Bobby to play,'—words
that jump out from the clatter
of teacups & illnesses. The piano
is huge, unforgettable.
It takes up the whole end wall
of the living room, faces me down
a short corridor of plump
knees, balanced saucers, hitched
trousers. 'Well when is
Bob going to play?'
one of them asks. My dad says,
'Come on, boy, they'd like you
to play for them,' & clears
a plate of cake
from the piano bench. I walk between
the knees & sit down

where the cake was, switch on
the fluorescent light
above the music. Right at the first notes
the conversation returns to long tales
of weddings, relatives bombed out again
in England, someone's mongoloid
baby, & there I am at the piano,
with no one listening or even
going to listen
unless I hit sour notes, or stumble
to a false ending.
I finish.
Instantly they are back to me. 'What a nice
touch he has,' someone interrupts
herself to say.
'It's the hands,' says another,
'It's always the hands, you can tell
by the hands,' & so I get up
& hide my fists
in my hands.

Dear Marsha

Judie Angell

Dear Anne Marie,   July 13

I guess this letter is probably a big surprise to you . . . I mean, you probably looked at the return address and signoff and all and saw that it's from nobody you ever heard of, right? Well, here's the reason I'm writing.

Maybe you remember this assignment that the kids in our English class got back in February. Our teacher (Ms. Bernardi, maybe that rings a bell) wrote to your English teacher and she asked him if he'd like to do this experiment: He would send a list of all the kids in your class with their names and addresses and we would pick those names out of a hat and write a letter to the name we picked. See, you all lived far away and the idea was to see if we could form a "relationship" (Ms. Bernardi grew up in the sixties) with a perfect stranger, using only pen and paper. (Or type-writer, I mean, *you* know.) Anyway, Ms. Bernardi said she wasn't going to grade the assignment, or even see it or anything because this assignment was personal, just for ourselves. You know, to "express ourselves" with a perfect stranger. Whatever. So naturally, if it didn't mean a grade or any-thing, I didn't do it.

But the thing is—I picked your name out of the hat and I just sort of kept it, you know, and now it's summer and hot and practically all of my friends are away, so . . . Here's a letter. You're a stranger even if you may not be perfect (or maybe you are perfect, I don't know), but here I am, trying to form this "relationship" using only two fingers on the typewriter (please excuse the mistakes, I'm taking Business Typing next semester) and you're the one I'm supposed to try it with.

Well, I'm not going to say anything more until I hear back from you—Hope you turn out to be cool.

> Your new pen pal (maybe)
> Marsha

Dear Marsha,   July 18
Your letter was great! It really picked up a slow summer for me.

I remember that assignment. Some of the kids really got into it when they got letters from your class and they're still writing back and forth. The friendships are terrific because everybody feels safe with them, you know? I mean, because we're so far away no one knows anyone the pen pal knows. And since you never have to meet, you feel freer to say whatever you want with no one coming down on you or whatever, you know.

So I'm glad you wrote and I'm also glad it's now instead of then, because back in Feb. I was really *wiped*, I mean really. See, my dad died, it wasn't sudden or anything, he was sick a long time, but still it was very hard on everybody as you can probably figure out. So now it's just my mom and my sister and me and . . . we miss Dad, so sometimes we get on each other's nerves.

I guess if you wanted me to be the first one to give out personal stuff I guess there's that. Plus . . . let's see. . . . If you're thinking about "m-e-n," I don't go out a whole lot, but there's one guy I like at school. The thing is, he's *younger* than I am and I get embarrassed about that and since he doesn't even know I like him . . . I guess you can't count it as a "relationship." (That word bugs me too.)

I hope this is enough for you to think that maybe we could be friends, and I like the idea of a pen pal.

> From
> Anne Marie

Dear Anne Marie,   July 21
You are *definitely* the coolest person! I couldn't wait to hear back from you so I'm writing you the same day I got your letter.

I'm sorry about your dad. That must be tough to deal with. I mean, I have both of my parents and it never occurred to me that one of them could die. I know that sounds stupid, but I just never thought about it.

They're okay most of the time, but really, I guess I just take them for granted, to be honest about it.

So now I'll tell you more about myself.

I'm a senior in high school, or at least I will be starting September. Which is okay, because the sooner I graduate the sooner I can start My Life. My dad says I could go to college if I want (*he's* the one who really wants me to go), but I'm not sure I could stand all that much school. I'm thinking about it more this summer, though, because I have this job at our local five-and-ten as a checkout girl and if anything is bor-ing, that is *it*! Here's what you get: "Mar-sha, last week you had green grosgrain in the sewing department and now it isn't there, why *not*?" And—"Mar-sha, you took ten minutes extra for lunch yesterday and it came off *my* time, so you better come back ten minutes early today." That kind of stuff. Borrrrr-ing.

Okay, well—I'm five feet five inches tall, which is about average, I guess, and I have black hair which in this weather I wear either in a chignon (sp?) or in a ponytail. It's pretty long and straight and I guess it's my nicest feature. I'm a cheerleader and I think my hair looks good flopping up and down when I jump. (I'm not really as conceited as that sounds!) Also I have brown eyes and no-more-BRACES. I'm pretty thin, which isn't too great when you wear a bathing suit. What do you look like? I picture Anne Marie as a blonde.

I don't have a boyfriend right now, although there's a very nice guy who works in the stockroom at the five-and-ten. Hmmm . . . maybe. . . .

Most of my friends got jobs at resorts and hotels in the mountains. I should have applied to one of them but as usual I was late and lazy, so here I am, bored at the five-and-ten. Write soon.

Your friend,
Marsha

Dear Marsha,   July 25

Boy, do I know what you mean about boredom! I'm working part time at my school—office stuff, and the rest of the time I'm at home because my mom and sister really need for us all to be together. Your town sounds like the same kind of hick burg mine is. You have one movie house and it's just got around to showing talkies, right? And: one Laundromat, a drugstore (NO BARE FEET, THIS MEANS YOU), a post office, and if you're real lucky, one of those no-alcohol bars for kids to hang out in on weekends.

One nice thing here, though—there is a lake we can go to. In fact, our family has always had a cabin there. It's called Lake Michigan, which was someone's idea of a joke because it's more of a pond than a lake and it has a lot more brambly woods than pond. But this summer no one in my house seems to have the energy for going up there a lot.

I'm a little shorter than you—five two exactly—and I do have blondish-brownish hair that's short and curly. I always wanted long black hair like yours. You sound really pretty and I bet that guy in the stockroom notices you pretty soon! I used to wear glasses but I got contacts finally and I think I look better now. Wish I had more to write but I don't, so let's hope things start to get more exciting for both of us!

Love
Anne Marie

Dear Anne Marie,   August 2

It took me a while before I could write again. It's not that I didn't want to, but some stuff happened and I've been kind of scared and depressed ever since.

What happened was, this girl at work—she's the one I was kidding about in

my last letter, the one who bitches about my coming back late from lunch. Her name is Claudia and we alternate shifts. Anyway, when I realized she was actually counting every one of my lunchtime minutes, I started coming back really on time, you know? Sometimes, even early. Well, last week when I relieved her, I counted up the receipts and the money in the register and stuff and it seemed to me that I was coming up short. The receipts and the money didn't check out, you know? But I figured it was me, I must've done something wrong. I mean, my math is hardly the greatest. So I let it go and when Claudia came back at four o'clock, I told her to check it out. So she did and said I was wrong and dumb and everything was okay and blah, blah, blah. But the next thing I know, Mrs. Handy, the manager, started checking everything between shifts because she said we were losing some money.

Listen, I won't drag this on, but accusations were thrown around and Claudia accused me of stealing. That was when I caught on that she was the one who was stealing and I knew that one time I got back too early for her to be able to hide it.

Well, of course she said I was the one and since it was her word against mine and she's a full-time worker and I'm only part time and no one noticed any shortage before I got there — naturally I got blamed. I wasn't arrested or anything because no one could prove I did it, but I did get fired. And as you put it so well, this *is* a hick burg, and I stand about as much chance of getting another job as I have of spreading wings and flying away. Which I'd sure like to do. I really didn't steal, Anne Marie. I hope you believe me. The cute boy in the stockroom sure doesn't. You should have seen the look he gave me.

So . . . things got exciting for a while, anyway.

Love
Marsha

Dear Marsha,   August 5
I got your letter and broke into tears, I swear I did. Of course I believe you didn't steal anything. But they will find out eventually. Claudia won't stop stealing and I bet she does the same thing with the next person they hire and they will all catch on.

I feel so bad for you, I don't know what to say. After I read your letter I told my mom and sister that I just had to get away for a while, so I took the bus up to our cabin and that's where I am now. I'm sitting on the porch and looking out at (ha-ha) Lake Michigan and thinking about you. People can be so mean. But I bet there are lots of people in the town who know you well enough to know it was all a lie and will be glad to hire you.

It's so peaceful up here, really. Just about an hour and fifteen minutes north of my house, but it feels like another world. Wait a minute, Marsha. . . .

You won't believe it! I'm back now, but I had to go inside and close the windows and doors and spray everything with Lysol! While I was sitting there describing all the peace and quiet, this SKUNK marches right up on the porch and lets me have some of what skunks do best! YUUUUCH! This is just AWFUL, did you ever get a whiff of skunk? They say tomato juice takes the smell away, but I don't have any and what are you supposed to do, bathe in it or what? PEEEEW!

So I'm sitting here in this locked cabin wondering which smells worse, the Lysol or the skunk or the mixture of both, and thinking of you.

Love
Anne Marie

Dear Anne Marie, August 10

Your letter gave me the first good laugh I've had in a while! I'm still laughing because I think I can smell that combination of stuff you mentioned on the pages of the letter! You can't imagine how much I wish I had a place to go like Lake Michigan (without the skunk!) but we're pretty far from any quiet place with water and woods. I mean, there's a pool at the town recreation center, but that's not exactly what I had in mind.  The closest I can get to coolness and peace and quiet is my basement, but *that* smells of cat litter and Clorox, *almost* as bad as your place!

Well, my mom and dad believe I didn't take any money or anything else, but it's hard for them because everyone they know heard about what happened. And so when people say, "Oh, Marsha, wasn't that awful, we just *know* you'd never" and all that, I somehow get the feeling they're really thinking Maybe she did, you know these kids today. . . .

Anyway, tell me something good to cheer me up. Your letters are the only nice thing to happen this whole stinking summer—NO PUN INTENDED!

Love
Marsha

Dear Marsha,   August 16

I hope by the time this gets to you that you're feeling better. I want you to know I really do think about you all the time.

Maybe this will cheer you up a little. . . . Did you ever have a carnival come to your town? Our firehouse sits on a tract of land of about twelve acres and every year they put on a really terrific carnival. Picture this: There's a high booth on wheels with a glass window where you can watch a boy spin pink cotton candy around and around. Close your eyes now, and you can smell it, all sickly sweet and gorgeous, and you can make mustaches and beards and eyebrows and earrings all over your face with it, you know? And they also have this huge plastic bubble, all different colors, with a foam bottom and you can go in there and jump your heart out. You fall over a lot, of course, but you don't get hurt even if you fall on your face because it's so soft. And there are these booths where you can throw baseballs at little Indian tepees and win neat stuff like plush polar bear dolls and clock radios and blow-dryers with three speeds and makeup mirrors and everything. And best of all is the Ferris wheel, because they stop it for a few minutes when you get to the top, and it's like you really are on top of the world. So picture yourself on top of the world and that's where you'll be.

That's where I was last night. And when I got to the top I thought about you and made a wish, so I know things will get better soon for you.

And also, guess what? At the shooting gallery, guess who I met? The younger guy I told you about. And we went on the Whip together. And I'm going back tonight, so . . . who knows?

Love
Anne Marie

Dear Anne Marie,   August 20

I have read your letter about eight hundred times. Where you live sounds so great. I pictured the carnival. I really tasted the cotton candy. I won a stuffed bear. I rode on the Ferris wheel with you and I think the "younger man" is cute. I liked being on top of the world, even if it was only for a few minutes.

Things here only seem to be getting worse. One of my girlfriends is back from her hotel job and you wouldn't believe how she sounded on the phone when I called her up. I feel like everyone's looking at me whenever I walk down the street.

Now I'm seriously starting to think about college, if only to get away from here. My dad says he's sorry it took something like this to get me thinking about it, but he's glad I am, he says. A blessing in disguise, he says. Ha, some blessing! But even if I do go to college, I still have a year of high school left and I honestly don't know how I'm going to stand it.

Tell me something else to smell and taste and ride on.

Love
Marsha

Dear Marsha,   August 25

I think it's neat you're thinking about college. If you're lucky enough to be able to go, I really think that's what you should do. It's just my opinion, but that's what I think.

Marsha, did you ever see kittens being born? You have *never* seen anything so incredible in your whole life! My Y-M (younger man) works at his dad's carpentry shop in the summer and they have this mama cat who was about to give birth and he asked me if I'd like to watch. Well, it took from six o'clock to around ten. The mama had a litter of seven kittens, and they came out two, two, one and two, over all those four hours. They each came out wrapped in a shiny silver cover, which the mama licked up and ate. I know it sounds really gross, but it was honestly beautiful. Their teeny eyes were shut tight and they made these little squeaky noises and they looked at first as if they had no fur, but they do. Y-M says I can have one.

Keep thinking about college and you'll see how quickly the year will go.

Love
Anne Marie

Dear Anne Marie,   September 1
It's Labor Day weekend and I'm spending it crying. The cheerleading squad is meeting Tuesday, the day before school starts and I'm "not welcome" on it anymore. I got the word straight from the captain herself. "Oh, I don't believe any of it, Marsha," she says, "but you know how people think of cheerleaders, they're supposed to represent the school's highest standards" and blah, blah, blah! "I know you'll sacrifice," she says, "for the good of the school." Right. Can you *believe* it? Anne Marie, it's *so* not fair!

Well, I can't handle it, Anne Marie, I really can't. I just can't spend an entire year at school like this. So I've made this decision, and I just know being the kind of person you are and with the kind of family you say you have, that you might be happy about it. This decision, I mean.

I know my mom and dad are on my side, but they're not, you know, the same as a *friend* or anything. And this summer, I guess you know that you became my very best friend.

I want to be where I can sit on top of the world on a Ferris wheel and watch little kittens being born and chase skunks away from a cabin porch. And spend all my time with a true friend, who's sensitive and caring and growing up with the same kinds of feelings I have. That stupid school assignment was the best thing that ever happened to me, Anne Marie, and I know I'm dragging this out, but here's my idea:

Could I spend the year with you? I swear on my own life I won't be any trouble, in fact, I'll be a help. With your dad gone, I can help make up for the work he did around the house. I'm very handy, I really am, I can do all kinds of things.

And best of all, we could go to school together, and do our homework together, and sit up nights and talk, and bake stuff and double date and go to the prom and make Senior Year everything it's supposed to be! And I'll bring my tapes—I bet I have the best rock and roll tape collection you ever heard!

Don't you think it would be great? Don't you? School's starting next week, Anne Marie. . . . Please let me know. . . .

Love
Marsha

WESTERN UNION NIGHT LETTER TUES SEPT 5
DEAR MARSHA—YOU MUST STAY IN SCHOOL, RIGHT THERE IN YOUR OWN TOWN—IT WILL BE HARD, VERY HARD, BUT YOU MUST DO IT—REMEMBER, YOU DIDN'T DO ANYTHING WRONG AND THEREFORE YOU MUST NOT RUN AWAY—YOU MUST NEVER LET STUPID AND CRUEL PEOPLE GET THE BEST OF YOU—I AM SURE YOUR MOM AND DAD HAVE TOLD YOU THE SAME—HOLD YOUR HEAD UP AS HIGH AS YOU CAN AND GIVE THAT CHEERLEADING SQUAD A GOOD RASP-BERRY—
MARSHA, I CANNOT TELL YOU HOW SORRY I AM FOR THIS—MY NAME WAS NOT SUPPOSED TO BE INCLUDED IN THAT LIST YOUR TEACHER RECEIVED FROM OUR TEACHER—SOMEONE MUST HAVE PUT IT IN AS A JOKE—BUT I DIDN'T MIND BECAUSE YOUR FIRST LETTERS WERE SUCH A JOY THAT I SIMPLY HAD TO ANSWER THEM IN KIND—THEN WHEN YOUR TROUBLE BEGAN, ALL I WANTED WAS TO MAKE YOU FEEL BETTER—MARSHA, I HOPE YOU WON'T MIND THIS—I HOPE IT DOESN'T MAKE ANY DIFFERENCE TO YOU—I HOPE WE CAN CONTINUE TO WRITE AND BE FRIENDS—
DEAR MARSHA, MY DAD DID DIE LAST WINTER AND I DO LIVE WITH MY MOTHER AND SISTER—THEY ARE EIGHTY-THREE AND SIXTY-THREE, RESPECTIVELY—I'M THE PRINCIPAL OF OUR SCHOOL AND I'M SIXTY-ONE YEARS OLD—

ALL MY BEST LOVE,
ANNE MARIE

A Sliver of Liver

Lois Simmie

Just a sliver of liver they want me to eat,
It's good for my blood, they all say;
They want me to eat just the tiniest sliver
Of yukky old slimy old slithery liver
I'm saying no thanks, not today.

No, I'll pass for tonight but tomorrow I might
Simply _beg_ for a sliver of liver;
"Give me liver!" I'll cry. "I'll have liver or die!
Oh _please_ cook me a sliver of liver!"
One piece might not do, I'll need two or a few,
I'll want tons of the wobbly stuff;
Of that quivery shivery livery pile
There may not be nearly enough.

Just a sliver, you say? No thanks, not today.
Tomorrow, I really can't say . . .
But today I would sooner eat slivers of glass,
Eat the tail of a skunk washed down with gas,
Slivers of sidewalks and slivers of swings,
Slivers and slivers of any old thing
Than a sliver of slimy old quivery shivery
Livery liver today.

Sonam...
Serenity and Concentration, Soccer and Video Games

Donna Douglas

Since he was eight years old, Sonam Puljor has been preparing himself mentally, physically and spiritually for life as a monk. Early evening as the sun begins to set on the Himalayan Mountains, the chanting of Sonam and his fellow monks can be heard for miles around. Sonam's dark brown eyes are fixed to his scriptures and his legs are crossed in a sitting position. To his left is Tashi, his best friend. Both are reading. Since they began their training at the age of eight, Sonam and Tashi have prayed, played, lived and studied together. Rumtek is their home and future.

Sonam is turning 16.

He's part of a young generation of Tibetans born and raised outside his own country. Since the Chinese occupied Tibet in the 1950's, Tibetan Buddhists have lived in exile, their monasteries and communities located in other countries, like little pockets of Tibet. Sonam is one of 200 monks living at the Rumtek monastery in Sikkim, a tiny independent state located near India's northeastern border. All of them are dedicated to Buddhism and developing their culture.

When he was eight years old, Sonam's parents bade him goodbye and gave him to the Tibetan Buddhists at the Rumtek Monastery.

For his parents, a Buddhist monk would bring good "karma" to the family. Like many Tibetans, Sonam's parents have lived in exile since the late 1950's. They have faced many hardships during their resettlement years when they crossed the Himalayas to seek refuge from Chinese communists.

Though he sees them only once a year, Sonam still feels close to his family.

His parents live 500 kilometres away, three days travel under difficult conditions. The family runs a small gift shop specializing in Tibetan handicrafts and goods.

For Sonam, the centre of his universe is Rumtek. His life's defined by the rules of the monastery . . . studies, meals, chores, co-operation, celibacy, non-violence, self reliance, and care of the poor and sick.

He was eight years old when he took his first Buddhist vows: celibacy, non-violence and the prohibition of alcohol. He follows a disciplined routine of study and meditation. He dresses in traditional red and yellow robes and lives at the Rumtek monastery on a full-time basis.

How has this shaped Sonam's values, his view of the world? His life as an adolescent?

A Typical Day for Sonam

- Rise before the sun, attend an early morning memorization course in the main temple
- Read and memorize sacred texts and follow the guidance of his teachers
- A long day of studies and work, including Tibetan writing, social studies, English, orals
- Music and dance courses prepare Sonam for special ceremonies or "Pujas"
- Sunset prayers, readings and chants
- A simple meal of rice and lentils
- Bed at 8:30 pm.

Reprinted with permission by TG Magazine and Adobe Foundations, 4519 Marquette, Montreal, PQ, H2J 3Y3, 514-526-5031.

What about Sonam, the individual? Smiling, mischievous, care-free, Sonam is a kid who loves soccer, badminton and video games. How does his life as a monk fit in with his life as a teenager? Does he ever think about girls, movies, big city lights? Will he continue along the path chosen for him by his parents? What does he value most in life and who does he want to be?

Sonam uses his free Wednesdays to play soccer, to learn video games at the Kunga restaurant in Rumtek, and to look at foreign magazines, activities not discouraged by the monastery as long as they don't conflict with his studies.

Sonam's hungry for the outside world, and curious about modern things like video games and cameras. He dreams of travelling to foreign countries, particularly to important Buddhist centres in Asia, Europe and America.

What Do I Remember of the Evacuation?

Joy Kogawa

What do I remember of the evacuation?
I remember my father telling Tim and me
About the mountains and the train
And the excitement of going on a trip.
What do I remember of the evacuation?
I remember my mother wrapping
A blanket around me and my
Pretending to fall asleep so she would be happy
Although I was so excited I couldn't sleep
(I hear there were people herded
Into the Hastings Park like cattle.
Families were made to move in two hours
Abandoning everything, leaving pets
And possessions at gun point.
I hear families were broken up
Men were forced to work. I heard
It whispered late at night
That there was suffering) and
I missed my dolls.
What do I remember of the evacuation?
I remember Miss Foster and Miss Tucker
Who still live in Vancouver
And who did what they could
And loved the children and who gave me
A puzzle to play with on the train.

And I remember the mountains and I was
Six years old and I swear I saw a giant
Gulliver of Gulliver's Travels scanning the horizon
And when I told my mother she believed it too
And I remember how careful my parents were
Not to bruise us with bitterness
And I remember the puzzle of Lorraine Life
Who said "Don't insult me" when I
Proudly wrote my name in Japanese
And Tim flew the Union Jack
When the war was over but Lorraine
And her friends spat on us anyway
and I prayed to the God who loves
All the children in his sight
That I might be white.

The Metaphor

Budge Wilson

Miss Hancock was plump and unmarried and over-enthusiastic. She was fond of peasant blouses encrusted with embroidery, from which loose threads invariably dangled. Like a heavy bird, she fluttered and flitted from desk to desk, inspecting notebooks, making suggestions, dispensing eager praise. Miss Hancock was our teacher of literature and creative writing.

If one tired of scrutinizing Miss Hancock's clothes, which were nearly always as flamboyant as her nature, one could still contemplate her face with considerable satisfaction. It was clear that this was a face that had once been pretty, although cloakroom discussions of her age never resulted in any firm conclusions. In any case, by now it was too late for simple, unadorned prettiness. What time had taken away from her, Miss Hancock tried to replace by artificial means, and she applied her makeup with an excess of zeal and a minimum of control. Her face was truly amazing. She was fond of luminous frosted lipsticks—in hot pink, or something closer to purple or magenta. Her eyelashes curled up and out singly, like a row of tiny bent sticks. Surrounding her eyes, the modulations of colour, toners, shadows could keep a student interested for half an hour if he or she were bored with a grammar assignment. Her head was covered with a profusion of small busy curls, which were brightly, aggressively golden—"in bad taste," my mother said, "like the rest of her."

However, do not misunderstand me. We were fond of Miss Hancock. In fact, almost to a person, we loved her. Our class, like most groups that are together for long periods of time, had developed a definite personality. By some fluke of geography or biology or school administration, ours was a

while about my metaphor—the one Miss Hancock had asked about—and then I decided to push it out of my head.

When I arrived home, I opened the door with my key, entered the front porch, took off my shoes, and read the note on the hall table. It was written in flawless script on a small piece of bond paper. It said: "At a Children's Aid board meeting. Home by 5. Please tidy your room."

The hall table was polished, antique, perfect. It contained one silver salver for messages and a small ebony lamp with a white shade. The floor of the entrance hall was tiled. The black and white tiles shone in the sunlight, unmarked by any sign of human contact. I walked over them carefully, slowly, having slipped and fallen once too often.

Hunger. I went into the kitchen and surveyed it thoughtfully. More black and white tiles dazzled the eye, and the cupboards and walls were a blinding spotless white. The counters shone, empty of jars, leftovers, canisters, appliances. The whole room looked as though it were waiting for the movers to arrive with the furniture and dishes. I made myself a peanut-butter sandwich, washed the knife and plate, and put everything away. Then I went upstairs to my room, walking up the grey stair carpet beside the off-white walls, glancing absently at the single lithograph in its black frame. "My home," I said aloud, "is a box. It is cool and quiet and empty and uninteresting. Nobody lives in the box." Entering my room, I looked around. A few magazines were piled on the floor beside my bed. On my dresser, a T-shirt lay on top of my ivory brush and comb set. Two or three books were scattered over the top of my desk. I picked up the magazines, removed the T-shirt, and put the books back in the bookcase. There. Done.

Then I called Julia Parsons, who was my best friend, and went over to her house to talk about boys. When I returned at six o'clock, my mother, who had been home only one hour, had prepared a complicated three-course meal—expert, delicious, nutritious. "There's food in the box," I mused.

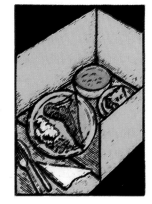

Since no one else had much to say at dinner, I talked about school. I told them about Miss Hancock's lesson on The Metaphor. I said what a marvellous teacher she was, how even the dumbest of us had learned to enjoy writing compositions, how she could make the poetry in our textbook so exciting to read and to hear.

My father listened attentively, enjoying my

enthusiasm. He was not a lively or an original man, but he was an intelligent person who liked to watch eagerness in others. "You're very fortunate, Charlotte," he said, "to find a teacher who can wake you up and make you love literature."

"Is she that brassy Miss Hancock whom I met at the home and school meeting?" asked my mother.

"What do you mean, brassy?"

"Oh. You know. Overdone, too much enthusiasm. Flamboyant. Orange hair. Is she the one?"

"Yes," I said.

"Oh," said my mother, without emphasis of any kind. "Her. Charlotte, would you please remove the dishes and bring in the dessert. Snow pudding. In the fridge, top left-hand side. Thank you."

That night I lay in the bath among the Estée Lauder bubbles (gift from my father on my last birthday) and created metaphors. I loved baths. The only thing nicer than one bath a day was two. Julia said that if I kept taking so many baths, my skin would get dry and crisp, and that I would be wrinkled before I was thirty. That was too far away to worry about. She also said that taking baths was disgusting and that showers were more hygienic. She pointed out that I was soaking in my own dirt, like bathers in the fetid Ganges. I thought this a bit excessive and said so. "For pete's sake!" I exclaimed. "If I have two baths a day, I can't be sitting in very much dirt. Besides, it's *therapeutic*."

"It's *what*?"

"Therapeutic. Water play. I read about it in *Reader's Digest* at the doctor's office. They let kids play with water when they're wild and upset. And now they're using warm baths to soothe the patients in mental hospitals."

"So?"

"So it could be useful if I happen to end up crazy." I laughed. I figured that would stop her. It did.

In the bath I always did a lot of things besides wash. I lifted up mounds of the tiny bubbles and held them against the fluorescent light over the sink. The patterns and shapes were delicate, like minute filaments of finest lace. I poked my toes through the bubbles and waved their hot pinkness to and fro among the static white waves. I hopefully examined my breasts for signs of sudden growth. If I lay down in the tub and brought the bubbles up over my body and squeezed my chest together by pressing my arms inward, I could

convince myself that I was full-breasted and seductive. I did exercises to lengthen my hamstrings, in order to improve my splits for the gymnastics team. I thought about Charles Swinimer. I quoted poetry out loud with excessive feeling and dramatic emphasis, waving my soapy arms around and pressing my eloquent hand against my flat chest. And from now on, I also lay there and made up metaphors, most of them about my mother.

"My mother is a white picket fence—straight, level. The fence stands in a field full of weeds. The field is bounded on all sides by thorny bushes and barbed wire."

"My mother is a lofty mountain capped by virgin snow. The air around the mountain is clear and clean and very cold." I turned on more hot water. "At the base of the mountain grow gnarled and crooked trees, surrounded by scrub brush and poison ivy."

Upon leaving the bath, I would feel no wiser. Then I would clean the tub very carefully indeed. It was necessary.

Not, mind you, that my mother ranted and raved about her cleanliness. Ranting and raving were not part of her style. "I know you will agree," she would say very oh ever so sweetly, implying in some oblique way that I certainly did not agree, "that it is an inconsiderate and really ugly thing to leave a dirty tub." Then she would lead me with a subtle soft-firm pressure into the bathroom so that we might inspect together a bathtub ringed with sludge, sprinkled with hair and dried suds. "Not," she would say quietly, "a very pretty sight."

And what, I would ask myself, is so terrible about that?" Other mothers—I know; I had heard them—nagged, yelled, scolded, did terrible and noisy things. But what was it about my mother's methods that left me feeling so depraved, so unsalvageable?

But of course I was thirteen by now, and knew all about cleaning tubs and wiping off countertops and sweeping up crumbs. A very small child must have been a terrible test to that cool and orderly spirit. I remember those days. A toy ceased to be a toy and began to be a mess the moment it left the toy cupboard. "I'm sure," she would say evenly, "that you don't want to have those blocks all over the carpet. Why not keep them all in one spot, over there behind Daddy's chair?" From time to time I attempted argument.

"But Mother, I'm making a garden."

"Then make a *little* garden. They're every bit as satisfying as large, sprawling unmanageable farms."

And since no one who was a truly nice person would want a large, sprawling unmanageable farm, I would move my blocks behind the chair and make my small garden there. Outside, our backyard was composed of grass and flowers, plus one evergreen tree that dropped neither fuzzy buds in the spring nor ragged leaves in the fall. No swing set made brown spots on that perfect lawn, nor was there a sandbox. Cats were known to use sandboxes as community toilets. Or so my mother told me. I assume she used the term *toilet* (a word not normally part of her vocabulary) instead of washroom, lest there be any confusion as to her meaning.

But in grade 7, you no longer needed a sandbox. My friends marvelled when they came to visit, which was not often. How serene my mother seemed, how lovely to look at, with her dark-blond hair, her flawless figure, her smooth hands. She never acted frazzled or rushed or angry, and her forehead was unmarked by age or worry lines. Her hair always looked as though a hairdresser had arrived at six o'clock to ready her for the day. "Such a peaceful house," my friends would say, clearly impressed, "and no one arguing or fighting." Then they would leave and go somewhere else for their snacks, their music, their hanging around.

No indeed, I thought. No fights in this house. It would be like trying to

down an angel with a BB gun—both sacrilegious and futile. My father, thin and nervous, was careful about hanging up his clothes and keeping his sweaters in neat piles. He certainly did not fight with my mother. In fact, he said very little to her at all. He had probably learned early that to complain is weak, to rejoice is childish, to laugh is noisy. And moving around raises dust.

This civilized, this clean, this disciplined woman who was and is my mother, was also, if one were to believe her admirers, the mainstay of the community, the rock upon which the town was built. She chaired committees, ran bazaars, sat on boards. When I first heard about this, I thought it a very exciting thing that she sat on boards. If my mother, who sat so correctly on the needlepoint chair with her nylon knees pressed so firmly together, could actually sit on *boards*, there might be a rugged and reckless side to her that I had not yet met. The telephone rang constantly, and her softly controlled voice could be heard, hour after hour, arranging and steering and manipulating the affairs of the town.

Perhaps because she juggled her community jobs, her housework, her cooking and her grooming with such quiet, calm efficiency, she felt scorn for those less able to cope. "Mrs. Langstreth says she is too *tired* to take on a table at the bazaar," she might say. It was not hard to imagine Mrs. Langstreth lounging on a sofa, probably in a turquoise chenille dressing gown, surrounded by full ashtrays and neglected children. Or my mother might comment quietly, but with unmistakable emphasis, "Gillian Munroe is having trouble with her children. And in my opinion, she has only herself to blame." The implication seemed to be that if Gillian Munroe's children were left in my mother's care for a few weeks, she could make them all into a perfectly behaved family. Which was probably true.

Certainly in those days I was well behaved. I spoke quietly, never complained, ate whatever was put before me, and obeyed all rules without question or argument. I was probably not even very unhappy, though I enjoyed weekdays much more than weekends. Weekends did not yet include parties or boys. It is true that Julia and I spent a lot of our time together talking

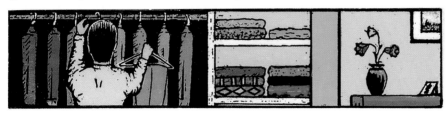

about boys. I also remember stationing myself on the fence of the vacant lot on Seymour Street at five o'clock, the hour when Charles Swinimer could be expected to return from high school. As he passed, I would be too absorbed in my own activity to look at him directly. I would be chipping the bark off the fence, or reading, or pulling petals from a daisy—he loves me, he loves me not. Out of the corner of my eye, I feasted upon his jaw line, his confident walk, his shoulders. On the rare days when he would toss me a careless "Hi" (crumbs to a pigeon), I would have to dig my nails into the wood to keep from falling off, from fainting dead away. But that was the extent of my thrills. No boys had yet materialized in the flesh to offer themselves to me. Whatever else they were looking for, it was not acne, straight, brown stringy hair or measurements of 32-32-32.

So weekdays were still best. Weekdays meant school and particularly English class, where Miss Hancock delivered up feasts of succulent literature for our daily consumption. *Hamlet* was the thing that spring, the spring before we moved into junior high. So were a number of poems that left me weak and changed. And our composition class gathered force, filling us with a creative confidence that was heady stuff. We wrote short stories, played with similes, created poems that did and did not rhyme, felt we were capable of anything and everything; if Shakespeare, if Wordsworth, could do it, why couldn't we? Over it all, Miss Hancock presided, hands fluttering, voice atremble with a raw emotion.

But *Hamlet* dominated our literature classes from April to June. Like all serious students, we agonized and argued over its meaning, Hamlet's true intent, his sanity, his goal. Armed with rulers, we fought the final duel with its bloody sequence, and a four-foot Fortinbras stepped among the dead bodies between the desks to proclaim the ultimate significance of it all. At the end, Miss Hancock stood, hands clasped, knuckles white, tears standing in her eyes. And I cannot pretend that all of ours were dry.

At the close of the year, our class bought an enormous tasteless card of thanks and affixed it to a huge trophy. The trophy was composed of two brass-coloured Ionic pillars that were topped by a near-naked athlete carrying a spiky wreath. On the plate below was inscribed: "For you and Hamlet with love. The grade 7 class. 1965."

When my mother saw it, she came close to losing her cool control.

"Who chose it?" she asked, tight-lipped.

"Horace Hannington," I answered. Oh, don't spoil it, don't spoil it.

"That explains it," she said, and mercifully that was all.

Junior high school passed, and so did innocence and acne. Hair curled, makeup intact, I entered high school the year that Charles Swinimer left for university. But there would be other fish to fry. Outwardly blasé, single-minded, and sixteen, I came into my first grade 10 class with a mixture of intense apprehension and a burning unequivocal belief that high school could and would deliver up to me all of life's most precious gifts—the admiration of my peers, local fame, boys, social triumphs. During August of that year, my family had moved to another school district.

I entered high school with a clean slate. It was terrifying to be so alone. I also knew that it was a rare and precious opportunity; I could approach life without being branded with my old failures, my old drawbacks. I was pretty; I had real curves; I was anonymous; I melted into the crowd. No one here would guess that I had once been such a skinny, pimply wretch.

Our first class was geography, and I knew enough of the material to be able to let my eyes and mind wander. Before the end of the period, I knew that the boy to pursue was Howard Oliver, that the most prominent and therefore the most potentially useful or dangerous girl was Gladys Simpson, that geography was uninteresting, that the teacher was strict. To this day I can smell the classroom during that first period—the dry and acrid smell of chalk, the cool, sweet fragrance of the freshly waxed floors, the perspiration that travelled back to me from Joey Elliot's desk.

The next period was English. My new self-centred and self-conscious sophistication had not blunted my love of literature, my desire to write, to play with words, to express my discoveries and confusions. I awaited the arrival of the teacher with masked but real enthusiasm. I was not prepared for the entrance of Miss Hancock.

Miss Hancock's marked success with fifteen years of grade 7 students had finally transported her to high places. She entered the classroom, wings spread, ready to fly. She was used to success, and she was eager to sample the pleasure of a group of older and more perceptive minds. Clad in royal blue velour, festooned with gold chains, hair glittering in the sun pouring in from the east window, fringed eyes darting, she faced the class, arms raised. She paused.

"Let us pray!" said a deep male voice from the back row. It was Howard Oliver. Laughter exploded in the room. Behind my Duo Tang folder, I snickered fiercely.

Miss Hancock's hands fluttered wildly. It was as though she were waving off an invasion of poisonous flies.

"Now, now, class!" she exclaimed with a mixture of tense jollity and clear panic. "We'll have none of *that*! Please turn to page seven in your textbook. I'll read the selection aloud to you first, and then we'll discuss it." She held the book high in the palm of one hand; the other was raised like an admonition, an artistic beckoning.

The reading was from Tennyson's "Ulysses." I had never heard it before. As I listened to her beautiful voice, the old magic took hold, and no amount of peer pressure could keep me from thrilling to the first four lines she read:

> *"I am a part of all that I have met;*
> *Yet all experience is an arch wherethro'*
> *Gleams that untravell'd world, whose margin fades*
> *For ever and for ever when I move."*

But after that, it was difficult even to hear her. Guffaws sprang up here and there throughout the room. Gladys Simpson whispered something behind her hand to the girl beside her and then broke into fits of giggles. Paper airplanes flew. The wits of grade 10 offered comments: "Behold the Bard!" "Bliss! Oh, poetic bliss!" "Hancock! Whocock? Hancock! Hurray!" "Don't faint, class! *Don't faint!*"

I was caught in a stranglehold somewhere between shocked embarrassment and a terrible desire for concealment. No other members of the class shared my knowledge of Miss Hancock or my misery. But I knew I could not hide behind that Duo Tang folder forever.

It was in fact ten days later when Miss Hancock recognized me. It could not have been easy to connect the eager skinny fan of grade 7 with the cool and careful person I had become. And she would not have expected to find a friend in that particular classroom. By then, stripped of fifteen years of overblown confidence, she offered her material shyly, hesitantly, certain of rejection, of humiliation. When our eyes met in class, she did not rush up to me to claim alliance or allegiance. Her eyes merely held mine for a moment, slid off, and then periodically slid back. There was a desperate hope in them that I could hardly bear to witness. At the end of the period, I waited until everyone had gone before I walked toward her desk on the way to the corridor. Whatever was going to happen, I wanted to be sure that it would not be witnessed.

When I reached her, she was sitting quietly, hands folded on top of her lesson book. I was reminded of another day, another meeting. The details were blurred; but I knew I had seen this Miss Hancock before. She looked at me evenly and said quietly, simply, "Hello, Charlotte. How nice to see you."

I looked at her hands, the floor, the blackboard, anywhere but at those searching eyes. "Hello, Miss Hancock," I said.

"Still writing metaphors?" she asked with a tentative smile.

"Oh, I dunno," I replied. But I was. Nightly, in the bathtub. And I kept a notebook in which I wrote them all down.

"Your writing showed promise, Charlotte." Her eyes were quiet, pleading. "I hope you won't forget that."

Or anything else, I thought. Oh, Miss Hancock, let me go. Aloud I said, "French is next, and I'm late."

She looked directly into my eyes and held them for a moment. Then she spoke. "Go ahead, Charlotte. Don't let me keep you."

She did not try to reach me again. She taught, or tried to teach her classes, as though I were not there. Week after week, she entered the room white with tension and left it defeated. I did not tell a living soul that I had ever seen her before.

One late afternoon in March of that year, Miss Hancock stepped off the curb in front of the school and was killed instantly by a school bus.

The next day, I was offered this piece of news with that mixture of horror and delight that so often attends the delivery of terrible tidings. When I heard it, I felt as though my chest and throat were constricted by bands of dry ice. During assembly, the principal came forward and delivered a short announcement of the tragedy, peppered with little complimentary phrases: "... a teacher of distinction ..." "... a generous colleague ..." "... a tragic end to a promising career ..." Howard Oliver was sitting beside me; he had been showing me flattering attention of late. As we got up to disperse for classes, he said, "Poor old Whocock Hancock. Quoting poetry to the angels by now." He was no more surprised than I was when I slapped him full across his handsome face, before I ran down the aisle of the assembly room, up the long corridor of the first floor, down the steps, and out into the parking lot. Shaking with dry, unsatisfying sobs, I hurried home through the back streets of the town and let myself in by the back door.

"What on earth is wrong, Charlotte?" asked my mother when she saw my stricken look, my heaving shoulders. There was real concern in her face.

"Miss Hancock is dead," I whispered.

"Miss *who*? Charlotte, speak up please."

"Miss Hancock. She teaches—*taught*—us grade 10 English."

"You mean that same brassy creature from grade 7?"

I didn't answer. I was crying out loud, with the abandon of a preschooler or someone who is under the influence of drugs.

"Charlotte, do please blow your nose and try to get hold of yourself. I can't for the life of me see why you're so upset. You never even told us she was your teacher this year."

I was rocking back and forth on the kitchen chair, arms folded over my chest. My mother stood there erect, invulnerable. It crossed my mind that no grade 10 class would throw paper airplanes in any group that *she* chose to teach.

"Well, then," she said, "why or how did she die?"

I heard myself shriek, "I killed her! I killed her!"

Halting, gasping, I told her all of it. I described her discipline problems, the cruelty of the students, my own blatant betrayal.

"For goodness' sake, Charlotte," said my mother, quiet but clearly irritated, "don't lose perspective. She couldn't keep order, and she had only herself to blame." That phrase sounded familiar to me. "A woman like that can't survive for five minutes in the high schools of today. There was nothing you could have done."

I was silent. I could have *said something*. Like thank you for grade 7. Or yes, I still have fun with The Metaphor. Or once, just once in this entire year, I could have *smiled* at her.

My mother was speaking again. "There's a great deal of ice. It would be very easy to slip under a school bus. And she didn't strike me as the sort of person who would exercise any kind of sensible caution."

"Oh, dear God," I was whispering, "I wish she hadn't chosen a *school bus*."

I cried some more that day and excused myself from supper. I heard my father say, "I think I'll just go up and see if I can help." But my mother said, "Leave her alone, Arthur. She's sixteen years old. It's time she learned how to cope. She's acting like a hysterical child." My father did not appear. Betrayal, I thought, runs in the family.

The next day I stayed home from school. I kept having periods of uncontrollable weeping, and even my mother could not send me off in that condition. Once again I repeated to her, to my father, "I killed her. We all killed her. But especially me."

"Charlotte."

Oh, I knew that voice, that tone. So calm, so quiet, so able to silence me with one word. I stopped crying and curled up in a tight ball on the sofa.

"Charlotte. I know you will agree with what I'm going to say to you. There is no need to speak so extravagantly. A sure and perfect control is what separates the civilized from the uncivilized." She inspected her fingernails, pushing down the quick of her middle finger with her thumb. "If you would examine this whole perfectly natural situation with a modicum of rationality, you would see that she got exactly what she deserved."

I stared at her.

"Charlotte," she continued, "I'll have to ask you to stop this nonsense. You're disturbing the even tenor of our home."

I said nothing. With a sure and perfect control, I uncoiled myself from my fetal position on the sofa. I stood up and left the living room.

Upstairs in my bedroom I sat down before my desk. I took my pen out of the drawer and opened my notebook. Extravagantly, without a modicum of rationality, I began to write.

"Miss Hancock was a birthday cake," I wrote. "This cake was frosted by someone unschooled in the art of cake decoration. It was adorned with a profusion of white roses and lime-green leaves, which drooped and dribbled at the edges where the pastry tube had slipped. The frosting was of an intense peppermint flavour, too sweet, too strong. Inside, the cake had two layers—chocolate and vanilla. The chocolate was rich and soft and very delicious. No one who stopped to taste it could have failed to enjoy it. The vanilla was subtle and delicate; only those thoroughly familiar with cakes, only those with great sensitivity of taste, could have perceived its true fine flavour. Because it was a birthday cake, it was filled with party favours. If you stayed long enough at the party, you could amass quite a large collection of these treasures. If you kept them for many years, they would amaze you by turning into pure gold. Most children would have been delighted by this cake. Most grown-ups would have thrown it away after one brief glance at the frosting.

"I wish that the party wasn't over."

A New World

Yvonne Chang

On January 23, 1990, my family and I waved goodbye to relatives, and friends at Taiwan's national airport. We weren't rich people, but my parents always tried their best to give us the best education and environment they could provide. After hours of flight, the plane finally landed at Pearson International Airport. My younger brother and I were both very excited. After another hour of interviewing we were finally out. The sky and atmosphere didn't seem to be any different from back home, but the weather was extremely cold.

We lived at a friend's house for a week and soon moved into an apartment. At that time, we only knew one family in the whole wide Canada! The first few weeks we were occupied with forms to fill, offices to register at, and places to know (where to buy food). We soon learned the way Canadians work was quite different from our ways. They have a fast living style; everything had to work instantly and effectively. You must make an appointment before you see doctors. Teachers won't stay after school if you don't have appointments with them. Computers aren't always available; you must book in if you wish to use one. I was glad that we didn't have to book in the food we wanted a day before in the cafeteria!

I was excited, anxious, scared, and shy on my first day of school. Canada wasn't totally new to me. My parents had been talking about it for the past two years. In my ideas, Canada not only had fresh air, open lands, but would also be filled with Whites and some Blacks. But I was wrong on the last idea. The minute I got into school, I saw a variety of skin, hair, and eye colours. I also saw a few people wearing special dresses that were different from others. I could see many oriental faces, too. Seeing those familiar faces made me relax.

A few days later, I began to realize that my school is filled with immigrants, and many people didn't speak fluent English. That took "scary" off my shoulder. I became daring and talked to people with my limited English. Although we didn't understand each other too well, we could always use body language and always have fun. But that is only with people who were in the same situation as I was. I found it hard to go into the real Canadian world. Language wasn't such a problem, but culture was. We have such different cultural baggage. The way we dress, the shows we watch, the food we eat, the books we read, the things we talk about, the way we think, and the jokes we play. We tried to be friendly and talk to each other, but the conversation often couldn't carry long.

I had always been in a girl's school in Taiwan. It feels so different to have boys in my classes. I didn't dare to talk to them, because I thought they would think that I was interested in them. But it didn't take me long to figure out that that wasn't the case at all!

Usually, people get into groups of the same country they came from. I remembered saying to myself, "I won't do that; I will try very hard to make friends with everyone," but I found out that there were many "natural walls" between us. Language was the first wall.

The fast life style which gave us just enough time to say "hi" and "bye" in the hallway was the second wall. The things we liked to talk about were sometimes quite different. That was the third wall. Walls were hard to break through and bridges were hard to build.

At first it was hard for me to understand what the teachers were talking about, especially those humorous teachers, because I almost never understood their jokes. I often am very quiet in classes. In Taiwan, students are expected to be very obedient, so in Canada, I never knew when we could cut in and give a little joke. I was afraid of asking questions because I was afraid that I may seem silly and I might waste the class time. And that is not like me at all. In Taiwan, I was notorious among classmates and friends for talking and never stopping. And I was also notorious for asking questions. But now I am only like myself when I'm in my E.S.L. class. I feel comfortable and at home in the class. My teacher says that she had always thought of Chinese being quiet and meek, and she never met someone who talks and asks as many questions as I do. Well, how can it not be since I've saved all my questions and energy for this class?

In Taiwan, we always wore uniforms to school, and I was quite excited

when I knew we could wear whatever we liked in Canada. But now it becomes a problem. I can't think how I could survive without a full length mirror in my room. I must get up early every morning to decide what to wear.

As time goes on, I learn the Canadian culture bit by bit. The more you know about something, the more easily you can become part of it. I've always admired Alexander the Great and his hope of getting the world into one. I think Canada is the perfect place to establish that hope, and I've always believed that together we're better.

Grandmother

Douglas Nepinak

in her dreams there is no television
speaking incessantly in a foreign language
of grand magnificent things
beyond her means

in her dreams everyone speaks Anishinabe
there is no confusion
no lapses into english
her grandchildren are not silent to her

the world is whole to her again
she walks through the bush collecting berries   roots
and stories off the great tree with a firm shake
the wind smells of seasons to come
they are good   full

Dances with History

Nathan Lee Chasing His Horse

My Indian name is Brown Eagle, the spiritual name I was given from my grandfather on my father's side, whose name was also Brown Eagle. He gave it to me in a ceremony called the Name-Giving Ceremony, which is a ritual performed when a child receives a spiritual name or Indian name. My legal name is Nathan Lee Chasing His Horse. Nathan Lee was given to me by my mother, and Chasing His Horse is the name I inherited from my father, Joseph Chasing His Horse. My movie name is Smiles A Lot.

Over a year ago my father and I went to Sinte Gleska, the Spotted Tail College, which is located on the Rosebud Indian Reservation in the state of South Dakota, where I live. He was doing research on Lakota treaty rights. Being interested in our history, I went along with him, not knowing an audition was taking place there for the part of Smiles a Lot in the movie *Dances With Wolves*. The chance to do a lot of horseback riding and archery interested me; to speak the Lakota language interested me most of all. The casting director especially wanted to see those of us with long hair. My tradition believes hair connects us to our spirit. My mother always took care of my hair, since I was a baby. It has never been cut in my life.

I have been very proud to do a part in a movie, especially with Kevin Costner. A good friend of mine, he put a smile on his face even when things got hard. I sure admire him. I know now acting has not only glamour and luxury.

I experienced a lot of hard work for a three-hour film and enjoyed making new friends, Indian and non-Indian. We all worked together as one big family. The movie had a lot of emotional parts, or maybe I should say mixed emotions because it addressed things about my culture and my people.

The way we were portrayed in *Dances* is real. It's the opposite of the old Hollywood stereotype of showing Indians as ignorant or savages (like the old John Wayne movies when he'd single-handedly defeat a bunch of Indians, or when they'd use non-Indians to play Indian roles). That was all unreal. The Lakota, one of three divisions of the Sioux, were a family of people with great respect for one another and nature. Very strong, humble, and wise, they fought and died courageously to defend their freedom and the sacred Black Hills—mountains on the South Dakota prairie—a fight that continues to this very day in the courts of the United States. (The land claims that have been ignored by Congress are now being reviewed by the United Nations.)

The experience of working on the movie made me even more proud to be what and who I am. I'm sixteen years old and a member of the Rosebud Sioux Tribe of the Great Sioux Nation, born in April on the twenty-eighth on the Rosebud Indian Reservation. I live with my parents, two sisters, and one brother. I am a descendant of the great Sioux chief Crazy Horse and many other great leaders of the Sioux. I am a sophomore at White River High School in South Dakota. My favorite sport is basketball.

I was raised learning the traditional ways of my people by the teachings of my father. I've always had a goal in life to follow my father's footsteps. He is a spiritual leader among my people and conducts the Seven Rites, or Seven Sacred Ceremonies, of the Lakota, which were brought to us thousands of years ago by a sacred being called the White Buffalo Calf Woman. The meaning of these ceremonies is that if one lives a full and happy life in this world, he will experience these seven phases of teachings in life: the Name-Giving Ceremony, Sweatlodge, Healing, Making-of-Relatives, Seeking-a-Vision, Marriage, and the Sundance Ceremony. They are conducted with utmost respect.

In the Sweatlodge Ceremony, a lodge or hut is built with willow sticks. Buffalo hides are tied over the sticks to form a dome shape, and a door is made to the west. Then about twenty-four circular stones are heated in a fire six feet from the door; when the stones are glowing hot, they are taken into the center of the lodge. Those who participate sit in a circle around the hot stones. The door is closed and water is poured on the hot stones, creating steam that causes the participants to perspire, which we believe purifies the body physically, mentally, and spiritually. Then the participants wipe themselves with sage, drink water, and pray and sing ancient songs. I've learned many things from the teachings of our ancient ceremonies: the Four Sacred Directions (west, north, east, south), which mean Four Sacred Virtues (honesty, humility, courage, and generosity); and the Four Phases of Life (childhood, youth, adulthood, and old age), taught through songs and example.

I've also learned that there were a lot of things that were outlawed in my culture. The Indian Religious Freedom Act wasn't passed until 1978. Last year a law was finally passed allowing our Lakota language to be taught in the schools.

I took part in the Reconciliation Ceremony they had at Crazy Horse Monument between whites and Indians of South Dakota. The governor of the state of South Dakota proclaimed 1990 as the Year of Reconciliation between Indians and whites. Both groups planned workshops and gatherings in order to better understand one another's culture and to counter racism. I led the singing of the Sacred Songs: the Filling-of-the-Pipe Song, the Four-Directions Song, and the Tree Song. The Filling-of-the-Pipe Song is sung while a medicine man fills the sacred pipe with tobacco to be smoked among the leaders of both races, and they all pray together. The Four-Directions Song is an ancient prayer sung toward all the Four Directions, beginning with the west. The Tree-Song sings of the tree of life and how all races are a part of the creation or nature.

It has been a big experience for me to be in a motion picture such as *Dances With Wolves*. Hardly any Indian children have the opportunity I've had. The money for education does not meet the needs of Indian children. Shannon County where many of the Indian actors in *Dances* live, is the second-poorest county in the nation. The high school dropout rate is 54 percent, higher than the national average. The life expectancy of Indian people is far below the national average; the suicide rate is triple. Unemployment and a lack of economic development hold my people in poverty. Alcohol and drug abuse is at an all-time high on my reservation.

The way I see alcohol and drugs is a pretending-to-be-happy thing for a lot of my friends and relatives, for the Lakota people. I was told by my grandpa that the Lakota people never had things like drugs and alcohol a long time ago. The white man brought it to the Lakota, and now the people use it to escape from problems; they depend on it. Maybe they do feel good for a while, but the problems are still there. There are a lot of young people my age who are into these things, too. I guess it's everywhere in this world, and it makes me sad and mad.

To the youth, let's continue our education and be a good example for the next generation without drugs and alcohol. It can be done. I was taught to learn who you were, who you are, and who you're going to be. For me, I'm learning my culture, and I believe in it. Let's prove things can work without the stuff. Our thoughts are as high as the eagle flies.

The Sleeper

Edward Field

When I was the sissy of the block who nobody wanted
on their team
Sonny Hugg persisted in believing that my small size
was an asset
Not the liability and curse I felt it was
And he saw a use for my swift feet with which I ran
away from fights.

He kept putting me into complicated football plays
Which would have been spectacular if they worked:
For instance, me getting clear in front and him
shooting the ball over—
Or the sensation of the block, the Sleeper Play
In which I would lie down on the sidelines near the
goal
As though resting and out of action, until the
scrimmage began
And I would step onto the field, receive the long
throw
And to the astonishment of all the tough guys in the
world
Step over the goal line for a touchdown.

That was the theory anyway. In practice
I had the fatal flaw of not being able to catch
And usually had my fingers bend back and the
breath knocked out of me
So the plays always failed, but Sonny kept on trying
Until he grew up out of my world into the glamorous
Varsity crowd, the popular kids of Lynbrook High.

But I will always have this to thank him for:
That when I look back on childhood
(That four psychiatrists haven't been able to help me
bear the thought of)
There is not much to be glad for
Besides his foolish and delicious faith
That, with all my oddities, there was a place in the
world for me
If only he could find the special role.

The Camel Dances

Arnold Lobel

The Camel had her heart set on becoming a ballet dancer.

"To make every movement a thing of grace and beauty," said the Camel. "This is my one and only desire."

Again and again she practiced her pirouettes, her relevés and her arabesques. She repeated the five basic positions a hundred times each day. She worked for long months under the hot desert sun. Her feet were blistered, and her body ached with fatigue, but not once did she think of stopping.

At last the Camel said, "Now I am a dancer." She announced a recital and danced before an invited group of camel friends and critics. When her dance was over, she made a deep bow.

There was no applause.

"I must tell you frankly," said a member of the audience, "as a critic and spokesman for this group, that you are lumpy and humpy. You are baggy and bumpy. You are, like the rest of us, simply a camel. You are not and never will be a ballet dancer!"

Chuckling and laughing, the audience moved away across the sand.

"How very wrong they are!" said the Camel. "I have worked hard. There can be no doubt that I am a splendid dancer. I will dance and dance just for myself."

That is what she did. It gave her many years of pleasure.

MORAL: Satisfaction will come to those who please themselves.

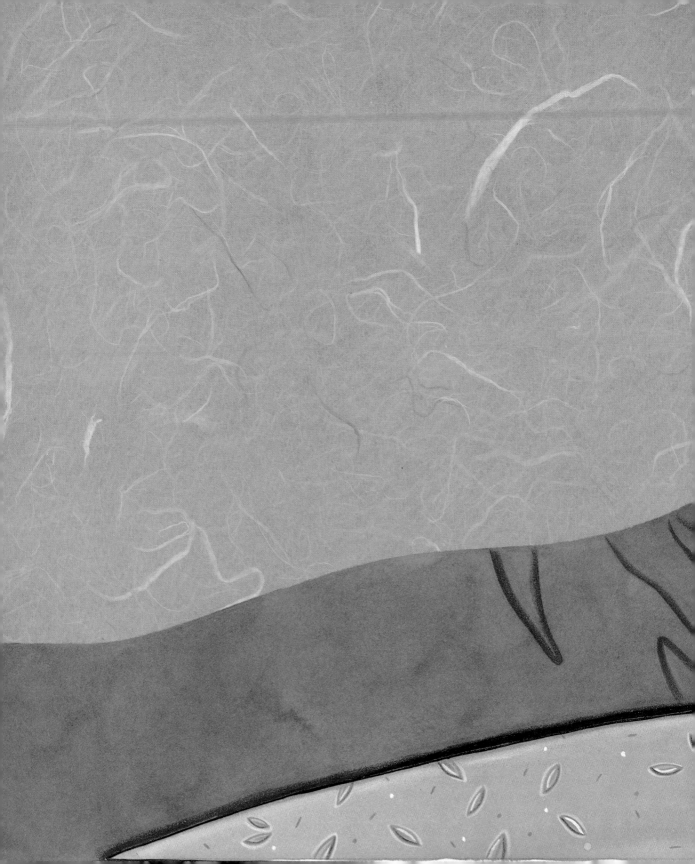

Side by Side

As It Is with Strangers

Susan Beth Pfeffer

For S.

It wasn't until right before I went to bed on Thursday that Mom bothered to tell me the son she'd given up for adoption twenty years earlier was coming over for supper the next day.

"What son?" I asked.

"I'm sure I've told you about him," Mom said. "You must have forgotten."

I figured I probably had. I'm always forgetting little things like my home-work assignments and being elected President of the United States. Having an older brother must have just slipped my mind. "How'd you two find each other?" I asked. Presumably Mom had never told me that.

"I registered with an agency," she said. "Put my name and address in a book, so if he ever wanted to find me, he could. I guess he did. Don't be late for supper tomorrow."

"I won't be," I promised. This was one reunion I had no intention of missing.

School the next day really dragged on. School never goes fast on Fridays, but when your mind is on some newly acquired half brother, it's real hard to care about Julius Caesar. I didn't tell anybody, though. It seemed to me it was Mom's story, not mine, and besides, my friends all think she's crazy anyway. Probably from things I've said over the years.

I went straight home from school, and was surprised, first to find the place spotless, and then to see Mom in the kitchen cooking away.

"I took a sick day," she informed me. "So I could prepare better."

"Everything looks great," I told her. It was true. I hadn't seen the place look so good since Great-Aunt Trudy came with the goat, but that's another story. "You look very pretty too."

"I got my nails done," Mom said, showing them off for me. They were coral colored. "And my hair."

I nodded. Mom had taught me that nothing was unbearable if your hair looked nice.

"Is that what you're planning to wear tonight?" she asked.

"I thought I'd shower and change into my dress," I said. I own a grand total of one dress, but this seemed to be the right kind of occasion for it.

Mom gave me a smile like I'd just been canonized. "Thank you," she said. "Tonight's kind of important for me."

I nodded. I wasn't sure just what to say anymore. Mom and I have been alone for eight years, and you'd figure by now I'd know how to handle her under any circumstances, but this one had me stumped. "What's for supper?" I finally asked.

"Southern fried chicken," Mom said. "At first I thought I'd make a roast, but then what if he doesn't like his meat rare? And turkey seemed too Thanksgivingish, if you know what I mean. Everybody likes fried chicken. And I made mashed potatoes and biscuits and a spinach salad."

"Spinach salad?" I asked. I could picture Mom pouring the spinach out of a can and dousing it with Wishbone.

"From scratch," Mom informed me. "Everything's from scratch. And I baked an apple pie too. The ice cream is store bought, but I got one of those expensive brands. What do you think?"

I thought that there obviously was something to that Prodigal Son story, since Mom never made anything more elaborate for me than scrambled eggs. "It smells great," I said. It did, too, the way you picture a house in a commercial smelling, all homey and warm. "I'm sure everything will go fine."

"I want it to," Mom said, as though I'd suggested that maybe she didn't.

There were a few things I knew I'd better clear up before Big Brother showed up. "What's his name?" I asked, for starters.

"Jack," Mom said. "That's not what I would have named him. I would have named him Ronald."

"You would have?" I asked. I personally am named Tiffany, and Ronald would not have been my first guess.

"That was my boyfriend's name," Mom said. "Ronny."

"Your boyfriend," I said. "You mean his father?"

Mom nodded. "You think of them as boyfriends, not fathers, when you're sixteen," she said.

Well that answered question number two. It had seemed unlikely to me that my father was responsible, but who knew? I wasn't there. Maybe he and Mom had decided they wanted a girl, and chucked out any boys that came along first.

Speaking of which. "There aren't any other brothers I've forgotten about?" I asked. "Is this going to be the first of many such dinners?"

"Jack's the only one," Mom replied. "I wanted to keep him, but Ronny wasn't about to get married, and Dad said if I gave him up for adoption then I could still go to college. I did the right thing, for him and for me. And I would have gone to college if I hadn't met your father. I don't know. Maybe because I gave up the baby, I was too eager to get married. I never really thought about it."

"Did Dad know?" I asked.

"I told him," Mom said. "He said it didn't matter to him. And it didn't. Whatever else was wrong in our marriage, he never threw the baby in my face."

I found myself picturing a baby being thrown in Mom's face, and decided I should take my shower fast. So I sniffed the kitchen appreciatively and scurried out. In the shower I tried to imagine what this Jack would look like, but he kept resembling Dad's high-school graduation picture, which made no sense biologically at all. So I stopped imagining.

When I went to my bedroom to change, though, I was really shocked. Mom had extended her cleaning ways to include my room. All my carefully laid out messes were gone. It would probably take me months to reassemble things. I considered screaming at Mom about the sanctity of one's bedroom, but I decided against it. Mom obviously wanted this guy to think she and I were the perfect American family, and if that meant even my room had to be clean, then nothing was going to stop her. I could live with it, at least for the evening.

Mom and I set the table three times before the doorbell finally rang. When it did, neither one of us knew who should answer it, but Mom finally opened the door. "Hello," this guy said. "I'm Jack."

"I'm Linda," Mom replied. "Come on in. It's nice to . . . well, it's good seeing you."

"Good to see you too," Jack said. He didn't look anything like my father.

"This is Tiffany," Mom said. "She, uh . . ."

"Her daughter," I said. "Your sister." I mean, those words were going to be used at some point during the evening. We might as well get them out of the way fast. Then when we got around to the big tricky words like *mother* and *son*, at least some groundwork would have been laid.

"It's nice to meet you," Jack said, and he gave me his hand to shake, so I shook it. They say you can tell a lot about a man from his handshake, but not when he's your long-lost brother. "I hope my coming like this isn't any kind of a brother. I mean bother."

"Not at all," Mom said. "I'm going to check on dinner. Tiffany, why don't you show Jack the living room? I'll join you in a moment."

"This is the living room," I said, which was pretty easy to show Jack, since we were already standing in it. "Want to sit down?"

"Yeah, sure," Jack said. "Have you lived here long?"

"Since the divorce," I said. "Eight years ago."

"That long," Jack said. "Where's your father?"

"He lives in Oak Ridge," I said. "That's a couple of hundred miles from here. I see him sometimes."

"Is he . . ." Jack began. "I mean, I don't suppose you'd know . . ."

"Is he your father too?" I said. "No. I kind of asked. Your father's name is Ronny. My father's name is Mike. I don't know much else about your father except he didn't want to marry Mom. They were both teenagers, I guess. Do you want to meet him too?"

"Sometime," Jack said. "Not tonight."

I could sure understand that one. "I've always wanted to have a big brother," I told him. "I always had crushes on my friends' big brothers. Did you want that—to have a kid sister, I mean?"

"I have one," Jack said. "No, I guess now I have two. I have a sister back home. Her name is Leigh Ann. She's adopted too. She's Korean."

"Oh," I said. "That's nice. I guess there isn't much of a family resemblance, then."

"Not much," Jack said, but he smiled. "She's twelve. How old are you?"

"Fifteen," I said. "Do you go to college?"

Jack nodded. "I'm a sophomore at Bucknell," he said. "Do you think you'll go to college?"

"I'd like to," I said. "I don't know if we'll have the money, though."

"It's rough," Jack said. "College costs a lot these days. My father's always griping about it. He owns a car dealership. New and used. I work there summers. My mom's a housewife."

I wanted to tell him how hard Mom had worked on supper, how messy the apartment usually was, how I never wore a dress, and Mom's nails were always a deep sinful scarlet. I wanted to tell him that maybe someday I'd be jealous that he'd been given away to a family that could afford to send him to college, but that it was too soon for me to feel much of anything about him. There was a lot I wanted to say, but I didn't say any of it.

"What's she like?" Jack asked me, and he gestured toward the kitchen, as though I might not otherwise know who he was talking about.

"Mom?" I said. "She's terrible. She drinks and she gambles and she beats me black and blue if I even think something wrong."

Jack looked horrified. I realized he had definitely not inherited Mom's sense of humor.

"I'm only kidding," I said. "I haven't even been spanked since I was five. She's fine. She's a good mother. It must have really hurt her to give you away like that."

"Have you known long?" Jack asked. "About me?"

"Not until recently," I said. It didn't seem right to tell him I'd learned less than twenty-four hours before. "I guess Mom was waiting until I was old enough to understand."

"I always knew I was adopted," Jack said. "And for years I've wanted to meet my biological parents. To see what they looked like. I love Mom and Dad, you understand. But I felt this need."

"I can imagine," I said, and I could too. I was starting to develop a real need to see what Jack's parents looked like, and we weren't even related.

"Tiffany, could you come in here for a minute?" Mom called from the kitchen.

"Coming, Mom," I said, and left the living room fast. It takes a lot out of you making small talk with a brother.

"What do you think?" Mom whispered as soon as she saw me. "Does he look like me?"

"He has your eyes," I said. "And I think he has your old hair color."

"I know," Mom said, patting her bottle red hair. "I almost asked them to dye me back to my original shade, but I wasn't sure I could remember it anymore. Do you like him? Does he seem nice?"

"Very nice," I said. "Very good manners."

"He sure didn't inherit those from Ronny," Mom declared. "Come on, let's start taking the food out."

So we did. We carried out platters of chicken and mashed potatoes and biscuits and salad. Jack came to the table as soon as he saw what we were doing.

"Oh, no," he said. "I mean, I'm sorry. I should have told you. I'm a vegetarian."

"You are?" Mom said. She looked as shocked as if he'd told her he was a vampire. Meat is very important to Mom. "You're not sick or anything, are you?"

"No, it's for moral reasons," Jack said. "It drives my mom, my mother, her name's Cathy, it drives Cathy crazy."

"Your mom," my mom said. "It would drive me crazy, too, if Tiffany stopped eating meat just for moral reasons."

"Don't worry about it," I told her. "I'll never be that moral."

"There's plenty for me to eat," Jack said. "Potatoes and biscuits and salad."

"The salad has bacon in it," Mom said. "I crumbled bacon in it."

"We can wash the bacon off, can't we Jack?" I said. "You'll eat it if we wash the bacon off, won't you?"

I thought he hesitated for a moment, but then he said, "Of course I can," and for the first time since we'd met, I kind of liked him. I took the salad into the kitchen and washed it all. The salad dressing went the way of the bacon, but we weren't about to complain. At least there'd be something green on Jack's plate. All his other food was gray-white.

Mom hardly ate her chicken, which I figured was out of deference to the

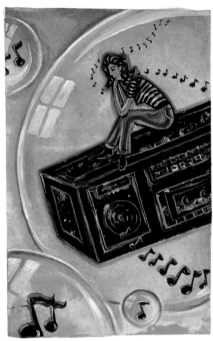

vegetarian, but I had two and a half pieces, figuring it might be years before Mom made it again. Jack ate more potatoes than I'd ever seen another human being eat. No gravy, but lots of potatoes. We talked polite stuff during dinner, what he was studying in college, where Mom worked, the adjustments Leigh Ann had had to make. The real things could only be discussed one on one, so after the pie and ice cream, I excused myself and went to Mom's room to watch TV. Only I couldn't make my eyes focus, so I crossed the hall to my room, and recreated my messes. Once I had everything in proper order, though, I put things back the way Mom had had them. I could hear them talking while I moved piles around, and then I turned on my radio, so I couldn't even hear the occasional stray word, like *father* and *high school* and *lawyer*. That was a trick I'd learned years ago, when Mom and Dad were in their fighting stage. The radio played a lot of old songs that night. It made me feel like I was seven all over again.

After a while Mom knocked on my door and said Jack was leaving, so I went to the living room and shook hands with him again. I still couldn't tell anything about his personality from his handshake, but he did have good manners, and he gave me a little pecking kiss on my cheek, which I thought was sweet of him. Mom kept the door open, and watched as he walked the length of the corridor to the stairs. She didn't close the door until he'd gotten into a car, his I assumed. Maybe it was a loaner from his father.

"You give away a baby," Mom said, "and twenty years later he turns up on your doorstep a vegetarian."

"He turns up a turnip," I said.

But Mom wasn't in the mood for those kinds of jokes. "Don't you ever make that mistake," she said.

"What mistake?" I asked, afraid she meant making jokes. If I couldn't make jokes with Mom, I wouldn't know how to talk with her.

"Don't you ever give up something so important to you that it breathes when you do," Mom said. "It doesn't have to be a kid. It can be a dream, an ambition, or a marriage, or a house. It can be anything you care about as deeply as you care about your own life. Don't ever just give it away, because you'll spend the rest of your life wondering about it, or pretending you don't wonder, which is the same thing, and you'll wake up one morning and realize it truly is gone and a big part of you is gone with it. Do you hear me, Tiffany?"

"I hear you," I said. I'd never seen Mom so intense, and I didn't like being around her. "I'm kind of tired now, Mom. Would you mind if I went to bed early?"

"I'll clean up tomorrow," Mom said. "You can go to bed."

So I did. I left her sitting in the living room and went to my bedroom and closed my door. But this time I didn't turn the radio on, and later, when I'd been lying on my bed for hours, not able to sleep, I could hear her in her room crying. I'd heard her cry in her room a hundred times before, and a hundred times before I'd gotten up and comforted her, and I knew she'd cry a hundred times again, and I'd comfort her then, too, but that night I just stayed in my room, on my bed, staring at the ceiling and listening to her cry. I think I did the right thing, not going in there. That's how it is with strangers. You can never really comfort them.

To a Sad Daughter

Michael Ondaatje

All night long the hockey pictures
gaze down at you
sleeping in your tracksuit.
Belligerent goalies are your ideal.
Threats of being traded
cuts and wounds
—all this pleases you.
O my god! you say at breakfast
reading the sports page over the Alpen
as another player breaks his ankle
or assaults the coach.

When I thought of daughters
I wasn't expecting this
but I like this more.
I like all your faults
even your purple moods
when you retreat from everyone
to sit in bed under a quilt.
And when I say 'like'
I mean of course 'love'
but that embarrasses you.
You who feel superior to black and
    white movies
(coaxed for hours to see *Casablanca*)
though you were moved
by *Creature from the Black Lagoon*.

One day I'll come swimming
beside your ship or someone will
and if you hear the siren
listen to it. For if you close your ears
only nothing happens. You will
    never change.

I don't care if you risk
your life to angry goalies
creatures with webbed feet.
You can enter their caves and castles
their glass laboratories. Just
don't be fooled by anyone but yourself.

This is the first lecture I've given you.
You're 'sweet sixteen' you said.
I'd rather be your closest friend
than your father. I'm not good at advice
you know that, but ride
the ceremonies
until they grow dark.

Sometimes you are so busy
discovering your friends
I ache with a loss
—but that is greed.

And sometimes I've gone
into *my* purple world
and lost you.

One afternoon I stepped
into your room. You were sitting
at the desk where I now write this.
Forsythia outside the window
and sun spilled over you
like a thick yellow miracle
as if another planet
was coaxing you out of the house
—all those possible worlds!—
and you, meanwhile, busy with
    mathematics.

I cannot look at forsythia now
without loss, or joy for you.
You step delicately
into the wild world
and your real prize will be

the frantic search.
Want everything. If you break
break going out not in.
How you live your life I don't care
but I'll sell my arms for you,
hold your secrets forever.

If I speak of death
which you fear now, greatly,
it is without answers,
except that each
one we know is
in our blood.
Don't recall graves.
Memory is permanent.
Remember the afternoon's
yellow suburban annunciation.
Your goalie
in his frightening mask
dream perhaps
of gentleness.

The Open Window

Saki

"My Aunt will be down presently, Mr. Nuttel," said a very self-possessed young lady of fifteen; "in the meantime you must try and put up with me."

Framton Nuttel endeavoured to say the correct something which should duly flatter the niece of the moment without unduly discounting the aunt that was to come. Privately he doubted more than ever whether these formal visits on a succession of total strangers would do much towards helping the nerve cure which he was supposed to be undergoing.

"I know how it will be," his sister had said when he was preparing to migrate to this rural retreat; "you will bury yourself down there and not speak to a living soul, and your nerves will be worse than ever from moping. I shall just give you letters of introduction to all the people I know there. Some of them, as far as I can remember, were quite nice."

Framton wondered whether Mrs. Sappleton, the lady to whom he was presenting one of the letters of introduction, came into the nice division.

"Do you know many of the people round here?" asked the niece, when she judged that they had had sufficient silent communion.

"Hardly a soul," said Framton. "My sister was staying here, at the rectory, you know, some four years ago, and she gave me letters of introduction to some of the people here."

He made the last statement in a tone of distinct regret.

"Then you know practically nothing about my aunt?" pursued the self-possessed young lady.

"Only her name and address," admitted the caller. He was wondering whether Mrs. Sappleton was in the married or widowed state. An undefinable something about the room seemed to suggest masculine habitation.

"Her great tragedy happened just three years ago," said the child; "that would be since your sister's time."

"Her tragedy?" asked Framton; somehow in this restful country spot tragedies seemed out of place.

"You may wonder why we keep that window wide open on an October afternoon," said the niece, indicating a large french window that opened on to a lawn.

"It is quite warm for the time of the year," said Framton; "but has that window got anything to do with the tragedy?"

"Out through that window, three years ago to a day, her husband and her two young brothers went off for their day's shooting. They never came back. In crossing the moor to their favourite snipe-shooting ground they were all three engulfed in a treacherous piece of bog. It had been that dreadful wet summer, you know, and places that were safe in other years gave way suddenly without warning. Their bodies were never recovered. That was the dreadful part of it." Here the child's voice lost its self-possessed note and became falteringly human. "Poor aunt always thinks they will come back some day, they and the little brown spaniel that was lost with them, and walk in at that window just as they used to do. That is why the window is kept open every evening till it is quite dusk. Poor dear aunt, she has often told me how they went out, her husband with his white waterproof coat over his arm, and Ronnie, her youngest brother, singing, 'Bertie, why do you bound?' as he always did to tease her, because she said it got on her nerves. Do you know, sometimes on still, quiet evenings like this, I almost get a creepy feeling that they will all walk in through that window—"

She broke off with a little shudder. It was a relief to Framton when the aunt bustled into the room with a whirl of apologies for being late in making her appearance.

"I hope Vera has been amusing you?" she said.

"She has been very interesting," said Framton.

"I hope you don't mind the open window," said Mrs. Sappleton briskly; "my husband and brothers will be home directly from shooting, and they always come in this way. They've been out for snipe in the marshes today, so they'll make a fine mess over my poor carpets. So like you menfolk, isn't it?"

She rattled on cheerfully about the shooting and the scarcity of birds, and the prospects for duck in the winter. To Framton it was all purely horrible. He made a desperate but only partially successful effort to turn the talk on to a

less ghastly topic; he was conscious that his hostess was giving him only a fragment of her attention, and her eyes were constantly straying past him to the open window and the lawn beyond. It was certainly an unfortunate coincidence that he should have paid his visit on this tragic anniversary.

"The doctors agree in ordering me complete rest, an absence of mental excitement, and avoidance of anything in the nature of violent physical exercise," announced Framton, who laboured under the tolerably widespread delusion that total strangers and chance acquaintances are hungry for the least detail of one's ailments and infirmities, their cause and cure.

"On the matter of diet they are not so much in agreement," he continued. "No?" said Mrs. Sappleton, in a voice which only replaced a yawn at the last moment. Then she suddenly brightened into alert attention—but not to what Framton was saying.

"Here they are at last!" she cried. "Just in time for tea, and don't they look as if they were muddy up to the eyes!"

Framton shivered slightly and turned towards the niece with a look intended to convey sympathetic comprehension. The child was staring out through the open window with a dazed horror in her eyes. In a chill shock of nameless fear Framton swung round in his seat and looked in the same direction.

In the deepening twilight three figures were walking across the lawn towards the window; they all carried guns under their arms, and one of them was additionally burdened with a white coat hung over his shoulders. A tired brown spaniel kept close at their heels. Noiselessly they neared the house, and then a hoarse young voice chanted out of the dusk: "I said, Bertie, why do you bound?"

Framton grabbed wildly at his stick and hat; the hall door, the gravel drive and the front gate were dimly noted stages in his headlong retreat. A cyclist coming along the road had to run into the hedge to avoid imminent collision.

"Here we are, my dear," said the bearer of the white mackintosh, coming in through the window, "fairly muddy, but most of it's dry. Who was that who bolted out as we came up?"

"A most extraordinary man, a Mr. Nuttel," said Mrs. Sappleton; "could only talk about his illnesses, and dashed off without a word of good-bye or apology when you arrived. One would think he had seen a ghost."

"I expect it was the spaniel," said the niece calmly; "he told me he had a horror of dogs. He was once hunted into a cemetery somewhere on the banks of the Ganges by a pack of pariah dogs, and had to spend the night in a newly dug grave with the creatures snarling and grinning and foaming just above him. Enough to make anyone lose their nerve."

Romance at short notice was her speciality.

Neighbour

Sadhu Binning

Triggered by the noise
from his lawn-mower
an old Indian saying
suddenly comes to mind
'you may often fight
with thy distant relatives
but never be cross with thy neighbour'

Standing on my porch
I imagine myself saying to him
"howdy pal, need some help?"
and he answers with a big smile
"thanks brother, have a seat,
let me finish this quickly
and we'll have a beer."

I feel an itch in my feet
to walk towards him
but forced by past memories I stop
re-examine my skin
as if hoping to find it changed

not willing to offer the other cheek
(never fully convinced by Gandhi)
I stand on my side of the line
he keeps mowing the lawn on the other side
he has such a nice friendly white face
he is my neighbour

Teenage Wasteland

Anne Tyler

He used to have very blond hair—almost white—cut shorter than the other children's so that on his crown a little cowlick always stood up to catch the light. But this was when he was small. As he grew older, his hair grew darker, and he wore it longer—past his collar even. It hung in lank, taffy-colored ropes around his face, which was still an endearing face, fine-featured, the eyes an unusual aqua blue. But his cheeks, of course, were no longer round, and a sharp new Adam's apple jogged in his throat when he talked.

In October, they called from the private school he attended to request a conference with his parents. Daisy went alone; her husband was at work. Clutching her purse, she sat on the principal's couch and learned that Donny was noisy, lazy, and disruptive; always fooling around with his friends, and he wouldn't respond in class.

In the past, before her children were born, Daisy had been a fourth-grade teacher. It shamed her now to sit before this principal, as a parent, a delinquent parent, who struck Mr. Lanham, no doubt, as unseeing or uncaring. "It isn't that we're not concerned," she said. "Both of us are. And we've done what we could, whatever we could think of. We don't let him watch TV on school nights. We don't let him talk on the phone till he's finished his homework. But he tells us he doesn't *have* any homework, or he did it all in study hall. How are we to know what to believe?"

From early October through November, at Mr. Lanham's suggestion, Daisy checked Donny's assignments every day. She sat next to him as he worked, trying to be encouraging, sagging inwardly as she saw the poor quality of the results—the sloppy mistakes in math, the illogical leaps in English themes, the history questions left blank if they required any research.

Daisy was often late starting supper, and she couldn't give much attention to Danny's younger sister. "You'll never guess what happened at . . ." Amanda would begin, and Daisy would tell her, "Not now, honey."

By the time her husband, Matt, came home, she'd be snappish. She would recite the day's hardships—the fuzzy instructions in English, the botched history map, the morass of unsolvable algebra equations. Matt would look surprised and confused, and Daisy would gradually wind down. There was no way, really, to convey how exhausting all this was.

In December, the school called again. This time, they wanted Matt to come as well. She and Matt had to sit on Mr. Lanham's couch like two bad children and listen to the news: Donny had improved only slightly, raising a D in history to a C, and a C in algebra to a B-minus. What was worse, he had developed new problems. He had cut classes on at least three occasions. Smoked in the furnace room. Helped Sonny Barnett break into a freshman's locker. And last week, during athletics, he and three friends had been seen off the school grounds, and when they returned, the coach had smelled beer on their breath. Daisy and Matt sat silent, shocked. Matt rubbed his forehead with his fingertips. Imagine, Daisy thought, how they must look to Mr. Lanham: an overweight housewife in a cotton dress and a too-tall, too-thin insurance agent in a baggy, frayed suit—the kind of people who were always hurrying to catch up, missing the point of things that everyone else grasps at once. She wished she'd worn nylons instead of knee socks.

It was arranged that Donny would visit a psychologist for testing. Mr. Lanham knew just the person. He would set this boy straight, he said.

When they stood to leave, Daisy held her stomach in and gave Mr. Lanham a firm, responsible handshake.

Donny said the psychologist was a jackass and the tests were really dumb, but he kept all three of his appointments, and when it was time for the follow-up conference with the psychologist and both parents, Donny combed his hair and seemed unusually sober and subdued. The psychologist said Donny had no serious emotional problems. He was merely going through a difficult period in his life. He required some academic help and a better sense of self-worth. For this reason, he was suggesting a man named Calvin Beadle, a tutor with considerable psychological training.

That night, Daisy lay awake pondering the term "self-worth." She had always been free with her praise. She had always told Donny he had talent, was smart, was good with his hands. She had made a big to-do over every little gift he had given her. In fact, maybe she had gone too far, although, Lord knows, she had meant every word. Was that his trouble?

She remembered when Amanda was born. Donny had acted lost and bewildered. Daisy had been alert to that, of course, but still, a baby keeps you so busy. Had she really done all she could have? She longed — she ached — for a time machine. Given one more chance, she'd do it perfectly — hug him more, praise him more, or perhaps praise him less. Oh, who can say . . .

The tutor told Donny to call him Cal. All his kids did, he said. Daisy thought for a second he meant his own children, then realized her mistake. He seemed too young, anyhow, to be a family man. He wore a heavy brown handlebar mustache. His hair was as long and stringy as Donny's, and his jeans as faded. Wire-rimmed spectacles slid down his nose. He lounged in a canvas director's chair with his fingers laced across his chest, and he casually, amiably questioned Donny, who sat upright and glaring in an armchair.

"So they're getting on your back at school," said Cal. "Making a big deal about anything you do wrong."

"Right," said Donny.

"Any idea why that might be?"

"Oh, well, you know, stuff like homework and all," Donny said.

"You don't do your homework?"

"Oh, well, I might do it sometimes but not exactly like they want it." Donny sat forward and said, "It's like a prison there, you know? You've got to go to every class; you can never step off the school grounds."

"You cut classes sometimes?"

"Sometimes," Donny said, with a glance at his parents.

Cal didn't seem perturbed. "Well," he said, "I'll tell you what. Let's you and me try working together three nights a week. Think you could handle that? We'll see if we can show that school of yours a thing or two. Give it a month; then if you don't like it, we'll stop. If *I* don't like it, we'll stop. I mean, sometimes people just don't get along, right? What do you say to that?"

"Okay," Donny said. He seemed pleased.

"Make it seven o'clock till eight, Monday, Wednesday and Friday," Cal told Matt and Daisy. They nodded. Cal shambled to his feet, gave them a little salute, and showed them to the door.

This was where he lived as well as worked, evidently. The interview had taken place in the dining room, which had been transformed into a kind of office. Passing the living room, Daisy winced at the rock music she had been hearing, without registering it, ever since she had entered the house. She looked in and saw a boy about Donny's age lying on a sofa with a book. Another boy and girl were playing Ping-Pong in front of the fireplace. "You have several here together?" Daisy asked Cal.

"Oh, sometimes they stay on after their sessions, just to rap. They're a pretty sociable group, all in all. Plenty of goof-offs like young Donny here."

He cuffed Donny's shoulder playfully. Donny flushed and grinned.

Climbing into the car, Daisy asked Donny, "Well? What do you think?"

But Donny had returned to his old evasive self. He jerked his chin toward the garage. "He's got a basketball net."

Now on Mondays, Wednesdays, and Fridays, they had supper early—the instant Matt came home. Sometimes, they had to leave before they were really finished. Amanda would still be eating her dessert. "Bye, honey. Sorry," Daisy would tell her.

Cal's first bill sent a flutter through Daisy's chest, but it was worth it, of course. Just look at Donny's face when they picked him up: alight and full of interest. The principal telephoned Daisy to tell her how Donny had improved. "Of course, it hasn't shown up in his grades yet, but several of the teachers have noticed how his attitude has changed. Yes, sir, I think we're onto something here."

At home Donny didn't act much different. He still seemed to have a low opinion of his parents. But Daisy supposed that was unavoidable—part of being fifteen. He said his parents were too "controlling"—a word that made Daisy give him a sudden look. He said they acted like wardens. On weekends, they enforced a curfew. And anytime he went to a party, they always telephoned first to see if adults would be supervising. "Don't you trust me?" he said.

"It isn't a matter of trust, honey . . ." But there was no explaining to him.

His tutor called one afternoon. "I get the sense," he said, "that this kid's feeling . . . underestimated, you know? Like you folks expect the worst of him. I'm thinking we ought to give him more rope."

"But see, he's still so suggestible," Daisy said. "When his friends suggest some mischief—smoking or drinking or such—why, he just finds it very hard not to go along with them."

"Mrs. Coble," the tutor said, "I think this kid is hurting. You know? Here's a serious, sensitive kid, telling you he'd like to take on some grown-up challenges, and you're giving him the message that he can't be trusted. Don't you understand how that hurts?"

"Oh," said Daisy.

"It undermines his self-esteem, don't you realize that?"

"Well, I guess you're right," said Daisy. She saw Donny suddenly from a whole new angle: his poor posture, that slouch so forlorn that his shoulders seemed about the meet his chin . . . oh, wasn't it awful being young? She'd had a miserable adolescence herself and had always sworn no child of hers would ever be that unhappy.

They let Donny stay out later, they didn't call ahead to see if parties were supervised, and they were careful not to grill him about his evenings. The tutor had set down so many rules! They were not allowed any questions at all about any aspect of school, nor were they to speak to his teachers. If a teacher had some complaint, she should phone Cal. Only one teacher disobeyed— the history teacher, Miss Evans. She called one morning in February. "I'm a little concerned about Donny, Mrs. Coble."

"Oh, I'm sorry, Miss Evans, but Donny's tutor handles these things now . . ."

"I always deal directly with the parents. You are the parent," Miss Evans said, speaking very slowly and distinctly. "Now here is the problem. Back when you were helping Donny with his homework, his grades rose overall from a D to a C, but now they've slipped back, and they're closer to an F."

"They are?"

"I think you should start overseeing his homework again."

"But Donny's tutor says . . ."

"I think it's nice that Donny has a tutor, but you should still be in charge of his homework. With you, he learned it. Then he passed his tests. With the

tutor, well, it seems the tutor is more of a crutch. 'Donny,' I say, 'a test is coming up on Friday. Hadn't you better be listening instead of talking?' 'That's okay, Miss Evans,' he says. 'I have a tutor now.' Like a talisman! I really think you ought to take over, Mrs. Coble."

"I see," said Daisy. "Well, I'll think about that. Thank you for calling."

Hanging up, she felt a rush of anger at Donny. A talisman! For a talisman, she'd given up all luxuries, so much time with her daughter, her evenings at home!

She dialed Cal's number. He sounded muzzy. "I'm sorry if I woke you," she told him, "but Donny's history teacher just called. She says he isn't doing well."

"She should have dealt with me."

"She wants me to start supervising his homework again. His grades are slipping."

"Yes," said the tutor, "but you and I both know there's more to it than mere grades, don't we? I care about the *whole* child—his happiness, his self-esteem. The grades will come. Just give them time."

When she hung up, it was Miss Evans she was angry at. What a narrow woman!

It was Cal this, Cal that, Cal says this, Cal and I did that. Cal lent Donny an album by The Who. He took Donny and two other pupils to a rock concert. In March, when Donny began to talk endlessly on the phone with a girl named Miriam, Cal even let Miriam come to one of the tutoring sessions. Daisy was touched that Cal would grow so involved in Donny's life, but she was also a little hurt, because she had offered to have Miriam to dinner and Donny had refused. Now he asked them to drive her to Cal's house without a qualm.

This Miriam had blurry lipstick and masses of rough red hair. She wore a short, bulky jacket that would not have been out of place on a motorcycle. During the trip to Cal's she was silent, but coming back, she was more talkative. "What a neat guy, and what a house! All those kids hanging out, like a club. And the stereo playing rock . . . gosh, he's not like a grown-up at all! Married and divorced and everything, but you'd think he was our own age."

"Mr. Beadle was married?" Daisy asked.

"Yeah, to this really controlling lady. She didn't understand him a bit."

"No, I guess not," Daisy said.

Spring came, and the students who hung around Cal's drifted out to the basketball net above the garage. Sometimes, when Daisy and Matt showed up

to pick up Donny, they'd find him there with the others—spiky and excited, jittering on his toes beneath the backboard. It was staying light much longer now, and the neighboring fence cast narrow bars across the bright grass. Loud music would be spilling from Cal's windows. Once it was The Who, which Daisy recognized from the time Donny had borrowed the album. "*Teenage Wasteland*," she said aloud, identifying the song, and Matt gave a short, dry laugh. "It certainly is," he said. He'd misunderstood; he thought she was commenting on the scene spread before them. In fact, she might have been. The players looked like hoodlums, even her son. Why, one of Cal's students had recently been knifed in a tavern. One had been shipped off to a boarding school in midterm; two had been withdrawn by their parents. On the other hand, Donny had mentioned someone who'd been studying with Cal for five years. "Five years!" said Daisy. "Doesn't anyone ever stop needing him?"

Donny looked at her. Lately, whatever she said about Cal was read as criticism. "You're just feeling competitive," he said. "And controlling."

She bit her lip and said no more.

In April, the principal called to tell her that Donny had been expelled. There had been a locker check, and in Donny's locker they found five cans of beer and half a pack of cigarettes. With Donny's previous record, this offense meant expulsion.

Daisy gripped the receiver tightly and said, "Well, where is he now?"

"We've sent him home," said Mr. Lanham. "He's packed up all his belongings, and he's coming home on foot."

Daisy wondered what she would say to him. She felt him looming closer and closer, bringing this brand-new situation that no one had prepared her

to handle. What other place would take him? Could they enter him in a public school? What were the rules? She stood at the living room window, waiting for him to show up. Gradually, she realized that he was taking too long. She checked the clock. She stared up the street again.

When an hour had passed, she phoned the school. Mr. Lanham's secretary answered and told her in a grave, sympathetic voice that yes, Donny Coble had most definitely gone home. Daisy called her husband. He was out of the office. She went back to the window and thought awhile, and then she called Donny's tutor.

"Donny's been expelled from school," she said, "and now I don't know where he's gone. I wonder if you've heard from him?"

There was a long silence. "Donny's with me, Mrs. Coble," he finally said.

"With you? How'd he get there?"

"He hailed a cab, and I paid the driver."

"Could I speak with him, please?"

There was another silence. "Maybe it'd be better if we had a conference," Cal said.

"I don't *want* a conference. I've been standing at the window picturing him dead or kidnapped or something, and now you tell me you want a—"

"Donny is very, very upset. Understandably so," said Cal. "Believe me, Mrs. Coble, this is not what it seems. Have you asked Donny's side of the story?"

"Well, of course not. How could I? He went running off to you instead."

"Because he didn't feel he'd be listened to."

"But I haven't even—"

"Why don't you come over and talk? The three of us," said Cal, "will try to get this thing in perspective."

"Well, all right," Daisy said. But she wasn't as reluctant as she sounded. Already, she felt soothed by the calm way Cal was taking this.

Cal answered the doorbell at once. He said, "Hi, there," and led her into the dining room. Donny sat slumped in a chair, chewing the knuckle of one thumb. "Hello, Donny," Daisy said. He flicked his eyes in her direction.

"Sit here, Mrs. Coble," said Cal, placing her opposite Donny. He himself remained standing, restlessly pacing. "So," he said.

Daisy stole a look at Donny. His lips were swollen, as if he'd been crying.

"You know," Cal told Daisy, "I kind of expected something like this. That's a very punitive school you've got him in—you realize that. And any half-decent lawyer will tell you they've violated his civil rights. Locker checks! Where's their search warrant?"

"But the rule is—" Daisy said.

"Well, anyhow, let him tell you his side."

She looked at Donny. He said, "It wasn't my fault. I promise."

"They said your locker was full of beer."

"It was a put-up job! See, there's this guy that doesn't like me. He put all these beers in my locker and started a rumor going, so Mr. Lanham ordered a locker check."

"What is the boy's name?" Daisy asked.

"Huh?"

"Mrs. Coble, take my word, the situation is not so unusual," Cal said. "You can't imagine how vindictive kids can be sometimes."

"Just tell me the boy's *name*," said Daisy, "so I can ask Mr. Lanham if that's who suggested the locker check."

"You don't believe me," Donny said.

"And how'd this boy get your locker combination in the first place?"

"Frankly," said Cal, "I wouldn't be surprised to learn the school was in on it. Any kid who marches to a different drummer, why, they'd just love an excuse to get rid of him. The school is where I lay the blame."

"Doesn't Donny ever get blamed?"

"Now, Mrs. Coble, you heard what he—"

"Forget it," Donny told Cal. "You can see she doesn't trust me."

Daisy drew in a breath to say of course she trusted him—a reflex. But she knew that cold-faced, wide-eyed look of Donny's.  He had worn that look when he was small, denying some petty misdeed with the evidence plain as day all around him. Still, it was hard for her to accuse him outright. She temporized and said, "The only thing I'm sure of is that they've kicked you out of school, and now I don't know what we're going to do."

"We'll fight it," said Cal.

"We can't. Even you must see that."

"I could apply to Brantly," Donny said.

Cal stopped his pacing to beam down at him. "Brantly! Yes. They're really into where a kid is coming from, at Brantly. Why, *I* could get you into Brantly. I work with a lot of their students."

Daisy had never heard of Brantly, but already she didn't like it. And she didn't like Cal's smile, which struck her now as feverish and avid—a smile of hunger.

On the fifteenth of April, they entered Donny in a public school, and they stopped his tutoring sessions. Donny fought both decisions bitterly. Cal, surprisingly enough, did not object. He admitted he'd made no headway with Donny and said it was because Donny was emotionally disturbed.

Donny went to his new school every morning, plodding off alone with his head down. He did his assignments, and he earned average grades, but he gathered no friends, joined no clubs. There was something exhausted and defeated about him.

The first week in June, during final exams, Donny vanished. He simply didn't come home one afternoon, and no one at school remembered seeing him. The police were reassuring, and for the first few days, they worked hard. They combed Donny's sad, messy room for clues; they visited Miriam and Cal. But then they started talking about the number of kids who ran away every year. Hundreds, just in this city. "He'll show up, if he wants to," they said. "If he doesn't, he won't."

Evidently, Donny didn't want to.

"It's been three months now and still no word. Matt and Daisy still look for him in every crowd of awkward, heart-breaking teenage boys. Every time the phone rings, they imagine it might be Donny. Both parents have aged. Donny's sister seems to be staying away from home as much as possible.

At night, Daisy lies awake and goes over Donny's life. She is trying to figure out what went wrong, where they made their first mistake. Often, she finds herself blaming Cal, although she knows he didn't begin it. Then at other times she excuses him, for without him, Donny might have left earlier. Who really knows? In the end, she can only sigh and search for a cooler spot on the pillow. As she falls asleep, she occasionally glimpses something in the corner of her vision. It's something fleet and round, a ball—a basketball. It flies up, it sinks through the hoop, descends, lands in a yard littered with last year's leaves and striped bars of sunlight as white as bones, bleached and parched and cleanly picked.

A Tanned Version

Hummarah Quddoos

And there is a huge immeasurable distance between us,
Between me and them.
They close their minds,
Ask the same repetitive questions,
Arranged marriages, strictness, trousers,
Same order.
Wherever I go.
What will they ask next:
Do you sleep, do you eat, can we touch?
I'm only a different colour
A tanned version of you.
They think we're all stereotypes
Carbon copies of each other.
We don't think they're all Princess Diana.
They're always amazed
When I can talk, can answer, have a mind,
As if to say this one's clever,
What other tricks do you do?
I'm not so very different
Just a tanned version of you.
How come I have to fight so hard
When you just have to show your face?

What I Want to Be
When I Grow Up

Martha Brooks

On the third Thursday afternoon of every month, I take my mother's hastily written note to the office where the school secretary, Mrs. Audrey Plumas, a nervous lady with red blotchy skin, looks at it and tells me I can go. Then I leave George J. Sherwood Junior High, walk down to the corner, and wait for the 2:47 bus which will get me downtown just in time for my four o'clock orthodontic appointment.

I hate taking the bus. It's always too hot even in thirty-below-zero weather. The fumes and the lurching make me sick. The people are weird.

Mom says with the amount of money she's forking out to give me a perfect smile I shouldn't complain. "Andrew," she says cheerfully, "taking the bus is an education. It's a rare opportunity for people of all types and from all walks of life to be in an enforced environment that allows them to really get a close look at one another." She then adds, meaningfully, "Think of it as research for your life's work." She goes on like that even though she can't possibly know what she's talking about because she's a business executive who drives a brand new air conditioned Volvo to work every day.

I made the mistake, a while ago, of telling her I want to be a journalist when I grow up. Out of all the things I've ever wanted to be—an undersea photographer, a vet for the London Zoo, a missionary in Guatemala—she feels this latest choice is the most practical and has latched onto it like it's the last boat leaving the harbour.

She feels that, at fourteen, I have to start making "important career choices." This, in spite of the fact that my teeth stick out from having stopped sucking my thumb only six years ago.

On the bus last month, I happened to sit across the aisle from a girl with pasty white skin and pale eyes lined in some kind of indigo gunk. We were right at the front, near the driver. The bus was so full there was no escape. She kept smiling like she had an imaginary friend. Every so often she'd lean forward and go, "Phe-ew," breathing right on me. The woman beside me wanted the whole bench to herself and edged me over with her enormous thighs until I was flattened against the metal railing. (I can't stand older women who wear stockings rolled, like floppy little doughnuts, down to their ankles.) She then took the shopping bag from her lap and mashed it between her ankles and mine as a further precaution that I wouldn't take up any more room than I had coming to me. Hot, numb with misery, and totally grossed-out, I closed my eyes and lost track of time. I went six extra stops and was fifteen minutes late for my appointment.

The old lady who runs the orthodontist's office also seems to run Dr. Fineman, who only appears, molelike, to run his fingers along your gums and then scurries off to other patients in other rooms. This old lady doesn't like kids unless they are with a parent. The first few months I went with my mother, Mrs. G. Blahuta, Receptionist (that's the sign on this dinosaur's desk) smiled and told me what a brave boy I was. She even exchanged recipes with my mother. That was four years ago. This past time, when I arrived late and gasping because I'm slightly asthmatic, Mrs. Blahuta (the orthodontist calls her Gladys; she has purple hair) scowled and asked me to come to the desk where I stood, wishing I could die, while she shrilled at me about inconsiderate teenagers who think of no one but themselves and show so little responsibility and motivation it's a wonder they can dress themselves in the morning.

Shaking with humiliation, I sat down to wait my turn beside a blonde girl with gold hairs on her beautiful tanned legs. She had been pretending to read a glamour magazine. Her eyebrows shot up as I sat down. She primly inched away and gave me her back like she was a cat and I was some kind of bug she couldn't even be bothered to tease.

On the trip home another gorgeous pristine-type girl swayed onto the bus two stops after mine. She sat down in the empty seat in front of me and opened the window I'd been too weak from my previous ordeals to tackle. This life-saving breeze hit my face, along with the sweet stirring scent of her

 musky perfume. Gratefully I watched the back of her neck. (She wore her hair up. The backs of girls' necks make me crazy.)

After about five more stops a sandy-haired man, whose stomach rolled like a pumpkin over the belt of his green work pants, got on the bus and sat down beside this breath-stopping girl. She didn't even seem to know he was there, and with great interest stretched her long neck to get a close look at a passing semi-trailer loaded with pigs. Their moist snouts poked at whatever air they could get at and you could tell they were on their way to the slaughterhouse. (Why else would pigs be spending a day in the city?)

The sandy-haired man readjusted his cap that was almost too small for his very large head. "Look at all them sausages!" he exclaimed, laughing really loudly at his dumb joke. The girl kept right on looking at the pigs. I could have died for her, but except for her nostrils that flared delicately and her slightly stiffened neck and shoulders, she didn't appear to be bothered at all.

The man playfully nudged her. "Hey!" he chortled, in a voice that could be heard all over the bus, "You like pork chops?"

She turned from the pigs (I noticed her incredibly long eyelashes that were light at the tips) and stared straight at him. His face went into a silly fixed smile. "Excuse me," she said coolly, and got up to leave.

"Oh, your stop comin' up, little lady?" he bellowed as he got up quickly. Pulling at his cap brim, he let her past.

She walked about four steps down the aisle and moved in beside an expensively dressed Chinese lady with bifocals who looked suspiciously back at us, then frowned. I frowned at the fat man so she'd know it had been him, and not me, causing all the commotion.

I couldn't believe it when the man, calling more attention to himself, leaned forward and poked at a business-type suit person! He said, in what possibly for him was a whisper, "Guess she don't like pigs." The suit person gave him a pained over-the-shoulder smile.

The man finally settled back. "I used to live on a farm. Yup. I did. I really did," he continued to nobody in particular because everybody near was pretending to look out of windows, or read, or be very concerned with what time their watches gave.

"Whew! It's hot!" He all of a sudden got up and reached over the suit person, ruffling his hair. "Oh sorry," he said. "Mind if I open this?" He tugged open the suit's window. The suit shot him a look that suggested he wasn't dealing with a full deck. Which he probably wasn't.

I prayed he would leave but ten minutes later the girl of my dreams got off the bus. I was left staring at the pork chop man's thick, freckled neck.

His stop wasn't until one before mine. As we pulled away I watched him walk over and strike up a conversation with another complete stranger who was too polite to ignore him.

Like I said, you have to put up with some very weird people when you take the bus.

Today, I pleaded with my mother to drive me downtown. She lay on the couch popping painkillers because yesterday she fell and twisted an ankle and suffered a very small fracture as well. She isn't in a cast or anything and it's her left foot so she doesn't need it to drive with. When I asked her nicely for the second time, explaining that she wouldn't even have to get out of the car, she glared at me a moment and burst into tears. I don't understand why she's so selfish. I hope she gets a migraine from watching soap operas all day.

Can you believe it? I was late again for my appointment. I tried to explain to the purple-haired dinosaur that I'd missed my bus on account of being kept late in science class. (I had to re-write a test I'd messed up the first time because I was away sick the day the teacher told us to study for it and my friend Gordon, the jerk, was supposed to tell me and forgot to.)

Mrs. Blahuta said snidely that she was surprised I was only twenty minutes late and did I intend to put in an appearance at my next monthly appointment or would they all be kept in suspense until the final moment of the working day which was five o'clock. Sharp!

She kept me until every last person, except myself, had been checked over. At five to five she ushered me into the orthodontist as his last appointment for the day. He processed me as if I were some dog in a laboratory and then Gladys dismissed me by holding out my next month's appointment slip like it was a bone I'd probably bury.

I got out onto the street, saw my bus departing,

and made a silent vow that for at least a month I wasn't going to speak to any person over the age of eighteen.

At five twenty-two I boarded my bus and all the seats were taken. As we got underway, I suddenly felt sick. I clung to the nearest pole while the bus lurched, braked, accelerated, and picked up three or four passengers at every stop. Heated bodies armed with parcels, babies, books, and briefcases pressed past me. Into his microphone, the driver ordered everyone to the back. I didn't budge. When his voice began to sound as if it were coming from inside a vacuum cleaner, another wave of nausea overcame me and my hands, hot and wet, slipped down the pole.

I hate getting motion-sickness. I'm sometimes so sensitive that just looking at, say, a movie of people going fast in a roller coaster can almost make me lose my last meal. Whenever I'm sick in the car, Mom says, "Fix your eyes on objects that are the furthest away. Don't look at anything that'll pass you by."

Remembering that, I turned to face the front of the bus. The furthest thing in my view was the pork chop man. As he was coming straight towards me, I shifted my gaze past his shoulder to a spot of blue that was, I guess, the sky. The bus took another shift and the sudden lurch swung me quickly around to where I'd been. I very nearly lost my battle with nausea to the skirts of a person wearing purple paisley.

Somebody gripped my arm, and said, "One of youse has to get up. This boy's going to be sick."

Immediately two people vacated their seats. Next thing I knew I was sitting beside a window with the pork chop man. He reached around behind me and tugged until wind hit my face.

"Hang your head out, now," he roared. "If you have to puke your guts out just go ahead and don't be shy." He patted my back in a fatherly way with one enormous hand while the other hung like a grizzly paw along the back end of my seat.

I did as I was told, breathed deeply for several seconds, and brought my head back in to have a look at him. I don't think I've ever seen such an enormous man. Up close, I realized he wasn't really so much fat as there was just an awful lot of him. "Name's Earl," he said, solemnly.

"Thanks, Earl," I said. "I'm Andrew."

"Don't have to thank me, Andrew. I joined A.A. two years ago. Haven't touched a drop since. I remember how it felt to be real sick."

I wanted to explain that I wasn't a drinker, but was overcome by another terrible feeling that I might lose control. Earl said, "Hold on, kid," and shoved my head out the window again.

We didn't talk much after that. It wasn't until my stop was coming up that I realized he'd just missed his.

I pulled the buzzer cord and said, "You missed your stop."

"How'd you know that?"

"I noticed you when you were on the bus one other time," I mumbled, embarrassed.

Earl sat back and looked straight ahead. He looked like a man who'd been struck by a thought that was almost too big to handle.

The bus arrived at my stop and Earl hurriedly got to his feet to let me past. I stepped off the bus with him right behind. On the street he said, still amazed, "You noticed me?"

The bus fumed noisily on past us.

"Yeah. Well—there was this girl, first. You came and sat beside her . . ." I trailed off.

"You know," said Earl, "just between you and me, city people aren't friendly. They don't notice nothing. See that old lady, there?"

At the light, an old girl tottered off the curb and started to cross the street. She carried two plastic Safeway bags full of groceries.

Out of the corner of his mouth, in a lisping whisper, Earl informed me, "If she was to fall and hurt herself just enough so she could still walk, not one person would stop and offer to help her home with those bags."

"That's true," I said, thinking that if they did, they'd probably turn around and help themselves to her purse.

We started across the street. I felt better, now that we were off the bus. I actually started to feel a little hungry. I wondered how I was going to say goodbye to Earl. I was afraid he might want to talk to me for a long time. He walked slowly and I felt obliged to keep pace with him.

We reached the other side and stopped on the sidewalk. All the while he kept going on about the time he'd taken some guy to emergency at the General Hospital. The guy had almost bled to death before they could get anybody's attention.

Without hardly pausing to breathe, Earl cornered me with his desperately lonely eyes and launched into another story. I made out like I was really interested but to tell the truth I was thinking about my favourite T.V. program, which would be on at that very moment, and about how Mom sits with me on the sofa, sometimes, while we eat our dinner and watch it together.

"Well," said Earl, too heartily, "I can see that you're going to be okay and I shouldn't keep you. Probably missed your supper, eh?"

He stuck out his hand, that massive freckled paw. Surprised, I took it and it surrounded mine in an amazingly gentle way. "Thanks," I said again.

"Told you not to mention it," said Earl. "We've all got to help each other out, don't we, buddy? But I can see I don't have to tell you that. You're different. You notice things."

My Name Is Masak

Alice French

In the spring of 1937 when I was seven years old my father told my brother and me that our mother had tuberculosis. We would have to go from Cambridge Bay to the hospital in Aklavik. So when the Hudson's Bay Company ship came in with supplies, my father and mother and my brother, Aynounik, and I, sailed back on it. We got measles on board and that made my mother even sicker. I didn't know how long it took us to make that trip but it seemed to last forever.

When we landed at Aklavik my mother went to the hospital and my brother and I were told we would be going to a boarding school, whatever that was. My father tried to explain that a boarding school was where children lived and went to school. He would not be able to take care of us while mother was in the hospital and we would have to stay there. I did not like the idea. My brother was only three years old and too young to understand.

Alone

How could there be so many people living in one building? I was so scared that I hung onto my father's hand. I did not like it there and I did not want my father to leave us. There were too many people. My brother was taken away by one of the supervisors. I tried not to cry in front of my father—he felt bad enough as it was.

An Eskimo girl, whose dialect I did not understand, took me to the playroom. She was talking to me in Eskimo, but it did not make sense. Thank goodness she spoke English too. She told me that we were having supper soon. I asked her if I would see my brother. She said yes, at supper time. Then she introduced me to the other girls by my Christian name—Alice. My Eskimo name was not mentioned and I did not hear my name Masak again until I went home.

Then I became aware of different languages. I asked my new friend what dialect the girls were speaking. I was told that it was the language of the Mackenzie Delta and that most of the Eskimo children were from there, except for a few from Coppermine and Cambridge Bay. There were a lot of Indian children from the upper Mackenzie. They were mostly Loucheux with some Dogribs and Slaveys.

Then a white lady came in to tell us it was supper time. Everyone got into line except me. She took my hand and told me her name was Miss Neville. I was taken to one of the lines and told that this would be my place from now on. We marched in single file to the dining-room. Suddenly, I saw my little brother. I started towards him, but I was told to stay in line. How little he looked, lost and lonesome. I felt like going over to tell him that everything was going to be all right, only I was not too sure of that myself.

After supper we went back to our side of the school. I did not even get to talk to my brother. We saw each other only at mealtimes. Sometimes we had the chance to shout at each other while playing outside but even outside the boys and girls were not allowed to mix.

Sometime later that fall Reverend H.S. Shepherd, our minister, came to the school to tell me that my mother had died. I did not believe him because I had visited her that morning. I went back to the hospital to find her but the bed she was been in was empty. How could she be there one day and not the next? I felt terribly alone. She was the only link I had with home and the life I had been used to. My father had gone back to his trap-line and we would not hear from him for a long time. It was not out of cruelty but out of necessity that he left us.

Boarding School

Inside the school we had four dormitories on the girls' side. I was in the youngest girls' dormitory for ages six to eight. The dormitories were joined by a big common washroom. There were towel hooks along both walls, wash basins, and jugs of water on a long table. Little brushes and tins of powder were on a shelf built into the middle of the table. I had to wait to see what the

other girls would use the little brushes for, so I watched what they did with them as we got ready for bed.

So that was what it was—to brush your teeth with. I wondered what that was supposed to do for you. Somebody told me that it was to keep you from having holes in your teeth. They certainly did have a lot of strange ideas. Another idea was combing your hair with coal oil when you first came to the school. That was to kill the head lice. I didn't have any but we all had to suffer through the coal-oil treatment whether we had lice or not.

Our house mother's name was Annie and she had a room just off the washroom. She told me that my mother was her cousin. That did not mean that I would be favoured above the other girls, but it felt good to know that I had a relative close at hand. She got us off to bed at night and woke us up in the morning.

The staff in our school slept in rooms off the hallway. Downstairs were two big classrooms, kitchen, staff dining-room, children's dining-room, principal's office, laundry room, a furnace room and two playrooms. The lavatory used to be outside until they had one built into the side of our playroom. The whole of the basement was a storeroom for school supplies and food was kept there, like a root cellar.

Our days started at seven in the morning. We dressed, washed, and brushed our teeth, made our beds and tidied our dorms. Then we went down to breakfast at eight o'clock.

Breakfast usually was porridge, sweetened with molasses, bread and jam, and tea to drink with sugar and milk. It never varied except on holidays. At nine we went to the classrooms. Then a break for lunch—soup, bread and powdered milk—and back to school again. Supper was the big meal of the day with fish, meat, potatoes, dessert, bread and tea. We had this at five-thirty, usually after a walk around town, or out into the country with our teacher. Bedtime was seven o'clock for the little ones, eight o'clock for the next lot and so on, until the oldest were in bed at ten and the lights were out. I expect it was the same for the boys.

While we were getting ready for bed we talked about the scary stories we would tell after the lights were out. I shivered thinking about them while I brushed my teeth. Betty, standing next to me at the sink, jabbed me in the ribs and scared me half to death.

"Hey Alice," she said. "Did you know that we have a ghost in our dorm? She always sits in the corner combing her hair and you can see the blue sparks flying in every direction." I started to shake because my bed was in one of the far corners of the room.

"Which corner?" I asked in a quavery voice.

"Your corner," she said, and went off to bed.

Then Miss Neville came in and I pleaded with her to tell us a story. As long as she was telling a story the lights would stay on and maybe the girls would go to sleep or be too tired to tell ghost stories.

"Not tonight, Alice," said Miss Neville. "All right, girls, time for bed. No talking after lights out, please."

She looked around to make sure that we were all under our covers and then she turned out the light and closed the door. It sure was dark in there then. I made certain that my bedding was loose so that I could jump out of bed fast if I had to.

Then they began to tell stories. Why did they always have to be scary ones —reindeer herders taking a coffin creaking through the woods on a sleigh, men reincarnated in dogs, rattling doors and the Devil's cloven hoof-prints on the snow?

Connie, whose bed was closest to the door, was posted as lookout. Her job was to tell us if someone was coming, but she was a most unlikely choice for the job. She talked more than any of us, and often she would forget that she was supposed to be listening for the supervisor's footsteps. As a result we were caught talking and were punished. We had to stand in the corner of the room for half an hour. This got to be very cold, for all we had on was our nightdresses.

One night I was punished in another way for using my bed as a trampoline. I was showing the girls how to go into a standing position from a belly-flop. As I came down the bed collapsed to the floor with a crash. Just as I disappeared from view into the bedding, the door opened and there stood Miss Melville.

"What is going on here?" she asked sternly.

There was a silence while I climbed from the ruins of my bed. She came over and grabbed my shoulder and gave me a good shaking.

"Alice, how many times have I told you not to jump on your bed?"

"Many times, Miss Melville," I answered with my teeth rattling in my head.

"That is correct," she said. "For being a naughty and disobedient child you shall sleep in your bed just as it is for a week. Now all of you settle down and no more nonsense."

I climbed into bed and found that it was quite comfortable. In the morning I woke up and realized that I had slept through the night without once waking up because of the cold. By the end of the week I had grown quite attached to my bed on the floor and hated to give it up for another.

Friday night was bath night. All one hundred and twenty-five of us were issued clean bedding and clothing. This consisted of one pair of long underwear, one pair of fleece-lined bloomers, one pair of black woollen stockings, a navy blue dress and clean towels. We took this with us and all headed for the laundry room. Inside there were eight galvanized tubs ready for use. These tubs were all filled by hand and had to be emptied the same way. We bathed two to a tub. Sometimes it got so steamed up that we could not see who our partners were. Our hair was washed by the bigger girls. Following this a jug of cold water was poured over us. This was to shrink our pores so that we would not catch cold, we were politely told.

Saturday was the most pleasant day of the week. We did all our housework in the morning—sweeping and dusting and tidying our dorms. After lunch, if we had parents in town, we could go home for the afternoon. I sometimes went home with my good friend who was called Peanuts because of her size. Her house was right in Aklavik. Then we went out to the Hudson's Bay store or to visit our other friends. Sometimes we just stayed at home enjoying the family atmosphere. After the crowded school life it felt good to be by ourselves for a while. Her mother would remind us that it was almost time to leave and we would collect some dried meat, bannock, butter, and sweets to take back to school with us.

Once a week, usually on Sunday, we were given seven candies by our supervisor. We were not allowed to eat them all at once. Instead we put them in a small box with our name on it and each night before bedtime we were allowed to have one candy. Sometimes we promised a friend a candy in return for a favour, and so that day we would have to go without.

Something else that we had each day was cod-liver oil, and it sure didn't taste good. It came in five-gallon cans on the boat during the summer. Before it was dished out it was poured into a two-pound can which our supervisor held. We would file past her each morning for a tablespoon and then dash to the toilet to spit it out. When our supervisor caught on to this we had to stay and open our mouths to show that we had swallowed the horrid stuff. I guess that was why we were so healthy. But by the time the five-gallon can was empty it was so rancid you could smell it a mile away I have never taken cod-liver oil since.

A Matter of Balance

W. D. Valgardson

He was sitting on a cedar log, resting, absentmindedly plucking pieces from its thick layer of moss, when he first saw them. They were standing on the narrow bridge above the waterfall. When they realized he had noticed them, they laughed, looked at each other, then turned their backs. In a moment, the short, dark-haired one turned around to stare at him again. His companion flicked a cigarette into the creek.

Bikers, he thought with a mixture of contempt and fear. He had seen others like them, often a dozen at a time, muscling their way along the road. These two had their hair chopped off just above the shoulders and, from where he sat, it looked greasy for it hung in tangled strands. They both had strips of red cloth tied around their heads. The dark-haired boy, he thought, then corrected himself, man, not boy, for he had to be in his middle twenties, was so short and stocky that he might have been formed from an old-fashioned beer keg. They both wore black leather vests, jeans, and heavy boots.

He was sorry that they were there but he considered their presence only a momentary annoyance. They had probably parked their bikes at the pull-off below the waterfall, walked up for god knows what reason—he could not imagine them being interested in the scenery—and would shortly leave again. He would be happy to see them go. He was still only able to work part time and had carefully arranged his schedule so that his Wednesdays were free. He didn't want anything to interfere with the one day he had completely to himself.

The tall blond man turned, leaned against the railing and stared up at Harold. He jabbed his companion with his elbow and laughed. Then he

raised his right hand, pointed two fingers like he would a pistol, and pretended to shoot.

The action, childish as it was, unsettled Harold and he felt his stomach knot with anxiety. He wished that he had been on the other side of the bridge and could simply have picked up his pack and walked back to his station wagon. The only way across the river, however, was the bridge and he had no desire to try to force his way past them. They reminded him of kids from his public school days who used to block the sidewalk, daring anyone to try to get by. He had been in grade two at the time and had not yet learned about fear. When he had attempted to ignore them and go around, they had shifted with him to the boulevard, then to the road and, finally, to the back lane. As his mother was washing off his scrapes and bruises and trying to get blood off his shirt, he had kept asking her why, why did they do it? Beyond saying that they were bad boys and that she would speak to the principal, she had no answers. Only later, when he was much older, had he understood that their anger was not personal and, so, could not be reasoned with.

Every Wednesday for the last six months, he had hiked to the end of this trail and then used his rope to lower himself to the river bank. Before the winter rains began and flooded the gorge, he wanted to do as much sniping as possible. The previous week, he had discovered a crack in the bedrock that looked promising but, before he had a chance to get out all the gravel, the day had started to fade and he had been forced to leave. The gorge was no place to spend the night. Even at noon, the light was filtered to a pale grey. He dressed warmly, wearing a cotton shirt, then a wool shirt and, finally, a wool jack-shirt; yet, within a few hours he was always shaking with cold. As strenuous as the panning was, it could not keep out the chill. The air was so damp that when he took a handful of rotting cedar and squeezed it, red water ran like blood between his fingers. On the tree trunks, hundreds of mushrooms grew. At first, because of their small size and dark grey colour, he thought they were slugs, but then he pried one loose with his fingernail and discovered its bright yellow gills.

Although he had been nowhere near the bottom of the crack, he had found a few flakes of gold which he meticulously picked out of his pan with tweezers. Panning in the provincial parks was illegal so he always went right to the end of the path, then worked his way along the river for another hundred yards. Recently, he had started taking as much as half-an-ounce of dust and small nuggets out of the river in a day and he wondered if someone had found out, but he immediately dismissed the idea. Only Conklin knew. When they met each Thursday he always showed Conklin his latest find. As far as his friends and colleagues were aware, he spent his days off hiking, getting himself back into shape after having been ill for over a year.

As he studied the two men below, he told himself he was letting his imagination run away with him again and to get it under control. There was no good in borrowing trouble. He stood up, swung his pack onto his shoulders and, being careful not to look like he was running away, resumed his hike.

From this point on, the trail was a series of switchbacks. If the two on the bridge were planning on following him and stealing his equipment or wallet, they would probably give up after a short distance and wait for easier prey. Unless they were in good condition, the steep climb would leave them gasping for breath.

Large cedars pressed close to the path, blocking out the light. Old man's beard hung from the branches. The ground was a tangle of sword fern, salal, and Oregon grape. In a bit of open space, an arbutus twisted toward the sun. Its bark, deep earth-red, hung in shreds. Here and there, the new pale green bark was visible. That was the way he felt, like a snake or an arbutus, shedding his old skin for a new, better one. The previous year, when nothing else had seemed to work, he had taken his pack and hiked from sunrise to sunset, exhausting himself so completely that he could not stay awake. The sniping, looking for gold in cracks, under rocks, among the roots of trees, had come when he had started to feel better.

At the next bend he stopped and hid behind a rotting stump. In a couple of minutes his pursuers—he told himself not to be foolish, not to be paranoid—appeared. They were walking surprisingly fast. If the trail had been even slightly less steep, they would have been running.

He wished there were a cutoff that would allow him to circle back. He could, he realized, use his equipment, if necessary, to lower himself to the river but to do so, he would need to gain enough of a lead to have time to untie and uncoil the rope, to set it around a tree, to climb down, and then to pull his rope down after him so that it could not be taken away or cut. He then would be faced with the problem of finding a route up. He had to be back by seven. It was the agreed upon time. Since their mother had been killed, the children became upset if he were even a few minutes late.

He looked at his watch. It was ten o'clock. It was a two-hour hike to the end of the trail, but he could hike out in an hour and a half. That did not leave him much time. First, he wanted to clean out the crack and, if possible, begin undercutting a large rock that sat in the centre of the river. Undercutting was dangerous. It could require that he move rocks and logs to divert the shallow water to either side of where he was going to work. Then he would need more logs to prop up the rock. He didn't want to get the work partly done and have half a ton of stone roll onto him. The nuggets that might be clustered around the base were worth some risk but there was no sense in taking more chances than necessary.

Ahead, through a gap in the trees, he saw the railway trestle. The two behind him would, he told himself, stop there. Hardly anyone went further. The trestle was an inexplicable focal point. Every weekend dozens of people hiked to it, then dared each other to cross over the gorge. Many, terrified of heights, balked after the first few steps and stood, rigid, unable to force themselves to go any further.

That, he reassured himself, was what those two were coming for. They would cross the trestle and scare each other by roughhousing like a couple of adolescents.

He had hoped, unreasonably, that there would be hikers or a railway crew on the tracks. Normally, it was a relief when there was no one there. Hikers were inclined to talk about their experiences and, in the past, he had been afraid that if he were frequently seen on the same trail his weekly visits might come to the attention of a park warden. To avoid that, he had deliberately arranged to come when the park was empty.

He did not stop but crossed over the tracks and entered the forest on the far side. The path dwindled to a narrow line of crushed ferns. The trees were shagged with wind-blown moss and deadfall was everywhere. It was old forest, and, in all the times he had come, he had never seen a bird or animal. As a child he had dreamed of living in the forest. In his dreams, his hunting had always been rewarded with game. The discrepancy between what he had hoped for and reality still astounded him.

While he was able to see the railway tracks he stopped and waited. His legs had begun to tire and cramp. He stretched them, then kneaded his right calf with his thumb and forefinger. Always before he had valued the silence and the isolation. Now, however, as he watched the two bikers look up and down the roadbed then cross to the path, Harold felt the forest close around him like a trap.

He hurried away. Even as he fled he reassured himself that they had done nothing. Anyone was free to hike wherever he wanted. If he just stopped, they would catch up and pass him by without paying any attention to him.

He kept his eyes on the path. He had no intention of tripping over a vine or slipping on a log. His fear, he chided himself, was not rational. If a mountie suddenly appeared and asked him what was the matter, what could he say? That he hadn't liked the way they had looked at him earlier? That they had threatened him? And how was that, sir? He could hear the question. And the answer? The blond one pointed his finger at me. Any mountie would think him mad.

The moss was so thick that his feet made no sound. There was only the creak of his pack, the harsh sound of his breathing. He would, he decided, abandon his plans, and when he got to the end of the granite ridge that ran along on his left, he would double back through the narrow pass on its far side. People don't assault other people without good reason, he told himself, but it did no good. His panic fluttered like dry leaves in a rising wind.

He wished that he had brought a hunting knife. It would have made him feel better to have had a weapon. His mind scurried over the contents of the pack as he tried to determine what he could use in a fight. The only possibility was his rack of chock nuts. It wasn't much. A dozen aluminum wedges, even clipped together on a nylon sling, would not be very effective.

As he came to the end of the ridge he turned abruptly to the left. The pass was nearly level and, unlike the area around it, contained only a few, scattered trees. There were, he remembered, circles of stone where people had made campfires. One day he had poked about and discovered used condoms, some plastic sandwich bags, and four or five beer bottles. A broken beer bottle, he thought, would serve as a weapon. He was just beginning to search for one when he saw a movement at the far end of the pass.

He became absolutely still. He felt so weak that he thought he was going to fall down. He craned his neck for a better look. If there were two of them, he could circle back the other way. In a moment, he realized that there was only one. That meant the other was on the path he had just left. He spun on his heel and ran back to the fork. No more than a quarter of a mile away the path ended. At that point, there was nothing to do but return the way he had come or descend to the river. In either case, he was trapped. His mouth, he realized, was so dry he could not swallow.

Behind him, he heard someone ask a question that sounded like "Where did he go?" and a muffled reply but he could not be sure of the words. The ground was nearly level. He was running when he burst out onto an area where the rock fell from the side of the trail like a frozen set of rapids. There were few places here for trees to root. Leaves and pine needles were swept from the pale green lichen by the winter rains. Rather than continue to what he knew was a dead end, he clambered down the slope. He had not explored this area. In the back of his mind was the hope that the rough rock continued all the way to the river. By the time they found out he was no longer on the path, he could have climbed the other cliff. All at once, he stopped. The rough, black rock turned into sixty feet of smooth slab.

There was no time to go back. He glanced over his shoulder, then at the slab. It was, he realized, deceptive. It angled down toward the river then stopped at a ragged edge. No steeper than a roof at the outset, it curved just enough that every few feet the angle increased. Patches of lichen and the smooth texture of the stone guaranteed that anyone who ventured out on it would be engaged in a test of balance.

There was a chance, because of his friction boots, that he could work his way onto the steepest part of the slope. If the two behind him were not pursuing him, they would pass by and he would never see them again. If they were, for whatever reason, meaning him some harm, they would have great difficulty reaching him.

Quickly, he unzipped the right hand pocket of his pack and pulled out a section of three-millimetre rope. He tied a figure eight knot in both ends, wrapped the rope around his left hand, then crept down to a small evergreen. Ten feet to the right, in a completely exposed area, there was a gnarled bush. Here and there, stunted trees, their trunks nearly as hard as the rock itself, protruded from cracks.

There was little room for error. If he began to slide, it would be difficult to stop before he went over the edge. At this part of the river, the fall would not be great, but height would not make any difference. Even a twenty-foot fall onto the scattered boulders of the river bed would certainly be fatal. He leaned out, brushed away some dust that had collected on the rock, then took his first step.

Above him someone whistled sharply. It startled him but he kept his eyes fixed on the surface of the rock. He fitted the toe of his boot onto a small nubbin, then his other toe onto a seam of cracked quartz. The greatest danger was that, for even a split second, he would allow himself to be distracted. For his next move, he chose a pebbled area no bigger than a silver dollar. From there, he moved to a depression that was only noticeable because of its slight shadow. He had crossed more difficult areas than this but always with the security of a harness and rope and a belayer he could trust. A fall in those circumstances meant no more than some scraped skin and injured pride.

When he was within two feet of the bush he felt a nearly overwhelming urge to lunge forward. He forced himself to stay where he was. On the rock

there could be no impetuous moves. Patience, above all else, was to be valued. There seemed to be no place for him to put his foot. He scanned the surface. Just below him there was a hairline crack. If he pressed down hard on it, it would hold him long enough for him to step to the side and up and catch hold of the bush.

Slowly, he pirouetted on his left foot, then brought his right foot behind it. He took a deep breath, forced the air out of his lungs, then in one fluid movement, stepped down, up and across. Even as his hand grasped the wooden stem, he felt his feet begin to slide.

While he unwrapped the three-millimetre rope from his arm, he sat with his legs on either side of the stem. He fitted a loop of rope around an exposed root, then slipped the second loop around his wrist. Unless the root gave way, the most he was going to fall was a couple of feet.

Only then did he allow himself to look back. There was still no sign of anyone. The area of tumbled rock ran on for a fair distance and, he realized, would take awhile to search. Realizing this, he cursed himself for not taking a chance and running back the way he had come.

He hooked his pack to the bush, took out the sling with the hardware on it, then eased himself out onto the steepest section of slab he could reach. Here he crouched, with his back to the trail, his hands splayed against the rock.

There was a sharp whistle above him. It was immediately answered from some distance back toward the trestle. With that, he realized that they had split up. One had blocked the trail while the other had done the searching.

He looked back again. Thirty feet behind him was the dark-haired biker. His blond companion was swinging down from the left. Both of them, Harold could see, were tired. He had, he thought with a distant kind of pleasure, given them a good run for their money. If they had been carrying packs, he would have outdistanced them.

They both stopped at the rough edge, some ten feet apart, looked at each other and smirked.

"Did you want something?" he asked. He had meant to make it a casual question, even offhand, as though he had no idea they had followed him, but panic sharpened his voice.

They both laughed as if at a joke.

"What do you want?" He was no longer sure that what he had planned would work. The blond-haired man had a small leather purse attached to his

belt. He unsnapped it and took out a bone-handled clasp knife. He pried out a wide blade.

"Are you crazy?" Harold cried. "What's the matter with you? I don't even know you."

They both grinned foolishly and studied their boots. They looked, he thought wildly, like two little boys caught in the middle of a practical joke.

Panic made him feel like he was going to throw up. "Are you nuts?" he shouted. "Are you crazy or something?"

Their answer was to start down the slab, one on each side of him. Their first steps were confident, easy. The surface of the rock was granular and bare at the edge and provided plenty of friction. He could see that neither was experienced. They both came down sideways, leaning into the rock, one hand pressed to the surface. He gripped the nylon sling in his right hand and concentrated on keeping his balance.

The dark-haired one was closest. He was coming down between the tree and the shrub, taking little steps, moving his left foot down, then his right foot, then his left, dangerously pressing all his weight onto the edge of his boot and, even more dangerously, leaning backwards, throwing off his centre of balance. Suddenly, a piece of lichen peeled away and his left foot slid out from under him. Instead of responding by bending out from the rock and pressing down with his toes, he panicked. He was sliding faster and faster. His body was rigid, his face contorted with fear, his eyes, instead of searching for a place he could stop his slide, were desperately fixed on the safe area he had just left behind. He made no sound. When he was finally even with Harold, he reached out his hand as though expecting it to be taken. There was, Harold saw, on the back of the hand, a tattoo of a heart pierced by a knife. A red and blue snake wound up the arm and disappeared beneath the sleeve. It was only by luck that his one foot struck a piece of root and he stopped. He was no more than a foot from the edge.

The blond man had come at an angle, picking his way along by fitting his knife blade into a crack. Just before his companion had lost control, the blond man had started to work his way across an area where there were no cracks. He seemed frozen into place.

"Why?" Harold shouted at him.

The sound seemed to wake the blond man from a stupor. He turned his head slowly to look at Harold. He squinted and formed his mouth into a small circle, then drew his chin down and ran his tongue along his lower lip. For a moment, Harold thought the biker was going to turn and leave.

"Get me out of here," his companion cried. Fear made his voice seem as young as a child's.

The blond man shook his head, then half-snarled, stood up, and tried to walk across the intervening space. It was as though momentum and will held him upright; then Harold swung the nylon sling over his head, lunged forward, and struck his opponent on the upper arm. The blow was not powerful and, normally, it would have been swept aside. But here, as they both teetered on the steep surface, it was enough to knock them both off balance.

As the blond man skidded down the rock, he jabbed at it with his knife, trying to find an opening. Six feet from the edge, he managed to drive the blade into a crack. The knife held. He jammed the tips of his fingers into the crack.

Harold had slipped, fallen, then been caught by the rope around his wrist. He pulled himself back to the shrub and knelt with his knee against the stem.

"Help us up," the dark-haired man begged. He looked like he was on the verge of weeping.

Harold loosened the rope, then untied it. Carefully, giving his entire attention to the task, he retraced his original route. Once at the evergreen, he knew he was safe. His sides were soaked with sweat and he could smell his own fear, bitter as stale tobacco. The two men never stopped watching him.

When Harold reached the top of the slab, the blond man called, in a plaintive voice, "For God's sake, don't leave us here."

Fear had softened their eyes and mouths but he knew it was only temporary. If he drew them to safety, they would return to what they had been.

"Pull us up," the dark-haired man whined. His red head-band had come off and was tangled in his hair.

Around them, the forest was silent. Not a bird called, not an animal moved. The moss that covered the rock and soil, the moss that clung thickly to the tree trunks, the moss that hung in long strands from the branches, deadened everything, muted it, until there were no sharp lines, no certainties. The silence pressed upon them. Harold had, for a moment, a mad image of all three of them staying exactly as they were, growing slowly covered in moss and small ferns until they were indistinguishable from the logs and rocks except for their glittering eyes.

"Tell somebody about us," the dark-haired man asked.

The words tugged at him like little, black hooks. He looked down. Their faces were bleached white with fear. He could tell someone, a park warden, perhaps, but then what would happen? If he had been certain they would be sent to prison he might have dared tell somebody, but he knew that would not happen. If charges were laid he would have to testify. They would discover his name and address. And, from then on, he would live in fear. Afraid to leave his house. Afraid to go to sleep at night. Afraid for his children. And what if they denied everything, turned it all around? He had the necessary equipment to rescue them and had refused. What if one of them had fallen by the time someone came? He could be charged with manslaughter and the children would be left without mother or father. No matter how he tried to keep Conklin out of it, he would become involved. Harold knew how people thought. His short stay in hospital for depression, his weekly visits to a psychiatrist to siphon off pain and, automatically, he was crazy.

"You bastard," the blond man screamed. "You bastard. Get us out of here." He kept shifting his feet about, trying to find a purchase where there was none. "If you don't, our friends will come. They'll get us out. Then we'll start looking for you. There's thousands of us. We'll find you."

The screaming startled him for a moment but then he thought about how soon the little warmth from the sun would disappear, of how the fog would drift down with the darkness, of how the cold would creep into everything, of how few people came this way.

"No," he said. He wondered if his wife had screamed like that. Six of her fingernails had been broken. *Unto the third generation*, Conklin had said. His children and his grandchildren, should he have any, would feel the effects. Alone on a dark parking lot, desperately fighting for her life, and he had been sitting in his study, reading. "Help never comes when it is most needed."

Then with real regret for the way things were but which couldn't be changed, he hefted his pack so that it settled firmly between his shoulders and returned the way he had come.

Equal Opportunity

Jim Wong-Chu

in early canada
when railways were highways

each stop brought new opportunities

there was a rule

> the chinese could only ride
> the last two cars
> of the trains

that is

until a train derailed
killing all those
in front

(the chinese erected an altar and thanked buddha)

a new rule was made

> the chinese must ride
> the front two cars
> of the trains

that is

until another accident
claimed everyone
in the back

(the chinese erected an altar and thanked buddha)

after much debate
common sense prevailed

the chinese are now allowed
to sit anywhere
on any train

Teens Make Their Own Peace

Leah Eskin

Carlos Hernandez grew up in El Salvador. But he never had a childhood there. "At seven years old I was working in the coffee plantations from six in the morning until six in the afternoon," says Carlos, now 19. "We were living in the worst conditions that a human being can have, eating the same things day after day. I also saw dead people in the street. In my country it is not a big deal to see a person that has been tortured and thrown on the street, in the middle of the street, every day. People, even children, get used to it."

But Carlos couldn't get used to the idea that 13-year-olds like himself were being forced into the army, to fight in El Salvador's civil war. In 1984, he and his family fled to Mexico and then crept across the border into the U.S. "We didn't want to leave," says Carlos. "We were forced to leave because of the conditions. I miss my country. I miss my people. I feel like I should be there sharing the trouble that they are going through. One day, all the dream of my family is to go back."

A Dream Deferred

Until that day, Carlos has devoted himself to sharing his story with other young people. In the fall of 1986, Carlos and 62 other young victims of violence spent a month telling American high school students about their experiences. The tour was sponsored by Children of War, an organization that hopes such encounters will help rid the world of wars.

"What we do is so simple," says program director Judith Thompson.

"We get people together and they talk to each other. You begin to see that human suffering is universal. One person may have experienced war, another from a middle-class background may have experienced drugs or a suicide attempt. But there is an underlying connection between their pain. You find, buried within you, new hope, optimism, and idealism."

When the Children of War tour came to Brookline High, in Brookline, Massachusetts, it sparked that kind of idealism in Autumn Bennett. "One at a time, each of the kids started talking about their experiences in war," says Autumn, then 16. "I never thought that war was something that affected people my own age, I thought it was fought by grown men. By the end, the whole room was just crying. It was unusual to see people who are usually very guarded against each other, just opening up and crying."

A Volunteer For Peace

The experience changed her life. Autumn began to notice—and befriend—refugees who attended her own school. She started thinking about warlike conditions young people face today: drugs, gang violence, and homelessness. She helped start a local chapter of Children of War. And she spent a year between high school and college helping plan the next Children of War tour.

"I want to educate my peers," says Autumn. "I want them to know that war does affect them. If you work to change adults or change the government, you'll get frustrated. But if you work to reach other youth, you feel powerful, you don't feel alone anymore."

Carlos agrees. "On the tour, I learned that it was not only me that had been through horrible things, that had pain inside. I learned about struggles in South Africa, Haiti, and Northern Ireland. Now every time I read a newspaper and see something from, say, South Africa, I feel like something over there is part of me. It is the same struggle that young people everywhere go through."

That knowledge, say both Autumn and Carlos, is the key to creating a more peaceful world. "I realized after the tour that I was a very powerful person," says Carlos. "I realized I can make change in the world."

Sherwood Forest Revisited

New adventures of Robin Hood

Val R. Cheatham

Characters

NARRATOR	SHERIFF OF ROTTINGHAM	MARIAN, *the King's daughter*
KING	ROBIN HOOD	MERRY MEN, *extras*

Scene 1

BEFORE RISE: NARRATOR *enters in front of curtain.*

NARRATOR: The story you are about to see is true. That is, it's a true account of a legend. Of course, it is true that legends cannot be verified—and it's also true that legends are sometimes invented to explain unknown events. But, generally speaking, they are supposed to be at least some of the time, partially, based on a little truth. Anyway, in this story, all the parts that are not true have very little to do with the true story anyway. This is the tale of the Great Humanitarian Hero, the Renowned Gentleman Thief, the Immortal Master Bandit, and all-around Hey-nonny-nonny Guy: Robin Hood! So, without further truths, let our story begin.

(*Exits. Curtains open.*)

TIME: *Long ago.*

SETTING: *King's throne room. Shields, swords, etc., hang on walls and there is a throne at center with bell rope hanging beside it.*

AT RISE: *The room is empty. Then* KING *enters with bag of money and sits on throne.*

KING: Suffering serfs, am I ever tired! It's been such a taxing day! Taxing knights, taxing damsels, taxing dragons. My subjects just don't realize how hard it is to think up all these new ways to collect taxes! (*Shifts position*) I need to get away and relax for several weeks and think of nothing. Too bad television hasn't been invented yet. Oh, well (*Pulls bell rope*), I can ring for the Jester and maybe have a few laughs. (ROBIN HOOD, *disguised as jester, enters, his head bowed, so the* KING *does not see his face.*)

ROBIN: You rang, Sire?

KING: Yes, Jester, amuse me with some of your traveling squire jokes. (*Suddenly*) Wait! (*Stands*) You're not the Jester—you're—

ROBIN (*Flinging off disguise, drawing sword and brandishing it with large sweeps*): Yes! Hey nonny-nonny, 'tis I, Robin Hood.

Here is my decree:

Ask not what your country can do for you,

But what you can give to me.

KING: You! Robin Hood! You dare to enter my castle? (*Composing himself*) Obviously you have forgotten about my guards. (*Mocking laugh*) Ha, ha, ha —at last Robin Hood has made a mistake!

ROBIN:

Alack, you are right,

A mistake has been made.

But, whose has it been?

Will you wager this blade?

(*Holds sword next to* KING'S *throat*)

KING: You fool! I'll wager nothing! All I have to do is pull on this (*Pulls bell rope*)— and my guards will be upon you before you can spout another "hey nonny-nonny!" (KING *smiles broadly. His expression begins to change as there is a long pause and no one comes.* KING *clears throat nervously.*)

ROBIN (*Folding arms nonchalantly*): Hey nonny-nonny . . .

KING (*Getting more nervous*): Just one pull (*Pulls again*) on this bell rope, and the Sheriff of Rottingham will arrive in full armor before you can say, "Stand and deliver!"

ROBIN (*Smiling*):

> Stand and deliver,
> O generous giver.

KING (*Pulling rope frantically*): I'm the King! You can't rob me in my own castle! It's . . . it's against the law!

ROBIN (*Stepping next to* KING):

> The poor will rejoice—
> For the King has no choice!

(*Holds out hand for money bag, which* KING *gives him*)

KING: I've heard of giving at the office, but this is ridiculous!

ROBIN (*Holding sword above head*):

> Hey nonny-nonny, a title I forswore,
> To rob from the rich and give to the poor!

(*Exits with flourish*)

KING (*Pulling rope vigorously*): Where are my guards? Modern technology— bah! (*Stops pulling cord*) I'll take old-fashioned lung power any day. (*Bellows*) Guards! (SHERIFF *enters. He speaks in manner of John Wayne and wears black patch over one eye.*)

SHERIFF: Let's get these cannons in a circle. Robin Hood is a-heading this way.

KING: You're too late, you silly sap. By this time Robin Hood is already heading that-a-way! (*Points toward exit*)

SHERIFF: Dad blast that varmint! I'd have had him with my fast draw if those little green Merry Men hadn't back-jumped me.

KING: Excuses! Excuses! That's all I hear! I want Robin Hood if you have to arrest every man in Sherwood Forest.

SHERIFF: We already did that! But Robin Hood escaped by dressing up like a woman.

KING: I want him if you have to burn down every tree in Sherwood Forest!

SHERIFF: We tried that, too, but those Merry Men of his picked up our flaming arrows and shot them right back at us. And oo — oh — did that ever smart!

Two against one
Is a scoundrel's ill creed.

KING: But, good sir, I am just a poor king, while this girl has all that money—see?

ROBIN (*To* MARIAN):

I say, good woman, can this be true?
Does all that money belong to you?

MARIAN: Yes! I'm . . . I'm rich!

ROBIN:

Well, hey nonny-nonny, alas and alack!
I rob from the rich, so give me your sack!
(*Takes money bag and gives it to* KING; MERRY MEN *exit.*)

MARIAN: Oh-oh! Did I ever goof on word choice that time!

KING (*To* ROBIN): Thank you, kind sir. You are a true gentleman of your chosen profession.

SHERIFF: Is it time to get the coachmen in a circle?

KING: No, you ignoble idiot, it's time to get out! (*Exits with* SHERIFF)

ROBIN (*Flourishing sword*):

Hey nonny-nonny and now I must go,
My country 'tis of thee.
I rob from the rich and give to the poor;
O say can the dawn's light you see?
(*Starts to exit*)

MARIAN: Now just hold on a minute, man. You're not the brainiest guy I ever met, but I really dig your dedication. How about the two of us tying the "I do" knot, then spending the happily-ever-after grooving in this greenery?

ROBIN:

Well, hey nonny-nonny. Sound drums and a fife!
Dost thou wish to be Maid Marian, my wife?

MARIAN: Well, I had *Ms.* Hood in mind, but if you promise you won't invite those little green Merry Men to dinner more than once a month, I'll O.K. it for the Maid Marian bit. (*Exits arm-in-arm with* ROBIN.)

KING (*Entering with* SHERIFF): Things do have a way of working out, don't they? This sure beats collecting taxes!

SHERIFF: You mean after all this I don't get to slap Robin Hood behind bars and collect the ree-ward?

KING: No. I have just solved three of my biggest problems! One, my daughter will get married and move out of the castle; and two, any time I need money I'll just send you out here disguised to look poor, and Robin Hood will give it to you.

SHERIFF (*Counting on fingers*): But I thought you said you had solved *three* problems.

KING: Yes! I did! *You* are going to be spending a lot of time out here looking poor!

(Curtain)

THE END

Production Notes

Characters: 3 male; 1 female; 1 male or female for Narrator; as many male or female extras as desired for Merry Men (non-speaking parts).

Playing Time: 15 minutes.

Costumes: Robin wears green and has sword. Merry Men are dressed similarly. King and Marian wear appropriate fairy tale costumes. Sheriff wears black eye patch, cowboy hat, and other Western accessories as desired.

Properties: Bag of money.

Setting: Scene 1: King's throne room, with throne, bell rope, and appropriate decorations as desired. Scene 2: Sherwood Forest, with backdrop of trees, if desired.

Lighting: No special effects.

Happy Dens or A Day in the Old Wolves' Home

Jane Yolen

Nurse Lamb stood in front of the big white house with the black shutters. She shivered. She was a brand-new nurse and this was her very first job.

From inside the house came loud and angry growls. Nurse Lamb looked at the name carved over the door: HAPPY DENS. But it didn't sound like a happy place, she thought, as she listened to the howls from inside.

Shuddering, she knocked on the door.

The only answer was another howl.

Lifting the latch, Nurse Lamb went in.

No sooner had she stepped across the doorstep than a bowl sped by her head. It splattered against the wall. Nurse Lamb ducked, but she was too late. Her fresh white uniform was spotted and dotted with whatever had been in the bowl.

"*Mush!*" shouted an old wolf, shaking his cane at her. "Great howls and thorny paws. I can't stand another day of it. The end of life is nothing but a big bowl of mush."

Nurse Lamb gave a frightened little bleat and turned to go back out the door, but a great big wolf with two black ears and one black paw barred her way. "Mush for breakfast, mush for dinner, and more mush in between," he growled. "That's all they serve us here at Happy Dens, Home for Aging Wolves."

The wolf with the cane added, "When we were young and full of teeth it was never like this." He howled.

Nurse Lamb gave another bleat and ran into the next room. To her surprise

it was a kitchen. A large, comfortable-looking pig wearing a white hat was leaning over the stove and stirring an enormous pot. Since the wolves had not followed her in, Nurse Lamb sat down on a kitchen stool and began to cry.

The cook put her spoon down, wiped her trotters with a stained towel, and patted Nurse Lamb on the head, right behind the ears.

"There, there, lambkin," said the cook. "Don't start a new job in tears. We say that in the barnyard all the time."

Nurse Lamb looked up and snuffled. "I . . . I don't think I'm right for this place. I feel as if I have been thrown to the wolves."

The cook nodded wisely. "And, in a manner of speaking, you have been. But these poor old dears are all bark and no bite. Toothless, don't you know. All they can manage is mush."

"But no one told me this was an old *wolves'* home," complained Nurse Lamb. "They just said 'How would you like to work at Happy Dens?' And it sounded like the nicest place in the world."

"And so it is. And so it is," said the cook. "It just takes getting used to."

Nurse Lamb wiped her nose and looked around. "But how could someone like *you* work here? I mean . . ." She dropped her voice to a whisper. "I heard all about it at school. The three little pigs and all. Did you know them?"

The cook sniffed. "And a bad lot they were, too. As we say in the barnyard, 'There's more than one side to every sty.'"

"But I was told that the big bad wolf tried to eat the three little pigs. And he huffed and he puffed and . . ." Nurse Lamb looked confused.

Cook just smiled and began to stir the pot again, lifting up a spoonful to taste.

"And then there was that poor little child in the woods with the red riding hood," said Nurse Lamb. "Bringing the basket of goodies to her sick grandmother."

Cook shook her head and added pepper to the pot. "In the barnyard we say, 'Don't take slop from a kid in a cloak.'" She ladled out a bowlful of mush.

Nurse Lamb stood up. She walked up to the cook and put her hooves on her hips. "But what about that boy Peter. The one who caught the wolf by the tail after he ate the duck. And the hunters came and —"

"Bad press," said a voice from the doorway. It was the wolf with the two black ears. "Much of what you know about wolves is bad press."

Nurse Lamb turned and looked at him. "I don't even know what bad press means," she said.

"It means that only one side of the story has been told. There is another way of telling those very same tales. From the wolf's point of view." He grinned at her. "My name is Wolfgang, and if you will bring a bowl of that thoroughly awful stuff to the table"—he pointed to the pot—"I will tell you *my* side of a familiar tale."

Sheepishly, Nurse Lamb picked up the bowl and followed the wolf into the living room. She put the bowl on the table in front of Wolfgang and sat down. There were half a dozen wolves sitting there.

Nurse Lamb smiled at them timidly.

They smiled back. The cook was right. Only Wolfgang had any teeth. Three, to be exact.

Wolfgang's Tale

Once upon a time (began the black-eared wolf) there was a thoroughly nice young wolf. He had two black ears and one black paw. He was a poet and a dreamer.

This thoroughly nice wolf loved to lie about in the woods staring at the lacy curlings of fiddlehead ferns and smelling the wild roses. He was a vegetarian —except for lizards and an occasional snake, which don't count. He loved carrot cake and was partial to peanut-butter pie.

One day as he lay by the side of a babbling brook, writing a poem that began

Twinkle, twinkle, lambkin's eye,
How I wish you were close by . . .

he heard the sound of a child weeping. He knew it was a human child because only they cry with that snuffling gasp. So the thoroughly nice wolf leaped to his feet and ran over, his hind end waggling, eager to help.

The child looked up from her crying. She was quite young and dressed in a long red riding hood, a lacy dress, white stockings, and black patent-leather Mary Jane shoes. Hardly what you would call your usual hiking-in-the-woods outfit.

"Oh, hello, wolfie," she said. In those days, of course, humans often talked to wolves. "I am quite lost."

The thoroughly nice wolf sat down by her side and held her hand. "There, there," he said. "Tell me where you live."

The child grabbed her hand back. "If I knew that, you silly growler, I wouldn't be lost, would I?"

The thoroughly nice wolf bit back his own sharp answer and asked her in rhyme:

> *Where are you going*
> *My pretty young maid?*
> *Answer me this*
> *And I'll make you a trade.*
>
> *The path through the forest*
> *Is dark and it's long,*
> *So I will go with you*
> *And sing you a song.*

The little girl was charmed. "I'm going to my grandmother's house," she said. "With this." She held up a basket that was covered with a red-checked cloth. The wolf could smell carrot cake. He grinned.

"Oh, poet, what big teeth you have," said the child.

"The better to eat carrot cake with," said the thoroughly nice wolf.

"My granny hates carrot cake," said the child. "In fact, she hates anything but mush."

"What bad taste," said the wolf. "I made up a poem about that once:

> *If I found someone*
> *Who liked to eat mush,*
> *I'd sit them in front of it,*
> *Then give a . . ."*

"Push!" shouted the child.

"Why, you're a poet too," said the wolf.

"I'm really more of a storyteller," said the child, blushing prettily. "But I do love carrot cake."

"All poets do," said the wolf. "So you must be a poet as well."

"Well, my granny is no poet. Every week when I bring the carrot cake over, she dumps it into her mush and mushes it all up together and then makes me eat it with her. She says that I have to learn that life ends with a bowl of mush."

"Great howls!" said the wolf, shuddering. "What a terribly wicked thing to say and do."

"I guess so," said the child.

"Then we must save this wonderful carrot cake from your grandmother," the wolf said, scratching his head below his ears.

The child clapped her hands. "I know," she said. "Let's pretend."

"Pretend?" asked the wolf.

"Let's pretend that you are Granny and I am bringing the cake to *you*. Here, you wear my red riding hood and we'll pretend it's Granny's nightcap and nightgown."

The wolf took her little cape and slung it over his head. He grinned again. He was a poet and he loved pretending.

The child skipped up to him and knocked upon an imaginary door.

The wolf opened it. "Come in. Come in."

"Oh, no," said the child. "My grandmother never gets out of bed."

"Never?" asked the wolf.

"Never," said the child.

"All right," said the thoroughly nice wolf, shaking his head. He lay down on the cool green grass, clasped his paws over his stomach, and made a very loud pretend snore.

The child walked over to his feet and knocked again.

"Who is it?" called out the wolf in a high, weak, scratchy voice.

"It is your granddaughter, Little Red Riding Hood," the child said, giggling.

"Come in, come in. Just lift the latch. I'm in bed with aches and pains and a bad case of the rheumaticks," said the wolf in the high, funny voice.

The child walked in through the pretend door.

"I have brought you a basket of goodies," said the child, putting the basket by the wolf's side. She placed her hands on her hips. "But you know, Grandmother, you look very different today."

"How so?" asked the wolf, opening both his yellow eyes wide.

"Well, Grandmother, what big eyes you have," said the child.

The wolf closed his eyes and opened them again quickly. "The better to see you with, my dear," he said.

"Oh, you silly wolf. She never calls me *dear*. She calls me *Sweetface*. Or *Punkins*. Or her *Airy Fairy Dee*."

"How awful," said the wolf.

"I know," said the child. "But that's what she calls me."

"Well, I can't," said the wolf, turning over on his side. "I'm a poet, after all, and no self-respecting poet could possibly use those words. If I have to call you that, there's no more pretending."

"I guess you can call me *dear*," said the child in a very small voice. "But I didn't know that poets were so particular."

"About *words* we are," said the wolf.

"And you have an awfully big nose," said the child.

The wolf put his paw over his nose. "Now that is uncalled-for," he said. "My nose isn't that big—for a wolf."

"It's part of the game," said the child.

"Oh, yes, the game. I had forgotten. The better to smell the basket of goodies, my dear," said the wolf.

"And Grandmother, what big teeth you have."

The thoroughly nice wolf sat up. "The better to eat carrot cake with," he said.

At that, the game was over. They shared the carrot cake evenly and licked their fingers, which was not very polite but certainly the best thing to do on a picnic in the woods. And the wolf sang an ode to carrot cake which he made up on the spot:

Carrot cake, o carrot cake
The best thing a baker ever could make,
Mushy or munchy
Gushy or crunchy
Eat it by a woodland lake.

"We are really by a stream," said the child.

"That is what is known as poetic license," said the wolf. "Calling a stream a lake."

"Maybe you can use your license to drive me home."

The wolf nodded. "I will if you tell me your name. I know it's not *really* Little Red Riding Hood."

The child stood up and brushed crumbs off her dress. "It's Elisabet Grimm," she said.

"Of the Grimm family on Forest Lane?" asked the wolf.

"Of course," she answered.

"Everyone knows where that is. I'll take you home right now," said the wolf. He stretched himself from tip to tail. "But what will you tell your mother about her cake?" He took her by the hand.

"Oh, I'm a storyteller," said the child. "I'll think of something."

And she did.

"She did indeed," said Nurse Lamb thoughtfully. She cleared away the now empty bowls and took them back to the kitchen. When she returned, she was carrying a tray full of steaming mugs of coffee.

"I told you I had bad press," said Wolfgang.

"I should say you had," Nurse Lamb replied, passing out the mugs.

"Me, too," said the wolf with the cane.

"You, too, what?" asked Nurse Lamb.

"I had bad press, too, though my story is somewhat different. By the by, my name is Oliver," said the wolf. "Would you like to hear my tale?"

Nurse Lamb sat down. "Oh, please, yes."

Oliver Wolf's Tale

Once upon a time there was a very clever young wolf. He had an especially broad, bushy tail and a white star under his chin.

In his playpen he had built tall buildings of blocks and straw.

In the schoolyard he had built forts of mud and sticks.

And once, after a trip with his father to the bricklayer's, he had made a tower of bricks.

Oh, how that clever young wolf loved to build things.

"When I grow up," he said to his mother and father not once but many times, "I want to be an architect."

"That's nice, dear," they would answer, though they wondered about it. After all, no one in their family had ever been anything more than a wolf.

When the clever little wolf was old enough, his father sent him out into the world with a pack of tools and letters from his teachers.

"*This* is a very clever young wolf," read one letter.

"Quite the cleverest I have ever met," said another.

So the clever young wolf set out looking for work.

In a short while he came to a crossroads and who should be there but three punk pigs building themselves houses and making quite a mess of it.

The first little pig was trying to build a house of straw.

"Really," said the clever wolf, "I tried that in the playpen. It won't work. A breath of air will knock it over."

"Well, if you're so clever," said the pig, pushing his sunglasses back up his snout, "why don't you try and blow it down."

The wolf set his pack by the side of the road, rolled up his shirt-sleeves, and huffed and puffed. The house of straw collapsed in a twinkling.

"See," said the clever wolf.

The little pig got a funny look on his face and ran one of his trotters up under his collar.

The wolf turned to the second little pig who had just hammered a nail into the house he was trying to build. It was a makeshift affair of sticks and twigs.

"Yours is not much better, I'm afraid," said the clever wolf.

"Oh, yeah?" replied the pig. "Clever is as clever does." He thumbed his snout at the wolf. "Let's see how you blow *this* house down, dog-breath."

The wolf sucked in a big gulp of air. Then he huffed and puffed a bit harder than before. The sticks tumbled down in a heap of dry kindling, just as he knew they would.

The second little pig picked up one of the larger pieces and turned it nervously in his trotters.

"Nyah, nyah nyah, nyah nyah!" said the third little pig, stretching his suspenders and letting them snap back with a loud twang. "Who do you think's afraid of you, little wolf? Try your muzzle on this pile of bricks, hair-face."

"That won't be necessary," said the clever wolf. "Every good builder knows bricks are excellent for houses."

The third little pig sniffed and snapped his suspenders once again.

"However," said the wolf, pointing at the roof, "since you have asked my opinion, I think you missed the point about chimneys. They are supposed to go straight up, not sideways."

"Well, if you're so clever . . ." began the first little pig.

"And have such strong breath . . ." added the second little pig.

"And are such a know-it-all and tell-it-ever . . ." put in the third little pig.

"Why don't you go up there and fix it yourself!" all three said together.

"Well, thank you," said the clever wolf, realizing he had just been given his very first job. "I'll get to it at once." Finding a ladder resting against the side of the brick house, he hoisted his pack of tools onto his back and climbed up onto the roof.

He set the bricks properly, lining them up with his plumb line. He mixed the mortar with care. He was exacting in his measurements and careful in his calculations. The sun was beginning to set before he was done.

"There," he said at last. "That should do it." He expected, at the very least, a thank-you from the pigs. But instead all he got was a loud laugh from the third little pig, a snout-thumbing from the second, and a nasty wink from the first.

The clever wolf shrugged his shoulders. After all, pigs will be pigs and he couldn't expect them to be wolves. But when he went to climb down he found they had removed the ladder.

"Clever your way out of this one, fuzz-ball," shouted the third little pig. Then they ran inside the house, turned up the stereo, and phoned their friends for a party.

The only way down was the chimney. But the wolf had to wait until the bricks and mortar had set as hard as stone. That took half the night. When at last the chimney was ready, the wolf slowly made his way down the inside, his pack on his back.

The pigs and their friends heard him coming. And between one record and the next, they shoved a pot of boiling mush into the hearth. They laughed themselves silly when the wolf fell in.

"That's how things end, fur-tail," the pigs shouted. "With a bowl of mush."

Dripping and unhappy, the wolf ran out the door. He vowed never to associate with pigs again. And to this day—with the exception of the cook—he never has. And being a well-brought-up wolf, as well as clever, he has never told his side of the story until today.

"Well, the pigs sure talked about it," said Nurse Lamb, shaking her head. "The way *they* have told it, it is quite a different story."

"Nobody listens to pigs," said Oliver Wolf. He looked quickly at the kitchen door.

"I'm not so sure," said a wolf who had a patch over his eye. "I'm not so sure."

"So you're not so sure," said Oliver. "Bet you think you're pretty clever, Lone Wolf."

"No," said Lone Wolf. "I never said I was clever. *You* are the clever little wolf."

Wolfgang laughed. "So clever he was outwitted by a pack of punk pigs."

The other wolves laughed.

"You didn't do so well with one human child," answered Oliver.

"Now, now, now," said the cook, poking her head in through the door. "As we say in the barnyard, 'Words are like wood, a handy weapon.'"

"No weapons. No fighting," said Nurse Lamb, standing up and shaking her hoof at the wolves. "We are supposed to be telling stories, not getting into fights."

Lone Wolf stared at her. "I never in my life ran from a fight. Not if it was for a good cause."

Nurse Lamb got up her courage and put her hand on his shoulder. "I believe you," she said. "Why not tell me about some of the good causes you fought for?"

Lone Wolf twitched his ears. "All right," he said at last. "I'm not boasting you understand. Just setting the record straight."

Nurse Lamb looked over at the kitchen door. The old sow winked at her and went back to work.

Lone Wolf's Tale

Once upon a time there was a kind, tender, and compassionate young wolf. He had a black patch over one eye and another black patch at the tip of his tail. He loved to help the under-dog, the under-wolf, the under-lamb, and even the under-pig.

His basement was full of the signs of his good fights. Signs like LOVE A TREE and HAVE YOU KISSED A FLOWER TODAY? and PIGS ARE PEOPLE, TOO! and HONK IF YOU LOVE A WEASEL.

One day he was in the basement running off petitions on his mimeo machine when he heard a terrible noise.

KA-BLAAAAAAM KA-BLOOOOOOOIE.

It was the sound a gun makes in the forest.

Checking his calendar, the kind and tender wolf saw with horror that it was opening day of duck-hunting season. Quickly he put on his red hat and red vest. Then he grabbed up the signs he had made for that occasion: SOME DUCKS CAN'T DUCK and EAT CORN NOT CORN-EATERS and DUCKS HAVE MOTHERS, TOO. Then he ran out of his door and down the path as fast as he could go.

KA-BLAAAAAAAM KA-BLOOOOOOOIE.

The kind and tender wolf knew just where to go. Deep in the forest was a wonderful pond where the ducks liked to stop on their way north. The food was good, the reeds comfortable, the prices reasonable, and the linens changed daily.

When the kind and tender wolf got to the pond, all he could see was one small and very frightened mallard in the middle of the pond and thirteen hunters around the edge.

"Stop!" he shouted as the hunters raised their guns.

This did not stop them.

The kind and tender wolf tried again, shouting anything he could think of. "We shall overcome," he called. "No smoking. No nukes. Stay off the grass."

Nothing worked. The hunters sighted their guns. The wolf knew it was time to act.

He put one of the signs in the water and sat on it. He picked up another sign as a paddle. Using his tail as a rudder, he pushed off into the pond and rowed toward the duck.

"I will save you," he cried. "We are brothers. Quack."

The mallard looked confused. Then it turned and swam toward the wolf. When it reached him, it climbed onto the sign and quacked back.

"Saved," said the kind and tender wolf triumphantly, neglecting to notice that their combined weight was making the cardboard sign sink. But when the water was up to his chin, the wolf suddenly remembered he could not swim.

"Save yourself, friend," he called out, splashing great waves and swallowing them.

The mallard was kind and tender, too. It pushed the drowning wolf to shore and then, hidden by a patch of reeds, gave the well-meaning wolf beak-to-muzzle resuscitation. Then the bird flew off behind the cover of trees. The hunters never saw it go.

But they found the wolf, his fur all soggy. "Look!" said one who had his name, *Peter*, stenciled on the pocket of his coat. "There are feathers on this wolf's jaws and in his whiskers. He has eaten *our* duck."

And so the hunters grabbed up the kind and tender wolf by his tail and slung him on top of the remaining sign. They marched him once around the town and threw him into jail for a week, where they gave him nothing to eat but mush.

"Now, wolf," shouted the hunter Peter when they finally let him out of jail, "don't you come back here again or it will be mush for you from now 'til the end of your life."

The kind and tender wolf, nursing his hurt tail and his aching teeth, left town. The next day the newspaper ran a story that read: PETER & THE WOLF FIGHT. PETER RUNS FOR MAYOR. VOWS TO KEEP WOLF FROM DOOR. And to this day no one believes the kind and tender wolf's side of the tale.

"I believe it," said Nurse Lamb looking at Lone Wolf with tears in her eyes. "In fact, I believe all of you." She stood up and collected the empty mugs.

"Hurray!" said the cook, peeking in the doorway. "Maybe this is one young nurse we'll keep."

"Keep?" Nurse Lamb suddenly looked around, all her fear coming back. Lone Wolf was cleaning his nails. Three old wolves had dozed off. Wolfgang was gazing at the ceiling. But Oliver grinned at her and licked his chops. "What do you mean, keep?"

"Do you want *our* side of the story?" asked Oliver, still grinning. "Or the nurses'?"

Nurse Lamb gulped.

Oliver winked.

Then Nurse Lamb knew they were teasing her. "Oh, you big bad wolf," she said and patted him on the head. She walked back into the kitchen.

"You know," she said to the cook. "I think I'm going to like it here. I think I can help make it a real *happy* HAPPY DEN. I'll get them to write down their stories. And maybe we'll make a book of them. Life doesn't *have* to end with a bowl of mush."

Stirring the pot, the cook nodded and smiled.

"In fact," said Nurse Lamb loudly, "why don't we try chicken soup for lunch?"

From the dining room came a great big cheer.

The Giant Bear

Kiakshuk

There once was a giant bear
who followed people for his prey.
He was so big he swallowed them whole:
Then they smothered to death inside him
if they hadn't already died of fright.

Either the bear attacked them on the run,
or if they crawled into a cave
where he could not squeeze his enormous body in,
he stabbed them with his whiskers like toothpicks,
drawing them out one by one,
and gulped them down.

No one knew what to do
until a wise man went out and let the bear swallow him,
sliding right down his throat into the big, dark, hot, slimy
stomach.

And once inside there, he took his knife
and simply cut him open,
killing him of course.

He carved a door in the bear's belly
and threw out those who had been eaten before,
and then he stepped out himself
and went home to get help with the butchering.

Everyone lived on bear meat for a long time.
That's the way it goes:
Monster one minute, food the next.

242

The "Close Your Eyes" Dance

Basil H. Johnston

Nanabush was very tired. He had walked all day and could go no farther. On the shore of a bay he stopped to drink and splash water on his face. Then he sat down on a large stone beneath a tree to rest his aching bones.

Near the shore on the far side of the bay there was a flock of ducks, swimming and diving and quacking loudly. Their noise drew Nanabush's attention. He squinted in the bright sunlight. Not having eaten all day, Nanabush was hungry as well as tired. The sight of the plump, juicy ducks sent pangs of hunger shooting through his empty stomach.

Nanabush knew there was no point in trying to catch the ducks. They were much too clever. He remembered with shame that once long ago some ducks had tricked him. He had swum underwater to catch them and tie their feet together with a rope so that he could pull them ashore. Instead the ducks had taken flight. Up into the sky they had soared, dragging Nanabush clinging hard to the rope behind them. Weak and frightened and dizzy, Nanabush had lost his grip on the rope and fallen—fortunately for him into the lake. From then on he had always kept away from ducks.

This time, no matter how hard he tried, Nanabush could not ignore the ducks. Their din and clatter carried across the bay. The ducks seemed to be mocking him. There they were eating and playing while he had not a bite to eat and not a single thing to cheer him.

As Nanabush watched the ducks, he began to grow angry. They were fat, and he was thin. They were happy, and he was sad. That did not seem fair. Why should some be well fed while others went hungry, and why should he be the hungry one? His needs were as great as those of others. His skills were equal to those of others. Game was abundant. And yet in the midst of plenty, Nanabush had to go hungry.

To comfort himself, Nanabush took out his drum and began to chant very softly. Almost immediately he began to feel better. Perhaps if he sang, Kitche Manitou would take pity on him. He closed his eyes and chanted a little louder. Then, much more cheerful, Nanabush stood up and began to dance. Perhaps a dance would bring a change in his fortunes.

"Hey, Nanabush!"

Startled, Nanabush shuffled to a halt. One plump little duck had crossed the bay and was now swimming close to Nanabush and looking at him curiously.

"What do you want?" Nanabush demanded.

"What are you doing?" the little duck asked, his eyes wide in wonder.

"Don't you know? I'm chanting and I'm dancing," Nanabush explained.

"May I dance? May I chant?" the young duck asked.

Nanabush laughed. "You! Dance!"

"But I want to dance," the little duck pleaded.

"Your feet are flat! They look like snowshoes," answered Nanabush.

"But I can run on top of water," the duck said.

"That's different," Nanabush answered. "Besides, you're too bow-legged."

"But I want to dance," the little duck begged.

Nanabush felt sorry for the little duck and he forgot about his hunger. "Well, if you want to," he said.

The little duck clambered out of the water. He slipped and slid and waddled over the stones. Even when he was standing, he went on wobbling.

"What do I do?" asked the duck.

"Just do what I do," answered Nanabush, and he began to drum and chant and dance. The little duck—wings outspread, beak open, feet scrunched—tripped and waddled behind Nanabush as if he were walking on hot coals. But all the while he quacked happily.

"Hey, Nanabush, may I dance too?" came another eager voice.

"If you want to," Nanabush muttered. And another duck joined the dance.

For Nanabush, chanting and dancing were forms of prayer. For the ducks, dancing was play and fun. Nanabush was sober and serious, but the ducks quacked and squawked in laughter.

"Hey, Nanabush, may we dance too?" came a chorus of voices.

All the ducks had swum over to the shore where Nanabush was. Nanabush stopped his chanting and dancing. An idea had just come to him.

"If you want to," he said. With a glint in his eye, he added, "I will teach you a new dance. It's called the 'close your eyes' dance."

All the young ducks cheered and flapped their wings, but one old duck grumbled, "I have never heard of that dance. How does it go?"

"It's easy," Nanabush explained, "one long gliding stride and two taps with the foot, one long gliding stride and two taps with the other foot, followed by a wiggle of the tail. You must close your eyes and chant as loud as you can. You must not peek. If you do, the dance is over."

"Good! Good! Good!" the ducks quacked.

Then Nanabush said, "We need a big fire for this dance. Before we begin, you must gather lots of wood."

The ducks did not need to be told twice. They wanted to dance. Off they went—some into the bush, others along the beach. They brought back twigs, branches, and dead wood. Soon there was a huge pile of wood on the beach, enough for a great bonfire.

Nanabush lit the pile of wood. "First, I want you to learn the step," he said.

"I will drum and chant. When you have learned the step and the beat, you can chant with me. Chant as loud as you want to, but remember you must not open your eyes. Do you understand?"

"Yes, yes," answered the ducks.

"Make a big circle," Nanabush ordered. And the ducks formed a great circle around the sizzling fire.

Nanabush began to chant. "Aaaayee, eeeeyae." The ducks waddled one long stride and two taps. They were very wobbly.

"Shorten your strides. Your legs are too short and too far apart," Nanabush commanded. After a couple of turns around the fire, Nanabush declared that they were ready to perform the dance.

"Remember," Nanabush said, "I chant and I drum. You chant with me, but keep your eyes closed. Are you ready?"

"Ready," came the reply.

Nanabush began to chant and drum. Soon the ducks were making such a din that Nanabush's voice was drowned out. Only the drum could be heard—and the scraping of feet.

Without losing a beat, Nanabush grabbed a duck, twisted his neck, and tossed him into the fire. The ducks had their eyes closed tight and did not see what was happening. Nanabush seized a second duck and then a third. The dancing and the squawking continued. Nanabush went on seizing ducks, one after another. The other ducks went right on quacking, and dancing, not daring to open their eyes, not wanting to spoil the dance by breaking the rule.

But the old duck was uneasy and opened one eye. To his horror, he saw Nanabush seize a duck, twist his neck, and stuff him into the embers.

"Nanabush is killing us. Fly! Fly! Fly!" the old duck screeched, and he flew off. The other ducks opened their eyes. When they saw what Nanabush was doing, they too flew off, squawking in terror.

Nanabush did not care. He had eight or nine fat ducks. He could not remember how many. As soon as they were cooked, he would eat. He laughed at how clever he had been—tricking the ducks who always had been so watchful.

Still laughing, Nanabush drew in a whiff of the roasting duck. He was hungry, hungrier than he had ever been, and he was tired. All the drumming and chanting and dancing had worn him out. He lay down to rest while the ducks cooked, and soon he was fast asleep.

As Nanabush slept, he began to dream about food, all kinds of food, but particularly roast duck. His dream was so real that he could even smell it.

He awoke with a start. He was no longer tired but he was starving. He rushed to the fire with a picture in his mind of sixteen beautiful drumsticks. With his mouth watering and his stomach telling him to hurry, hurry, Nanabush reached into the fire for the nearest duck.

But all he got was a handful of charred, black bones! While he had slept, the ducks had burnt to a crisp.

Overhead the ducks were screeching. "Have a feast, Nanabush. Shall we have another dance? Will you drum and chant for us while we dance the 'dance of hunger'?"

Our World

With a Little Gold Pencil

Barbara Girion

I had been a reporter for Union High's paper since my freshman year. Now, as a junior, I was features editor and doing everything possible to make sure I was appointed editor-in-chief for my senior year.

I knew that the way to keep ahead of the competition was to come up with super ideas, and this year I'd hit on a winner. I had started a personality news column called "Shelby Sez," with my picture at the top. That's me, Shelby Dreighton, age seventeen. I thought of myself as a high-school-age Barbara Walters, getting juicy interviews with a cross-section of the student body. No one was safe from me: jocks, cheerleaders, grinds, intellects, freaks. I would quote them and then write my own opinion of their activities.

Of course I wasn't always kind, and some of the things I said were slightly controversial. As a result, almost every week I had a fight with Mr. Harrington, our adviser — like the time he read my column on class do-gooders. I had said that do-gooders would even mop up the bathroom floors if they could put it on their college applications and get credit for being well-rounded students.

"Are you sure you want to write this, Shelby?" That was Mr. Harrington's favorite remark.

"Are you telling me I can't write it, Mr. Harrington?"

"Just remember, Shelby, you can do a lot of damage to a person with a little gold pencil."

He was referring to a *real* little gold pencil. It had been a gift to me from Mom and Dad. It was attached by a chain to a tiny refillable notebook, and I carried it everywhere. I try to make the person I'm interviewing feel

comfortable. No tape recorders or big notebooks—just this tiny pencil and pad that fit neatly into my pocket. It's amazing, but when people see the pencil they're caught off guard. I don't think they realize you can write just as much with a little pencil as with a big one.

Of course I *did* get plenty of "Why don't you drop dead and save us the trouble of drowning you?" letters after the publication of some of my columns. But if that was the price of freedom of the press, so be it.

Now I was angling for a column on L. Mark Compton, super-jock, *the* athlete at Union High. A six-foot-two senior with incredible black eyes and eyelashes, he had letters in football, basketball, and track.

When I cornered L. Mark after his basketball practice one evening, he said he'd give me a couple of minutes. He had just showered, and there were still some drops of water sparkling in his hair. We sat in the bleachers and talked about sports and team spirit, and he told me how great it was to play for good old Union. But that isn't what Barbara Walters would settle for, and neither would I.

"Mark," I said. "Really, the kids like to read personal stuff. You know, your favorite foods, rock stars, TV programs . . . stuff like that."

He hesitated. When he did speak, his voice was low and soft. But I wasn't

 supposed to be lulled by his voice. I was supposed to be concentrating on his words. If I didn't, Larry would say, "I told you so."

That's Larry Williams. He's a senior and editor-in-chief. We've been sort of going together this year. He keeps saying I've got the best chance at editor-in-chief because I'm completely professional. He also said I was the only one he'd trust to interview L. Mark Compton, because every other girl on the paper would immediately fall in love with him.

Mark stood up. "Listen, Shelby Dreighton, I've read some of the interviews you've done with other kids. I'm not about to give you any ammunition."

That annoyed me. Besides, I was beginning to feel uncomfortable. He was just so big standing there. Every once in a while our knees would touch, and those beautiful eyelashes were very distracting.

I looked down at my notebook. My little gold pencil had been drawing flower petals. I *never* doodle during interviews. I flipped to a fresh page.

"Everybody calls you Mark, but your name is L. Mark. Tell me, what's the first initial for?"

"No, you don't. That's my secret." He reached for his gym bag. "But I'm starving, and I'll buy you a burger. My car's in the lot."

That's how the interview began. In fact, it took a while for it to end. It lasted through three evenings—*great* evenings, I should add. Of course I got a razzing from Larry, especially when I broke our weekly Friday night date to watch Channel 10's movie greats so I could sit in the bleachers and cheer for Union High and L. Mark Compton.

"I think you're falling for that guy, like every other girl in this school," Larry said.

"Wrong!" I retorted. "Didn't you ever hear of research?"

"Research at a basketball game?"

"If you want me to write about L. Mark Compton, I've got to observe him in his natural habitat, don't I?"

That Friday, after the game, I waited for L. Mark. When he came out of the locker room, he steered me out of the gym and out to the parking lot—through a maze of kids, including the cheerleaders, who lifted their eyebrows. I felt quite aglow from all the looks we got.

After going for pizza, we sat in front of my house in Mark's car and talked. He had his arm draped over the back of the seat and was talking in that low voice, and Barry Manilow was singing something on the radio—I don't know what. All I knew was that L. Mark was awfully near and that the music was making me feel very drifty. Mark was talking about the ocean, saying that he was a certified scuba diver and that every summer he worked on a university oceanography project. He wanted to major in marine biology in college. It really surprised me.

I don't know how I concentrated, though. The music kept sending vibrations through the car. Or maybe *I* was sending them. All of a sudden L. Mark leaned over and kissed me.

There are some things you can't report even if you *are* a super-objective reporter. I floated into the house, and all I know is that for the next few days, every time I heard Barry Manilow on the radio, my mind just seemed to drift away from whatever I was trying to concentrate on. Of course Larry noticed and started to kid me about it, and about the fact that I hadn't yet done my "Shelby Sez" column on L. Mark Compton.

"Don't worry," I said. "You'll have it on your desk by Friday."

The next day I waited for Mark outside the gym even though we didn't have a definite date. He walked out with some of the guys and sort of lit up when he saw me. "Hi, Shelby!" he said. "Hey, grab this, will you?" He had his gym bag in one hand and tossed me his loose-leaf notebook with the other—expecting *me* to carry it! I couldn't believe it! That did it. I'd had enough of Larry's taunts, for one thing, but for another I realized maybe Larry was right: Mark just took it for granted that every girl would fall for him. But not me.

He drove me home, and right in the middle of a Barry Manilow record, I leaned over and said, "C'mon, L. Mark. You know all my ambitions, and I know yours. Aren't you ever going to tell me what the L. stands for?"

He didn't even hesitate. Big, strong L. Mark trusted me. "Lancelot," he said.

"What? I don't believe it! Lancelot, like in King Arthur?"

"The same. My mother was a nut on lovers in literature. You know, Lancelot and Guinevere. So she promised herself that her first son would be named Lancelot. Luckily, my father insisted on adding Mark, too."

"Fantastic story." I leaned back against my seat. "Maybe you're lucky she didn't fall in love with *Gone With the Wind*. She could have named you Rhett."

"I've thought of that. Or Cyrano, from *Cyrano de Bergerac.*"

"Or Count Vronsky, from *Anna Karenina?*"

We played this game all the way home. I should have realized that we were picking only ill-fated lovers.

Lancelot Mark Compton never said a word when the "Shelby Sez" column appeared. It began with a question:

"Guess what a fantastic, three-letter athletic hero's first initial, L, stands for? Not love—though you'd think so, from the lineup of girls at the locker room —but for Lancelot! Please tell us, Lancelot Mark Compton: Could it be that Mark is really for Mark Antony, as in *Antony and Cleopatra*?"

He never said a word when he stood on the foul line that night and missed because the opponent's crowd was hooting, "Lancelot, Lancelot, trot back home to Camelot. . . ."

He never said a word when his locker was decorated with big red paper kisses and a sign saying, "To Lancelot, love from Guinny and all the other maids-in-waiting." As a matter of fact, he never said a word about it because Lancelot Mark Compton apparently had decided never to speak to me again.

I resumed my Friday nights at the TV movies with Larry, but it wasn't the same. First of all, Larry's kisses were getting a little too demanding. And frankly, they were boring. Kissing Larry had never been boring before. But of course I hadn't had L. Mark's kisses to compare them with. Larry couldn't help but notice. I tried to kiss him good-night with a little enthusiasm, but I couldn't manage it.

"Look, Larry," I finally said, "let's cool it a little, okay? I mean, we work well together on the paper, and I don't think we should mess up the relationship with all this other stuff."

"What's up, Shelby? Is it still Mark Compton? I thought that Lancelot column meant your crush was all over."

"There's nothing to be over 'cause there was never anything to begin with. Right now I'm just interested in becoming editor-in-chief and doing a good job for the paper."

"Okay by me." He zipped up his jacket.

I leaned over and kissed him on the cheek. Larry really was a nice guy, and I

didn't want him to be mad. "You know, Larry, I'll tell you something if you promise not to laugh. Ever since I was a little girl, I've just wanted to be another Brenda Starr."

"Brenda Starr . . . like in the comics?"

"I know it's silly, but I always thought she was a real person and I wanted to be just like her, writing fabulous stories, being a famous reporter, traveling, wearing glamorous clothes, meeting mysterious men—the whole bit."

He opened the door. "Just think," he said. "When I was a little kid, I only wanted to be a fireman."

The next week, besides my column—in which I got in a dig about all the expensive student cars in the parking lot—I had to write a long, boring story about the guidance department. Larry excused me from putting the paper to bed, since I was already swamped with all the data from my research.

On Friday morning, when the paper came out, I didn't get to pick up my copy because I was busy making up labs I had missed while trying to make sense out of the guidance department. After lab, as I walked down the hall to my locker, I heard a lot of snickers and also noticed Paul Mann, one of the school's biggest nerds, standing near my locker with a bunch of his pals. They were all talking at once. I knew they were still mad about my story on them, in which I remarked that they gave Union some of the trashy aura of the New York Bowery.

"Well, if it isn't Brenda Starr. . . ." "Yeah, how ya doin', Brenda?" "Say, looking for a mystery man, Brenda?" "How about me?"

Paul got down on his knees. "Hey, Brenda, I'll put a patch on my eye if it'll turn you on."

"What are you talking about?" I asked, really annoyed. I took a step toward my locker. On the door was a note the size of a poster: "Dear Brenda: Never realized you wanted a little love in your life. I'll meet you tonight. Your mystery man."

The hoots got louder. One of the girls from the paper was going by, and I pulled her over. My cheeks were getting hot. I didn't like being laughed at. "Hey, Gail, what's going on?"

"Oh Shelby!" she said, laughing. "Didn't you see your interview? It was a fabulous idea!"

"My interview? What are you talking about?"

Gail handed me the school paper and pointed to the "Shelby Sez" column. Instead of my story on the cars in the parking lot, there was a story about me! "That famous Union High School girl reporter—who, with her little gold pencil, cuts down personalities like a machete in a sugarcane field—has revealed to your editor-in-chief that she's always dreamed of being Brenda Starr. In fact, this girl reporter, obviously still arrested in an adolescent state, has even shown evidence lately that she would be receptive to a mystery man! Any mystery men out there? Your reporter awaits you. . . ." And so on. I felt sick. How could Larry take something I had told him privately and print it like that? And how could he distort it so much and make me look and sound like such a fool? I found my way to the girls' room. I didn't want to cry, but I couldn't help it. I flushed the toilet every time someone walked in so no one would hear me. I made myself wash my face, smile, grit my teeth, and last through a horrible day of taunts.

Late in the afternoon I passed Mark Compton. Well, I thought, I'm surely going to hear from him. He just smiled and said, "Hi, Shelby," as he passed by. That was the first time he had spoken to me since his interview.

I couldn't sleep the whole night. I had a lot of thinking to do: about interviewing people and making news at the expense of others.

Monday afternoon we had a newspaper staff meeting. I knew everyone was watching me, especially Larry and Mr. Harrington. I didn't say anything, except when Larry asked if anyone had some new ideas to offer.

I raised my hand. "I've got one, Larry." I looked around the table. "I'd like to do something different for the 'Shelby Sez' column. I'd like to spend some time each week actually participating in the activity of the person I'm writing about—like working with the prom committee, or practicing with the fencing club, or studying with the grinds." There were murmurs around the table. Larry leaned over and whispered something to Mr. Harrington and then looked back at me.

"What exactly is the point, Shelby? First of all, it'd take an awful lot of extra time, and second, I don't see how it could have any real impact on the column." Some of the other kids nodded.

I cleared my throat. "Well, what I have in mind is giving the column a new slant, some new life. But even more important, well . . . I've been doing a lot of thinking, and I have a feeling that if I were more *involved* in what I wrote about, maybe I'd really understand the things other kids are interested in—instead of just putting them down."

Mr. Harrington smiled, and I knew I had another winner.

"Okay, sounds good to me," Larry said. "Go to it."

When the meeting ended Larry walked over to me and held my arm. "So, what's the first 'new' column going to be about, Shelby?"

"It's going to be a surprise," I answered. I pulled my arm away, but gently. "I'll tell you this much, though: It *is* going to take lots of 'practice.' But don't worry about my meeting the deadline—I'm starting the story right away."

"Okay, I'm counting on you!" Larry said with a smile. He headed down the hall.

Before starting for my next class, I pulled out my little gold pencil and wrote a reminder to myself: "Talk to L. Mark's basketball coach about getting hold of an extra uniform, my size." Then I drew a little flower petal next to the note.

Televising the Three R's in New Glasgow, N.S.

Don Cayo

Members of the New Glasgow High School environment club know all about Boat Harbour, a notorious environmental hot spot near their homes in Pictou County, N.S. It is where waste from the Scott Maritimes Ltd. pulp and paper mill is treated—after a fashion—before flowing into Northumberland Strait. A lot of people gripe about it, but until teacher Len Pelerine and his student television crew hiked to the site last spring, none of them had ever seen it.

The crew was there to document the waste-treatment process for "Earth Watch," the club's weekly cable television show. It is a half-hour mix of studio interviews, on-the-scene reports (done when the students can borrow the station's only portable camera), features and commentaries. It is sometimes amateurish, unceasingly enthusiastic, and always an unabashed advocate for reducing, reusing and recycling.

As Pelerine and five students crested a small hill and spied the five-metre-wide brook frothing forth from an underground conduit, the verdict was clear. Cries of "Oh gross!" rose as a chorus. They grew almost to a chant as wreaths of foul-smelling steam enveloped them.

It was equally "gross!" when producer Charles Watters gingerly took a water sample; when cameraman Chris Strathdee stooped for a close-up of gunk floating on the water; when somebody's foot nearly slipped into the slime; and when the crew came upon a landfill choked with two decades' accumulation of pulp fibres dredged from settling ponds.

But if judgment was swift, it was also thorough. Crew members examined and discussed every aspect of the controversial waste-treatment facility, operated not by Scott Maritimes but by the Nova Scotia Department of the

Environment. They noted that in the growth-oriented late 1960s the province had committed itself to treat the waste for 25 years as an incentive to attract the mill to Pictou County; they speculated that the government might be unwilling to renew the unpopular agreement; they wondered what will happen then.

The TV show is something quite new for the club, itself less than two years old. Like most such school activities in a province with no curriculum courses devoted specifically to environmental issues, it sprang from the interest of a teacher. Pelerine's subject is chemistry and his passion is sports, but it was the impending birth of his first child that created the spark.

"My wife and I were talking about what kind of diapers we should use," he said. "She did quite a bit of research. I thought it was something students might be interested in."

It was. And so, not long before his cotton-diapered son arrived home from the hospital, the New Glasgow High School environment club was born.

The club's early activities were energetic but traditional—cleaning up a beach, lobbying local and provincial politicians, holding an open house to promote environmental concerns, and launching a school-wide recycling program that has continued despite problems finding places to take some recyclable materials.

The television show came about almost by accident. Club members were looking for ways to share their enthusiasm, and Pelerine wondered if they might do a show or two on cable. Last December he checked with the local station. "They said, 'Sure. You can have half an hour a week. You can start Monday.'"

And so, with instruction from the station's two-person staff amounting to little more than how to turn on the equipment, "Earth Watch" began.

The show involves fewer than 20 of the up to 70 students who have come out for some club projects. For that reason alone—not to mention the broad interests of the most active members—the club continues to seek new activities, such as "adopting" a stretch of Trans-Canada Highway that members pledge to keep clean, and developing peer education programs to take into junior high and elementary schools.

At a Saturday breakfast meeting, Chris Meadows, supervisor of math and science for Pictou School District, enthusiastically suggests the club's projects could be the focus of future "Earth Watch" programs.

Meadows' comment sparks the sharpest debate of the morning. Heather MacDonald, a Grade 11 student and a member of the technical crew rarely seen on-camera, worries that people could misinterpret club members' motives. She is adamant that the club should not do things just to get material for "Earth Watch." The nods and murmurs of agreement as she speaks confirm that the majority see their first interest as the environment. Interest in television is a distant second. While they acknowledge that the show is a powerful tool to arouse the interest of others, no one wants to do anything that leads people to think they are motivated by the publicity rather than genuine environmental concern.

A key goal underlying everything club members do is to educate others and motivate them to adopt environmentally sound activities of their own.

"If we can get the public out to pull debris from a stream or to plant trees, they'll remember that a lot more than five minutes of TV with some guy from a fast-food chain saying he won't sell foam packaging any more," says Pelerine.

That process of education and involvement starts with club members themselves.

"We've learned a lot about the subjects we've covered," says Watters who, as a Grade 12 student, was in his last year in the club. "But there's an awful lot of things around here that we haven't covered and that we still have to learn about."

"Most of the topics we've studied have been suggested by Mr. Pelerine," adds MacDonald. "But now that we're getting out and doing these things, we're also getting a lot more ideas of our own about other projects we could do."

Specimen 2001, Probably 21 C

Jeni Couzyn

(on an ancient manuscript)

Dear Aunty May,
Last week after the news I sent off some
express letters.
I sent them to

The Human Inhabitant, The White House, USA,
The Human Inhabitant, The Kremlin, USSR and
The Human Inhabitant, 10 Downing Street, UK.

Inside the letters I wrote: You must not send
people to the wars because they have told me
they don't want to kill a species they

haven't seen.
          The Post Office
returned the letters to me unopened.

On the envelope they wrote: Address Unknown.

So then I sent express letters to all the Human
Inhabitants, in all the houses in the world.
Inside the letters I wrote:
STOP PRESS: If you don't want to go to the wars
(like you keep telling me) then you needn't.
There are no longer Human Inhabitants

governing the world.
                    The Post Office
returned all those letters to me as well:
Address Unknown.

That's how I discovered it.
The Post Office wouldn't lie.
There aren't any Human Inhabitants in the world.

There are a lot of explosions around the stars.
I feel lonely.

In case of miracles like you used to believe in
I am going to put this letter into a bottle
and throw it into the sea. Love from Eve.

He Came from *The Far Side*

Elizabeth Keyishian

A group of scientists leave their microscopes and mathematical formulas behind as they race each other to the ice cream truck. It's not the way you'd expect scientists to act. But it happens all the time in *The Far Side*, a popular cartoon series by Gary Larson.

The Far Side appears in the comics section of newspapers all across North America. In *The Far Side*, dogs wear glasses, and snakes live in houses and have funny hairdos. Scientists act just like kids. And animals act just like people.

And that may explain why millions of people find Gary Larson cartoons so funny. Humans and animals trade places. But that doesn't keep the animals from acting like animals—even though they wear pointy glasses and sit on couches.

The Far Side first appeared about 10 years ago. Back then, a lot of people just didn't understand them. They thought the cartoons were weird. But Gary Larson kept drawing. And *The Far Side* won a loyal following. Today there are *The Far Side* calendars, T-shirts, mugs and books.

Among *The Far Side's* many fans is a group of people who Larson loves to poke fun at—scientists.

"His cartoons keep crossing my desk, sent around by other scientists," says Dr. Mike Smith, a research scientist at the Museum of Natural History in New York City. Why is Larson so popular with scientists? He's one of the few cartoonists who makes jokes about scientists and their work, explains Dr. Smith. "He's poking fun at us, and we like that."

Most people think of scientists as very serious-minded people. In real life, scientists make models of dinosaurs to help them study what dinosaurs were

really like. In *The Far Side*, scientists play with their dinosaur-models as if they were toys.

"Science is all about playing a game, to try and see things in a different way," explains Dr. Charles Whitney, a scientist at Harvard University. "And Gary Larson knows this." As a scientist, Dr. Whitney plays games like thinking about stars as if they were balloons instead of balls of gas. "Scientists take a bizarre attitude about things in order to understand them," says Dr. Whitney. "And that's just what Gary Larson does."

Swamp Thing

Larson took a lot of science classes in college, but he isn't a professional scientist. Nevertheless, he seems to have an insider's understanding of the way scientists think and act. According to Larson, he has loved science since he was a child.

"My real love was biology," he says. When he was nine or ten, he got a plastic microscope for Christmas. "It was the coolest thing I ever got. The microscope came with a few sample slides—a piece of leaf and other things." Gary Larson wanted to study more than leaves. He immediately went out and started collecting other stuff to look at through the microscope. "Within an hour, I was looking at the heads of flies.

"But my most exciting discovery was what I found in a drop of swamp water." Looking at the drop under the microscope, Gary Larson found a whole new world of tiny creatures. "This was as exciting to me as if I had been stalking tigers in the jungle."

Although their parents weren't crazy about the idea, Gary and his brother Dan would occasionally flood their backyard to make a swamp. This provided a good temporary home for the snakes, lizards, frogs and salamanders that he and Dan collected.

Fear of the Dark

As a child, Gary Larson was very afraid of the dark. Alone in the dark, he had to think of some way to keep from getting too scared. He forced himself to think about the monster he was so afraid of. And then he realized that the monster might be just as afraid of him as he was of it.

And that's really what many of Gary Larson's cartoons are about. What do "monsters" and animals think of us? And what would happen if animals behaved like humans? Gary Larson puts himself in someone else's shoes, whether they are bear shoes, deer shoes or bug shoes.

Virtual Reality

Brianna Politzer

You're sitting in your living room, playing a video game. You pull the joystick to the left, and the plane you're flying swoops over a river valley.

Suddenly — zap!! — you blink your eyes and you're no longer in the room, but sitting inside the cockpit of the plane. You see the dark, purple mountains on either side of you, the river below, the clouds above. You hear the wind rushing over the wings, the hum of the engine. You no longer need the joystick. To fly higher, you look upwards. By simply moving your head, you send the plane left or right.

Sounds like a science-fiction movie, right? Wrong!

New computer technology makes it possible to experience flying a plane, travelling through space or even visiting imaginary worlds — without ever leaving the room. Scientists call it virtual reality, because it feels so close to being real.

With virtual reality (or artificial reality, as it's sometimes known), the user wears a special glove called a data glove and a pair of goggles. Inside the glove and goggles are tiny, electronic sensors. When you move your head or your hand, the sensors tell the computer to respond. (This is how you controlled the plane's movements.)

The computer interprets your movements as commands. In a virtual world, you reach your hand toward an object and close your fingers. The computer understands the motion as a command to pick up the object.

The goggles make virtual reality more . . . real. In each eyepiece of the goggles is a tiny computer screen that displays a computer image. The image on each screen is slightly different. When you see both screens at the same time, the image looks three-dimensional. It's so lifelike, it's almost like being there.

Is It Live or . . . ?

"It feels like you're inside a cartoon," says Jaron Lanier. A pioneer in artificial reality, Lanier is the head of a company called VPL in Redwood City, CA. VPL makes gloves and goggles for virtual reality programs. "Everything feels real, although it doesn't quite seem natural."

In one project Lanier is working on, you put on gloves and goggles and step into a world where there are strange vines and bushes growing everywhere. "When you pick up the plants, they change shape and make music." Lanier says.

In another virtual world, created by scientists at a company called Autodesk in Sausalito, California, you sit on a real bicycle, put on goggles and begin to pedal. As you pedal faster, something incredible happens: It seems as if the bicycle is rising into the air. Soon, you feel you're flying above the Earth, just like the kids in *E.T.*

"It's like being in a dream, a vivid dream," says Randal Walser, a scientist at Autodesk. "You feel as if your entire self is in another place."

Autodesk has also developed a virtual reality racquetball game. Two people play together. Both see the imaginary ball and their imaginary racquets. They control their racquets by the motion of their gloved hands. They even hear a "thwack!" as the racquet hits the ball.

Sometimes artificial reality can be produced without gloves and goggles. This happens at an exhibit called "Videoplace" at the Connecticut State Museum of Natural History. Visitors stand in front of a screen. Below the screen is a video camera. Walk in front of the camera and your shadow appears on the screen.

As you face the shadow, a strange green, insect-like creature darts onto the screen and dances on the shadow's head. Hold out your hands and the creature crawls onto the shadow's fingers. Capture the creature between the shadow hands and it explodes!

In another game at Videoplace (games are changed by walking away from the camera, then walking back in front of it), a person's finger leaves different-colored trails on the screen. When all five fingers are spread out, the trails disappear, as if a chalkboard had been erased.

These and other games at Videoplace are made possible by 14 separate computers. Each computer is connected to the video camera, explains Myron Krueger, the exhibit's inventor.

"The computers analyze your silhouette 30 times every second," says Krueger. "It can tell what part of your body is where on the screen. If you hold up one finger, the computer knows that it's one finger. If you hold up all five fingers, the computer also knows that."

Inside the Body

But virtual reality isn't all fun and games. The technology has serious uses, too.

Scientists are now making virtual reality programs that allow a surgeon to travel inside an enlarged, three-dimensional computer image of a patient's body. The graphics are made from very detailed pictures similar to X-rays. If a patient had a cancerous tumor, for example, a surgeon could travel inside a picture of his body to get a better view of how to operate.

Architects are even strolling through virtual reality buildings. If they don't like the way things are laid out, they can change the building *before* it's actually built.

And in Japan, a company uses virtual reality to sell its kitchens. Before ordering a real kitchen, customers walk through a virtual version, opening virtual cabinets and checking out virtual appliances. They can even pick up virtual dishes—carefully. If dropped, they'll "virtually" break!

Perhaps the most exciting use of virtual reality is to get a bird's-eye view of planets and galaxies. Users of a virtual reality project at NASA—the U.S. space agency—can "fly" through outer space.

Spaced Out

Michael McNeill, a scientist at the University of Illinois, is helping NASA with this project. "You really feel like you're floating in space," he says. "You move around, in and out, just by moving your head. It's much different from just looking into a computer screen. It's like you're there. Space is all around you."

One current program lets you zoom through the Valles Marineris, one of the longest canyons on Mars. This wild ride is based on real photos taken by *Viking* spacecraft. Also, NASA scientists hope that, one day, astronauts will see a planet's surface through the eyes of a roving robot. They will use goggles and data gloves to command the robot from the safety of a space ship or home base.

Virtual reality may sound like a thing of the future, but some kids are already experiencing a version of it. The Power Glove for Nintendo is similar to expensive data gloves. With the Power Glove, you don't actually enter the video game world. But it does let you move things around the screen by pointing instead of using a joystick.

And recently, Meredith Bricken, a scientist at the University of Washington, taught kids at local schools how to program their own virtual worlds. She gave the kids software that allowed them to create 3-D drawings on the computer. Some of their projects included a pool you could dive into, a space station on the moon and a mountain that could be explored from inside out.

"Virtual reality brings out your sense of adventure," Bricken says. "Adults have mapped the real world pretty thoroughly. But now there are new worlds to explore."

Market Day

Dionne Brand

Early Sunday morning,
before the sun comes up,
before the dew stops falling,
when eyelids are still shut.
We go to market laden
baskets on our heads,
walk down empty narrow streets
to the village square.
Across from the gas station,
around the round-a-bout,
down by the busy corner,
the sun begins to grin.
Then suddenly the air is filled
with myriad sounds and smells,
with laughing, bartering,
exchanging greetings,
on Sunday market day.

Self-Employment: A Dream That Can Become a Reality

from *Canada Prospects*

More than half of the people in a recent survey shared the dream of starting their own business.

In 1989, 166,000 of them took the plunge in what has become the fastest-growing part of the Canadian economy.

In 1988–89, entrepreneurs accounted for 8 of every 10 new jobs that were created. They also generated about 30 per cent of the economic activity in Canada even though self-employed people make up about 13 per cent of the work force.

An entrepreneur is defined as someone who organizes and manages a business undertaking, assuming the risk for the sake of profit and success.

Whether it is independence, a thirst for success or simply a way of earning a living, those people who have been self-employed are likely to stay with it through thick and thin. It certainly isn't easy street: 40 per cent of new businesses disappear in the first three years of operation through failure or, in some cases, through mergers. Most entrepreneurs, however, pick themselves up and begin again.

The attractions of self-employment are only partly explained by earnings which, on average, are higher than traditional jobs. The lure may be more to do with the less tangible benefits—the opportunity to control one's own destiny, to achieve one's full potential, to define and achieve one's personal sense of success.

Self-employment is also often a practical solution for people who may have been unsuccessful in their traditional workplace. For example:

- 11 per cent of those self-employed are members of visible minorities;
- 17 per cent are people with disabilities; and
- 34 per cent are women, reflecting a trend where more women than men are starting new businesses.

In many cases, the road to self-employment begins with seeing an opportunity in an area in which the individual is familiar or there appears to be an obvious need. Both the possibilities and opportunities are endless with countless stories of success.

Greig Clark painted his way to wealth and success when, with a friend, he turned his profitable summer job into College Pro Painters. In less than 15 years, the organization has grown to about 270 franchises in Canada and the United States.

Hilary Kyro from Thunder Bay turned her artistic talents and love of jazz into a successful business in downtown Toronto. "Sometimes I wonder if I can keep up," she says in discussing the demand for her paintings and drawings.

Every community has examples.

Industry, Science and Technology Canada lists 10 steps to help turn a good idea into a business:

- **Recognize opportunity.** Look for ways that you can offer a product or service that people are looking for.
- **Take the initiative.** Find something practical you can do—right now—to start making your idea work. Don't wait for someone else to give you a push.
- **Define your goals.** Make sure you have a clear idea about what you want to achieve in the long run. If you don't know where you want to go, it is a lot harder to get there.
- **Find your market niche.** Define how the product or service you can offer is different from everything else in the marketplace.
- **Understand your market.** Find out who will buy your unique product or service, how much they will pay and how other factors might affect their decision to buy from you.
- **Seek advice.** Lawyers and accountants can provide expert advice in areas where you might need it so that you can concentrate on your own area of expertise.
- **Communicate with your staff.** When you become your own boss, you may have employees. Make sure they know exactly what you want from them in their jobs.

- **Be willing to make sacrifices.** When you are your own boss, the sacrifices you will have to make are really investments in your future.
- **Maintain high energy levels.** When you are the boss, you are in charge of the action. You need to muster the energy and enthusiasm to keep things moving.
- **Believe in your venture.** You are the only one who can make it work.

Wings of Mercy

Markoosie

In Baffin Island Fiord, Constable Swart scribbled Charlie Delta's position across a yellow message pad. Once again he tried to contact pilot Norris Mann in his stricken aircraft. There was no reply.

Norris opened the side window and tried to see ahead and below. He saw a large icepan, before the extreme cold forced his eyes shut. He pulled his head back inside and as calmly as possible fought to keep control of the aircraft.

Constable Swart continued to try and make contact with the plane without success. Then he switched his frequency and said; "Devon Island Base. This is Baffin Island Fiord. Do you copy?" After several repeats he received an answer.

"Go ahead Baffin Island Fiord."

"Charlie Delta has been forced down."

"Oh my God! Did you get his position?"

"Yes, when I got his May Day, he was at latitude 74 degrees, longitude 80."

The pilot's face lost all feeling as he strained his freezing eyeballs for a glimpse of the icepan. It was rough surfaced as he had feared. As soon as the tires touched the ice, he pulled the power all the way back and turned off the power switch at the same time. The plane bounced once, came down hard and bounced off the ice again. It came down hard the third time and everything seemed to break apart. Norris heard a muffled cry from Nurse Moore, before he blacked out.

"Baffin Island Fiord this is Devon Island Base. Do you copy?"

"Go ahead, Devon Island Base, I hear you."

"Did Norris say he was ditching in the water or on the ice?"

"He said he was going to try for an icepan."

"OK. Baffin Island Fiord, we will contact National Defence for rescue service."

"Is there anything we can do to help from this side?"

"Afraid not, we will do everything possible from here."

Constable Jim Coleman was called to the radio shack. The radio operator outlined the situation.

"We have a downed aircraft in about here," he explained, tracing the location on the map tacked to the wall. "There is a very slim chance that they are still alive. Norris Mann is a skilled pilot but I don't think he has had much winter experience. Nurse Moore was tending the wounded boy and I understand his father Mannik is aboard. We called National Defence for rescue service and an aircraft is on the way from Frobisher with a doctor and supplies."

"I hope he made it to an icepan. But even so, how can a doctor get there this time of the year?" the constable asked.

"The doctor will be a member of the Royal Canadian Air Force parachute team. We are hoping he can make the jump. Those Air Force boys know their business."

"They are our only hope," the constable replied quietly.

"Not quite, Jim," said the radioman. "You could organize the Eskimo rescue party."

"I can try that," said the constable, still scanning the map. "That is about two hundred miles away and four days by dog team. Keep me posted on events. I am going to the settlement and talk to the people."

Norris slowly opened his eyes. Slowly his memory returned and the terrible realization of their predicament. His head was pounding with pain as he turned it around without moving his body. He lay beside his seat. Slowly he got into sitting position. A sharp pain shot through his left leg. His boot was torn and a trace of blood showed through. "Broken," he thought to himself. He found a flashlight and flicked it on.

He looked to where his passengers had been and saw the nurse prostrate over the body of Seeko while Mannik seemed to be pinned against the wall. Norris tried to stand, but his legs refused to co-operate. "Could both be broken," he thought, surprised at his own calmness. He dragged himself toward the nurse with his hands. She was still and did not respond when he pushed her from Seeko. The boy was still breathing. He called for Mannik and was answered by a low moan. Mannik, bleeding from a cut on his forehead, began to crawl toward him and knelt beside Seeko. "He is still alive," he said gratefully. Nurse Moore began to moan and then opened her eyes. "Is everyone alright? How long have we been down?" The questions all came at once as she sought to understand the situation.

"I think my legs are broken, but there is no pain," said Norris.

"Let me get those boots off. Have you got a knife?"

Norris pointed to the survival kit box. The nurse crawled toward the box, stopping to look at Seeko on the way. She listened to his breathing and was satisfied that his condition remained stable.

Doreen began to cut the laces on the pilot's torn boot. He clenched his teeth to keep from crying out as she removed it and the sock. A bone protruded. Quickly and skillfully, in spite of the cramped conditions, she applied a splint and bandage. She wrapped the leg in a blanket to protect it from the cold that she realized for the first time was creeping into the aircraft. She unlaced the boot from the other leg. A quick examination showed that no bones were broken but it was badly sprained and swelling. She wrapped it as best she could from the limited resources in the first aid box. Turning to Mannik she next wiped his wound clean and bandaged it.

"Anywhere else hurt?" she asked. She was relieved when Mannik shook his head and grinned.

They began to survey the damage and the full realization of their situation came to them. The aircraft door was broken off. One wing was broken and the nose buried in the snow and ice. The tiny finger of light from the flashlight disappeared in the blowing snow. How far they were from land or the size of the icepan was unknown to them. Above the wind they could hear the growing thunder of crushing ice.

"How long do you think it will be before we are rescued?" the nurse asked Norris.

He did not want to tell her that the chances were slim. He tried to be cheerful. "It might take several days, depending on the weather. The only way to get off here will be by helicopter, and the nearest is about a thousand miles away. There is almost no daylight this time of the year. I hope they got the bearings I sent as we came down. We have to get out of here before we freeze."

"I must build a shelter for us," said Mannik. "I will build an igloo." He opened his pack and took out a snow-knife and a rifle, the hunter's tools.

When Mannik left the plane Doreen put an extra blanket around Seeko. "I did not want to say it in front of his father, but I don't think he can live much longer without a doctor." Norris nodded. He was thinking about it and about the food supply. He always carried emergency food—enough for one man for

a week. He had a small pressure cooker and fuel for one man for two days. But there were four people. They sat in silence, listening to the beating of the wind and the distant grinding of the ice. Weak daylight crept into the plane with the cold.

Mannik returned to announce that the igloo was finished and he needed blankets to cover the floor. They could move in. He took the blankets and the heater and soon had the little shelter warm. With the help of the nurse, he moved Seeko into it first. Together they returned and helped Norris down from the plane and dragged him through the small opening.

"We will make tea first," Mannik said, "and then I will go and see how big this icepan is. There is a chance I might get a seal. A seal will keep us fed and provide enough fat to keep Seeko and Norris warm." There was something in his calm and determined manner that gave strength to all of them.

Far away from the little igloo and the wrecked aircraft Constable Coleman was explaining the situation to a group of Inuit hunters.

"We have no way of knowing if they are alive. They could be on the ice and it would be impossible for a plane to land near them. That is why I am asking for volunteers to make up a rescue party. Are there any questions?" Coleman asked.

"You think they are about two hundred miles away?" asked one of the men who was called Nuki.

"Yes, but we are not sure if that is the correct position." The constable returned to the map, and pointed to the probable spot. "It's somewhere here, between Kikitalook and Toononik."

"That is a lot of land and water from here," answered Nuki. Turning to the other men for approval, he said simply: "We will go."

Nuki turned again to the hunters in the room and began to give instructions in their own language. "We will start in two hours. We will need twenty men and if possible, make up fifteen dog teams. We should take the six kayaks because there is still a lot of open water. Pack enough food for a week for ourselves and the dogs. We may have to hunt later but our first job is to get to the site." The men stood up when he stopped talking and went to their homes to prepare themselves.

Four hours after the call for help went out, and RCAF Boxcar landed on the Devon Island Base strip. The first person down the ladder was a tall man in a flight suit, carrying a bag. "Hi!" he greeted the constable. "I'm Doctor Carl Poole. I would like to speak to the radioman who has been talking to Baffin Island Fiord."

Inside the radio hut over a cup of hot coffee Doctor Poole gathered all the details of the accident.

"Can you tell me what really happened. How long ago and what has been done?"

The radioman outlined the situation. "The boy is young. He shot himself in the stomach area. The bullet is .22 calibre. The nurse said he lost a lot of blood. It has been about ten hours since the accident and we have no way of knowing what his condition is now. Just that he is somewhere out there if he is alive," he said, pointing to the map on the wall.

Thirty minutes later the Boxcar was refuelled and again airborne. At two thousand feet they lost visual contact with the ground. The doctor studied a map with the navigator.

"Let's go up to nine thousand feet and then descend under the cloud when we get over Lancaster Sound," the navigator said. "That will be in forty-five minutes."

Over the Sound, the plane dropped to 800 feet. Fog rolled up to meet them, blocking out the thousands of floating icepans, except in a few spots. For two hours they flew a pattern over the area, all eyes straining for signs of wreckage. "There is no hope of finding them under these conditions," the pilot said. "We will return to base and try again later." The big plane gained altitude and headed back to Devon Island Base.

On the icepan the three people heard the plane passing over them but they could not see it. When the sound faded away for the last time, Doreen Moore began to cry.

"At least they are looking for us," Norris said, trying to comfort her. "They made a good try but the clouds are too low. They will be back."

"Don't worry, nurse," Mannik said. "They will come again and again until

they find us. We have a saying that no matter how sadly a day ends, another new day will come to the land tomorrow."

Inside the igloo, which was warm but cramped, Norris was making plans. "Mannik, look in the baggage compartment of the plane. Collect all the rags or anything else that will burn. There is gasoline in the belly tank. Push up the drain valve and fill up a bottle or oilcan with it. Soak the rags and leave them outside in the open and the next time you hear a plane run out and light fire to it."

"I will give you a hand," said Doreen. Together she and Mannik crawled out of the igloo.

Back at Devon Island Base the pilot and navigator listened to the latest weather reports. They were not good. The meteorologist charted the path of an approaching storm. "It is now over Melville Island and was over Prince Patrick Island yesterday. That means it is moving pretty fast. You won't have much time before you are grounded."

The ice was rugged and made travelling slow. The barking of the dogs and the creaking of the sleds were the only sounds in the darkness. Nuki was ahead of the party, because he remembered the way from his early hunting years. They had been travelling for several hours and the dogs were growing tired when Nuki called a halt.

"We will stop a while and eat," he said to Shinak, his closest companion.

"Are we going to keep on all night?" Shinak asked.

"We will have to go as far as the dogs can last. It is going to be rough but lives depend on us," Nuki answered.

Inside the small igloo, the shadows of three silent people were cast upon the ice walls. They all looked anxiously at Seeko who was fighting for breath. Doreen decided she had to say the words that she hoped she would never have to say.

"Mannik," she began, "I have to tell you the truth. There is nothing more I can do. I don't think he will live till morning."

Mannik looked into the eyes of the nurse and said: "I have been expecting those words for some time. I am old enough to know when death is near." Then he turned away and wept quietly. For many hours that was the only sound in the silent cell, while the wind mourned outside.

"Listen," Norris said suddenly. "Hear it? It's an aircraft up there! Quick Mannik, light the fire!"

Norris dragged himself out after Mannik. The fire was already blazing. Norris lay on his back on the ice and looked at the sky. The clouds were patchy now and the sound of motors was getting closer.

The pilot was the first to see the pinpoint of light on the floating ice island. "Look over there!" he shouted to his co-pilot. "We have found them! Tell the doctor to prepare to jump. Get the engineer to prepare to drop supplies."

The big aircraft circled wide and turned back toward the welcoming light on the ice below. They were at 700 feet with the clouds above them. It was too low for the doctor to jump and he would have to go "blind." Directly over the fire he turned and went up to two thousand feet and into the darkness of the clouds. The turn continued for three minutes, then he signaled for the supplies to be dropped.

"OK, Doc. If you're ready we will do that again. I will go in over the fire and then climb and circle. We can let you go at two thousand feet in three minutes."

The doctor signaled that he was ready. He wanted to look at his watch for some reason. He went to the back of the aircraft and stood in his bulky clothes under the blue light to wait for the signal. "I hope that this is one big icepan," he thought to himself.

Foul Shot

Edwin A. Hoey

With two 60's stuck on the scoreboard
And two seconds hanging on the clock,
The solemn boy in the centre of eyes,
Squeezed by silence,
Seeks out the line with his feet,
Soothes his hands along his uniform,
Gently drums the ball against the floor,
Then measures the waiting net,
Raises the ball on his right hand,
Balances it with his left,
Calms it with fingertips,
Breathes,
Crouches,
Waits,
And then through a stretching of stillness,
Nudges it upward.
The ball
Slides up and out,
Lands,
Leans,
Wobbles,
Wavers,
Hesitates,
Exasperates,
Plays it coy
Until every face begs with unsounding screams—
And then

      And then

        And then,

Right before ROAR-UP,
Dives down and through.

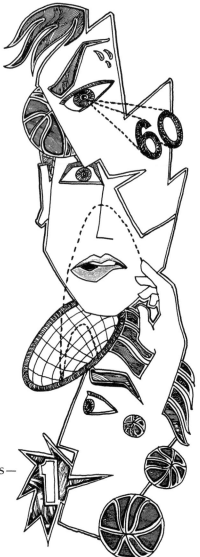

282

The Pond

Mervyn Morris

There was this pond in the village
and little boys, he heard till he was sick,
were not allowed too near.
Unfathomable pool, they said,
that swallowed men and animals just so;
and in its depths, old people said,
swam galliwasps and nameless horrors;
bright boys kept away.

Though drawn so hard by prohibitions,
the small boy, fixed in fear, kept off;
till one wet summer, grass growing lush,
paths muddy, slippery, he found himself
there at the fabled edge.

The brooding pond was dark.
Sudden, escaping cloud, the sun
came bright; and, shimmering in guilt,
he saw his own face peering from the pool.

galliwasps: Various lizards of Central America and the West Indies.

Can We Make Basketball Canada's National Sport?

Jeffrey Reed

Basketball, bouncing into its second century, is on a rebound in Canada. Things are changing. But it's going to take hard work to keep our talented Canadian players, men and women, at home.

High school basketball is as popular in Canada as it is in the United States. This is where the similarity ends.

Bill Pargeter, a respected basketball coach in London, ON (where he is assistant coach at University of Western Ontario) teaches the finer points of the game to players aged 8–24. "The Americans play a lot better basketball," says Pargeter, "especially the men. They have so many big players, and the coaching is really intense."

Really, basketball is to Americans what hockey is to Canadians.

Pargeter exposes his teams to American talent in tournaments, and says high-profile tourneys are the only way to be noticed. One of his prize student grads, 21 year old Heather Hart of London, listened closely to his advice. She played basketball all year long, seriously since grade 7, and eventually made the Ontario provincial team. She earned a full scholarship at the University of North Carolina.

Hart is thrilled that her education is being paid for because of her dedication to perfection. She's a 6′3″ starter on her team in her second university year.

Hart's discovery by North Carolina was accidental. A Toronto school sent a video tape of a game involving Heather's London John Paul II High School to the university; Heather was noticed, recruited and signed.

A Dream in Gold: Jennifer Krempien

The game was a cliff-hanger. With less than seven minutes left in the basketball final at Barcelona, the Canadian women held only a one-point lead over their US opponents, the defending champions. But the underdogs rallied to win 35–26, clinching Canada's first gold medal in the sport. And for 17-year-old Jennifer Krempien, a guard on that winning wheelchair basketball team at September's 1992 Paralympic Games, it was a victory that she says she will never forget. "Being on the podium with the gold medal around my neck, looking at the flag and hearing the national anthem will always stick out in my mind," she says. "There was a lot of pride being Canadian at that moment and a real sense of accomplishment."

For Krempien, the youngest player on the 12-member team, playing in the Paralympics fulfilled a dream. Paralysed from the waist down at age 5 after she fell off a picnic table and developed a blood clot in her spine, she started playing basketball, floor hockey and volleyball in an elementary school recreation program.

Her advice to teens? "Believe in yourself and in what you can do. Even if people are telling you, 'No, no, you can't do that,' just try it anyway. Even if you fail, you are still going to learn."

"It wasn't until offers came in that I started thinking about scholarships," explains Hart. "I visited five schools." She says she chose to play in the US because of a better brand of ball, plus the fully-paid education.

Hart's advice: "You have to pick a place where you feel comfortable, but your first decision has to be education."

North Carolina head coach Ed Baldwin scouts regularly in Canada, looking for talented players like Hart. "The skill level is a little bit better," Baldwin says of the US where children play basketball at a very young age, much like Canadian kids begin hockey.

"I look for someone with a real nice shot," says Baldwin.

There are important steps to introducing yourself to an American college or university. Baldwin says a student should begin with a game video tape.

There are Canadian organizations which help high school students become noticed, both in Canada and the US.

The larger US schools' athletic programs are governed by the National Collegiate Athletic Association (NCAA). Its director of communications, Jim Marchiony, says though each college recruits where it wants, there are national scouting guidelines. "Someone cannot be actively recruited until their senior year in high school," says Marchiony.

Unlike American schools, Canadian financial aid covers partial costs and varies from province to province. Places like the Canadian Interuniversity Athletic Union give a breakdown of what's available from across the country. Scholarship and grant money includes trust funds operated by private organizations and government grants, but none offers nearly as much money as American schools.

So, how do we keep our best players in Canada? Enter Basketball Canada, based in Victoria, BC. Basketball Canada oversees our men's and women's national programs, fielding teams in international competitions, including the Summer Olympics.

Men's program manager John Affleck identifies the problem: our best

---

James Naismith

James Naismith, a Canadian, was a phys-ed instructor in 1891, at the Young Men's Christian Association Training School in Springfield, Massachusetts, when he was struck by the need for a good indoor team game that would combine the most exciting parts of several outdoor games and yet could be played in a gymnasium.

The game he came up with called for two teams who tried to score points by getting a large, light-weight ball into a wall basket. For the first game, two peach baskets were borrowed from the school janitor to serve as goals. To make the game challenging and playable on an indoor court, he outlawed running with the ball except while bouncing it. And because it was played on a hard floor, he didn't allow tackling. He called this new game basketball.

Naismith's students loved the new game—even though it did have some problems. For instance, there was the overcrowding problem. Teams were huge—some had as many as 50 players. That meant a lot of jostling and bumping. And then there was the basket problem. When a team scored a point, the ball sat in the basket and everyone had to wait around until someone got a ladder to get it down. Gradually these problems were worked out. Teams were limited to five players and a hole was cut in the bottom of the bushel basket so that the ball would fall right through. In 1906, hoops with bottomless nets took the place of baskets.

players are scattered around the world, in American universities and professional leagues in the US and Europe. Only a handful of world-class players (like U of BC's J.D. Jackson, a national team member) stays in Canada.

Canada does not have a national basketball league. The US has the NBA and other professional leagues for men and women. In Europe and elsewhere, men and women play professional basketball.

An American group, with Basketball Canada's co-operation, has plans to start Pro Basketball Canada. Eight teams would have to include at least five Canadians each—a step in the right direction.

Currently the World Basketball League includes some Canadian cities, but the rosters are full of Americans.

Our national men's program includes a junior, student, and national team. Perhaps future players will come out of the Toronto high school scene, a North American hotbed of high school basketball.

Bob Maydo, coach at Toronto's Bathurst Heights SS, has sent players to the US on scholarship and says interest is continual. But there are rules, even in the high school ranks. Ryan Fabricius, a Barrie, ON high school basketball star, was just this year banned from playing basketball for Martingrove Collegiate in Toronto.

Fabricius has been one of the top Canadian high school basketball players. The Ontario Federation of School Athletic Associations rules that he transferred to the Toronto school from Barrie Central Collegiate in order to gain recognition to earn a US college scholarship. OFSAA doesn't allow transfers purely for athletic reasons.

Clearly, academics rule.

Reprinted with permission by TG Magazine,
202 Cleveland St., Toronto, ON, M4S 2W6, 416-487-3204.

A Sound of Thunder

Ray Bradbury

The sign on the wall seemed to quaver under a film of sliding warm water. Eckels felt his eyelids blink over his stare, and the sign burned in this momentary darkness:

> TIME SAFARI, INC.
> SAFARIS TO ANY YEAR IN THE PAST.
> YOU NAME THE ANIMAL.
> WE TAKE YOU THERE.
> YOU SHOOT IT.

A warm phlegm gathered in Eckels' throat; he swallowed and pushed it down. The muscles around his mouth formed a smile as he put his hand slowly out upon the air, and in that hand waved a check for ten thousand dollars to the man behind the desk.

"Does this safari guarantee I come back alive?"

"We guarantee nothing," said the official, "except the dinosaurs." He turned. "This is Mr. Travis, your Safari Guide in the Past. He'll tell you what and where to shoot. If he says no shooting, no shooting. If you disobey instructions, there's a stiff penalty of another ten thousand dollars, plus possible government action, on your return."

Eckels glanced across the vast office at a mass and tangle, a snaking and humming of wires and steel boxes, at an aurora that flickered now orange, now silver, now blue. There was a sound like a gigantic bonfire burning all of Time, all the years and all the parchment calendars, all the hours piled high and set aflame.

A touch of the hand and this burning would, on the instant, beautifully reverse itself, Eckels remembered the wording in the advertisements to the letter. Out of chars and ashes, out of dust and coals, like golden salamanders, the old years, the green years, might leap; roses sweeten the air, white hair turn Irish-black, wrinkles vanish; all, everything fly back to seed, flee death, rush down to their beginnings, suns rise in western skies and set in glorious easts, moons eat themselves opposite to the custom, all and everything cupping one in another like Chinese boxes, rabbits in hats, all and everything returning to the fresh death, the seed death, the green death, to the time before the beginning. A touch of a hand might do it, the merest touch of a hand.

"Hell and damn," Eckels breathed, the light of the Machine on his thin face. "A real Time Machine." He shook his head. "Makes you think. If the election had gone badly yesterday, I might be here now running away from the results. Thank God Keith won. He'll make a fine President of the United States."

"Yes," said the man behind the desk. "We're lucky. If Deutscher had gotten in, we'd have the worst kind of dictatorship. There's an anti-everything man for you, a militarist, anti-Christ, anti-human, anti-intellectual. People called us up, you know, joking but not joking. Said if Deutscher became President

they wanted to go live in 1492. Of course it's not our business to conduct Escapes, but to form Safaris. Anyway, Keith's President now. All you got to worry about is—"

"Shooting my dinosaur," Eckels finished it for him.

"A *Tyrannosaurus rex*. The Thunder Lizard, the damnedest monster in history. Sign this release. Anything happens to you, we're not responsible. Those dinosaurs are hungry."

Eckels flushed angrily. "Trying to scare me!"

"Frankly, yes. We don't want anyone going who'll panic at the first shot. Six Safari leaders were killed last year, and a dozen hunters. We're here to give you the damnedest thrill a *real* hunter ever asked for. Traveling you back sixty million years to bag the biggest damned game in all Time. Your personal check's still there. Tear it up."

Mr. Eckels looked at the check for a long time. His fingers twitched.

"Good luck," said the man behind the desk. "Mr. Travis, he's all yours."

They moved silently across the room, taking their guns with them, toward the Machine, toward the silver metal and the roaring light.

First a day and then a night and then a day and then a night, then it was day-night-day-night-day. A week, a month, a year, a decade! A.D. 2055. A.D. 2019. 1999! 1957! Gone! The Machine roared.

They put on their oxygen helmets and tested the intercoms.

Eckels swayed on the padded seat, his face pale, his jaw stiff. He felt the trembling in his arms and he looked down and found his hands tight on the new rifle. There were four other men in the Machine. Travis, the Safari leader, his assistant, Lesperance, and two other hunters, Billings and Kramer. They sat looking at each other, and the years blazed around them.

"Can these guns get a dinosaur cold?" Eckels felt his mouth saying.

"If you hit them right," said Travis on the helmet radio. "Some dinosaurs have two brains, one in the head, another far down the spinal column. We stay away from those. That's stretching luck. Put your first two shots into the eyes, if you can, blind them, and go back into the brain."

The Machine howled. Time was a film run backward. Suns fled and ten million moons fled after them. "Good God," said Eckels. "Every hunter that ever lived would envy us today. This makes Africa seem like Illinois."

The Machine slowed; its scream fell to a murmur. The Machine stopped.

The sun stopped in the sky.

The fog that had enveloped the Machine blew away and they were in an old time, a very old time indeed, three hunters and two Safari Heads with their blue metal guns across their knees.

"Christ isn't born yet," said Travis. "Moses has not gone to the mountain to talk with God. The Pyramids are still in the earth, waiting to be cut out and put up. *Remember* that, Alexander, Caesar, Napoleon, Hitler—none of them exists."

The men nodded.

"That"—Mr. Travis pointed—"is the jungle of sixty million two thousand and fifty-five years before President Keith."

He indicated a metal path that struck off into green wilderness, over steaming swamp, among giant ferns and palms.

"And that," he said, "is the Path, laid by Time Safari for your use. It floats six inches above the earth. Doesn't touch so much as one grass blade, flower, or tree. It's an antigravity metal. Its purpose is to keep you from touching this world of the past in any way. Stay on the Path. Don't go off it. I repeat. *Don't go off.* For *any* reason! If you fall off, there's a penalty. And don't shoot any animal we don't okay."

"Why?" asked Eckels.

They sat in the ancient wilderness. Far birds' cries blew on a wind, and the smell of tar and an old salt sea, moist grasses, and flowers the color of blood.

"We don't want to change the Future. We don't belong here in the Past. The government doesn't *like* us here. We have to pay big graft to keep our franchise. A Time Machine is damn finicky business. Not knowing it, we might kill an important animal, a small bird, a roach, a flower even, thus destroying an important link in a growing species."

"That's not clear," said Eckels.

"All right," Travis continued, "say we accidentally kill one mouse here. That means all the future families of this one particular mouse are destroyed, right?"

"Right."

"And all the families of the families of that one mouse! With a stamp of your foot, you annihilate first one, then a dozen, then a thousand, a million, a *billion* possible mice!"

"So they're dead," said Eckels. "So what?"

"So what?" Travis snorted quietly. "Well, what about the foxes that'll need those mice to survive? For want of ten mice, a fox dies. For want of ten foxes, a lion starves. For want of a lion, all manner of insects, vultures, infinite billions of life forms are thrown into chaos and destruction. Eventually it all boils down to this: fifty-nine million years later, a cave man, one of a dozen on the *entire* world, goes hunting wild boar or saber-tooth tiger for food. But you, friend, have *stepped* on all the tigers in that region. By stepping on *one* single mouse. So the cave man starves. And the cave man, please note, is not just *any* expendable man, no! He is an *entire future nation*. From his loins would have sprung ten sons. From *their* loins one hundred sons, and thus onward to a civilization. Destroy this one man, and you destroy a race, a people, an entire history of life. It is comparable to slaying some of Adam's grandchildren. The stomp of your foot, on one mouse, could start an earthquake, the effects of which could shake our earth and destinies down through Time, to their very foundations. With the death of that one cave man, a billion others yet unborn are throttled in the womb. Perhaps Rome never rises on its seven hills. Perhaps Europe is forever a dark forest, and only Asia waxes healthy and teeming. Step on a mouse and you crush the Pyramids. Step on a mouse and you leave your print, like a Grand Canyon, across Eternity. Queen Elizabeth might never be born, Washington might not cross the Delaware, there might never be a United States at all. So be careful. Stay on the Path. *Never* step off!"

"I see," said Eckels. "Then it wouldn't pay for us even to touch the *grass*?"

"Correct. Crushing certain plants could add up infinitesimally. A little error here would multiply in sixty million years, all out of proportion. Of course maybe our theory is wrong. Maybe Time *can't* be changed by us. Or maybe it can be changed only in little subtle ways. A dead mouse here makes an insect imbalance there, a population disproportion later, a bad harvest further on, a depression, mass starvation, and, finally, a change in *social* temperament in far-flung countries. Something much more subtle, like that. Perhaps only a soft breath, a whisper, a hair, pollen on the air, such a slight, slight change that unless you looked close you wouldn't see it. Who knows?

Who really can say he knows? We don't know. We're guessing. But until we do know for certain whether our messing around in Time *can* make a big roar or a little rustle in history, we're being damned careful. This Machine, this Path, your clothing and bodies, were sterilized, as you know, before the journey. We wear these oxygen helmets so we can't introduce our bacteria into an ancient atmosphere."

"How do we know which animals to shoot?"

"They're marked with red paint," said Travis. "Today, before our journey, we sent Lesperance here back with the Machine. He came to this particular era and followed certain animals."

"Studying them?"

"Right," said Lesperance. "I track them through their entire existence, noting which of them lives longest. Very few. How many times they mate. Not often. Life's short. When I find one that's going to die when a tree falls on him, or one that drowns in a tar pit, I note the exact hour, minute, and second. I shoot a paint bomb. It leaves a red patch on his hide. We can't miss it. Then I correlate our arrival in the Past so that we meet the Monster not more than two minutes before he would have died anyway. This way, we kill only animals with no future, that are never going to mate again. You see how *careful* we are?"

"But if you came back this morning in Time," said Eckels eagerly, "you must've bumped into *us*, our Safari. How did it turn out? Was it successful? Did all of us get through—alive?"

Travis and Lesperance gave each other a look.

"That'd be a paradox," said the latter. "Time doesn't permit that sort of mess—a man meeting himself. When such occasions threaten, Time steps aside. Like an airplane hitting an air pocket. You felt the Machine jump just before we stopped? That was us passing ourselves on the way back to the Future. We saw nothing. There's no way of telling *if* this expedition was a success, *if* we got our monster, or whether all of us—meaning *you*, Mr. Eckels—got out alive."

Eckels smiled palely.

"Cut that," said Travis sharply. "Everyone on his feet!"

They were ready to leave the Machine.

The jungle was high and the jungle was broad and the jungle was the entire world forever and forever. Sounds like music and sounds like flying tents filled the sky, and those were pterodactyls soaring with cavernous gray wings, gigantic bats out of a delirium and a night fever. Eckels, balanced on the narrow Path, aimed his rifle playfully.

"Stop that!" said Travis. "Don't even aim for fun, damn it! If your gun should go off—"

Eckels flushed. "Where's our *Tyrannosaurus?*"

Lesperance checked his wrist watch. "Up ahead. We'll bisect his trail in sixty seconds. Look for the red paint, for Christ's sake. Don't shoot till we give the word. Stay on the Path. *Stay on the Path!*"

They moved forward in the wind of morning.

"Strange," murmured Eckels. "Up ahead, sixty million years, Election Day over. Keith made President. Everyone celebrating. And here we are, a million years lost, and they don't exist. The things we worried about for months, a lifetime, not even born or thought about yet."

"Safety catches off, everyone!" ordered Travis. "You, first shot, Eckels. Second, Billings, Third, Kramer."

"I've hunted tiger, wild boar, buffalo, elephant, but Jesus, this is *it*," said Eckels. "I'm shaking like a kid."

"Ah," said Travis.

Everyone stopped.

Travis raised his hand. "Ahead," he whispered. "In the mist. There he is. There's His Royal Majesty now."

The jungle was wide and full of twitterings, rustlings, murmurs, and sighs.

Suddenly it all ceased, as if someone had shut a door.

Silence.

A sound of thunder.

Out of the mist, one hundred yards away, came *Tyrannosaurus rex*.

"Jesus God," whispered Eckels.

"Sh!"

It came on great oiled, resilient, striding legs. It towered thirty feet above half of the trees, a great evil god, folding its delicate watchmaker's claws close to its oily reptilian chest. Each lower leg was a piston, a thousand pounds of white bone, sunk in thick ropes of muscle, sheathed over in a gleam of pebbled skin like the mail of a terrible warrior. Each thigh was a ton of meat, ivory, and steel mesh. And from the great breathing cage of the upper body those two delicate arms dangled out front, arms with hands which might pick up and examine men like toys, while the snake neck coiled. And the head itself, a ton of sculptured stone, lifted easily upon the sky. Its mouth gaped, exposing a fence of teeth like daggers. Its eyes rolled, ostrich eggs, empty of all expression save hunger. It closed its mouth in a death grin. It ran, its pelvic bones crushing aside trees and bushes, its taloned feet clawing damp earth, leaving prints six inches deep wherever it settled its weight. It ran with a gliding ballet step, far too poised and balanced for its ten tons. It moved into a sunlit arena warily, its beautifully reptile hands feeling the air.

"My God!" Eckels twitched his mouth. "It could reach up and grab the moon."

"Sh!" Travis jerked angrily. "He hasn't seen us yet."

"It can't be killed." Eckels pronounced this verdict quietly, as if there could be no argument. He had weighed the evidence and this was his considered opinion. The rifle in his hands seemed a cap gun. "We were fools to come. This is impossible."

"Shut up!" hissed Travis.

"Nightmare."

"Turn around," commanded Travis. "Walk quietly to the Machine. We'll remit one-half your fee."

"I didn't realize it would be this *big*," said Eckels. "I miscalculated, that's all. And now I want out."

"It sees us!"

"There's the red paint on its chest!"

The Thunder Lizard raised itself. Its armored flesh glittered like a thousand green coins. The coins, crusted with slime, steamed. In the slime, tiny insects wriggled, so that the entire body seemed to twitch and undulate, even while the monster itself did not move. It exhaled. The stink of raw flesh blew down the wilderness.

"Get me out of here," said Eckels. "It was never like this before. I was always sure I'd come through alive. I had good guides, good safaris, and safety. This time, I figured wrong. I've met my match and admit it. This is too much for me to get hold of."

"Don't run," said Lesperance. "Turn around. Hide in the Machine."

"Yes," Eckels seemed to be numb. He looked at his feet as if trying to make them move. He gave a grunt of helplessness.

"Eckels!"

He took a few steps, blinking, shuffling.

"Not *that* way!"

The Monster, at the first motion, lunged forward with a terrible scream. It covered one hundred yards in four seconds. The rifles jerked up and blazed fire. A windstorm from the beast's mouth engulfed them in the stench of slime and old blood. The Monster roared, teeth glittering with sun.

Eckels, not looking back, walked blindly to the edge of the Path, his gun limp in his arms, stepped off the Path, and walked, not knowing it, in the jungle. His feet sank into green moss. His legs moved him, and he felt alone and remote from the events behind.

The rifles cracked again. Their sound was lost in shriek and lizard thunder. The great lever of the reptile's tail swung up, lashed sideways. Trees exploded in clouds of leaf and branch. The Monster twitched its jeweler's hands down to fondle at the men, to twist them in half, to crush them like berries, to cram them into its teeth and its screaming throat. Its boulder-stone eyes leveled with the men. They saw themselves mirrored. They fired at the metallic eyelids and the blazing black iris.

Like a stone idol, like a mountain avalanche, *Tyrannosaurus* fell. Thundering, it clutched trees, pulled them with it. It wrenched and tore the metal Path. The men flung themselves back and away. The body hit, ten tons of cold flesh and stone. The guns fired. The Monster lashed its armored tail, twitched its snake jaws, and lay still. A fount of blood spurted from its throat. Somewhere inside, a sac of fluids burst. Sickening gushes drenched the hunters. They stood, red and glistening.

The thunder faded.

The jungle was silent. After the avalanche, a green peace. After the nightmare, morning.

Billings and Kramer sat on the pathway and threw up. Travis and Lesperance stood with smoking rifles, cursing steadily.

In the Time Machine, on his face, Eckels lay shivering. He had found his way back to the Path, climbed into the Machine.

Travis came walking, glanced at Eckels, took cotton gauze from a metal box, and returned to the others, who were sitting on the Path.

"Clean up."

They wiped the blood from their helmets. They began to curse too. The Monster lay, a hill of solid flesh. Within, you could hear the sighs and murmurs as the furthest chambers of it died, the organs malfunctioning, liquids running a final instant from pocket to sac to spleen, everything shutting off, closing up forever. It was like standing by a wrecked locomotive or a steam shovel at quitting time, all valves being released or levered tight. Bones cracked; the tonnage of its own flesh, off balance, dead weight, snapped the delicate forearms, caught underneath. The meat settled, quivering.

Another cracking sound. Overhead, a gigantic tree branch broke from its heavy mooring, fell. It crashed upon the dead beast with finality.

"There." Lesperance checked his watch. "Right on time. That's the giant tree that was scheduled to fall and kill this animal originally." He glanced at the two hunters. "You want the trophy picture?"

"What?"

"We can't take a trophy back to the Future. The body has to stay right here where it would have died originally, so the insects, birds, and bacteria can get at it, as they were intended to. Everything in balance. The body stays. But we *can* take a picture of you standing near it."

The two men tried to think, but gave up, shaking their heads.

They let themselves be led along the metal Path. They sank wearily into the Machine cushions. They gazed back at the ruined Monster, the stagnating mound, where already strange reptilian birds and golden insects were busy at the steaming armor.

A sound on the floor of the Time Machine stiffened them. Eckels sat there, shivering.

"I'm sorry," he said at last.

"Get up!" cried Travis.

Eckels got up.

"Go out on that Path alone," said Travis. He had his rifle pointed. "You're not coming back in the Machine. We're leaving you here!"

Lesperance seized Travis' arm. "Wait—"

"Stay out of this!" Travis shook his hand away. "This s.o.b. nearly killed us. But it isn't *that* so much. Hell, no. It's his *shoes!* Look at them! He ran off the Path. My God, that *ruins* us! Christ knows how much we'll forfeit. Tens of thousands of dollars of insurance! We guarantee no one leaves the Path. He left it. Oh, the damn fool! I'll have to report to the government. They might revoke our license to travel. God knows *what* he's done to Time, to History!"

"Take it easy, all he did was kick up some dirt."

"How do we *know*?" cried Travis. "We don't know anything! It's all a damn mystery! Get out there, Eckels!"

Eckels fumbled his shirt. "I'll pay anything. A hundred thousand dollars!"

Travis glared at Eckels' checkbook and spat. "Go out there. The Monster's next to the Path. Stick your arms up to your elbows in his mouth. Then you can come back with us."

"That's unreasonable!"

"The Monster's dead, you coward. The bullets! The bullets can't be left behind. They don't belong in the Past; they might change something. Here's my knife. Dig them out!"

The jungle was alive again, full of the old tremorings and bird cries. Eckels turned slowly to regard the primeval garbage dump, that hill of nightmares and terror. After a long time, like a sleepwalker, he shuffled out along the Path.

He returned, shuddering, five minutes later, his arms soaked and red to the elbows. He held out his hands. Each held a number of steel bullets. Then he fell. He lay where he fell, not moving.

"You didn't have to make him do that," said Lesperance.

"Didn't I? It's too early to tell." Travis nudged the still body. "He'll live. Next time he won't go hunting game like this. Okay." He jerked his thumb wearily at Lesperance. "Switch on. Let's go home."

1492. 1776. 1812.

They cleaned their hands and faces. They changed their caking shirts and pants. Eckels was up and around again, not speaking. Travis glared at him for a full ten minutes.

"Don't look at me," cried Eckels. "I haven't done anything."

"Who can tell?"

"Just ran off the Path, that's all, a little mud on my shoes—what do you want me to do—get down and pray?"

"We might need it. I'm warning you, Eckels, I might kill you yet. I've got my gun ready."

"I'm innocent. I've done nothing!"

1999. 2000. 2055.

The Machine stopped. "Get out," said Travis.

The room was there as they had left it. But not the same as they had left it. The same man sat behind the same desk. But the same man did not quite sit behind the same desk.

Travis looked around swiftly. "Everything okay here?" he snapped.

"Fine. Welcome home!"

Travis did not relax. He seemed to be looking at the very atoms of the air itself, at the way the sun poured through the one high window.

"Okay, Eckels, get out. Don't ever come back."

Eckels could not move.

"You heard me," said Travis. "What're you *staring* at?"

Eckels stood smelling of the air, and there was a thing to the air, a chemical taint so subtle, so slight, that only a faint cry of his subliminal senses warned him it was there. The colors, white, gray, blue, orange, in the wall, in the furniture, in the sky beyond the window, were . . . were . . . And there was a *feel*. His flesh twitched. His hands twitched. He stood drinking the oddness with the pores of his body. Somewhere, someone must have been screaming one of those whistles that only a dog can hear. His body screamed silence in return. Beyond this room, beyond this wall, beyond this man who was not quite the same man seated at this desk that was not quite the same desk . . . lay an entire world of streets and people. What sort of world it was now, there was no telling. He could feel them moving there, beyond the walls, almost, like so many chess pieces blown in a dry wind. . . .

But the immediate thing was the sign painted on the office wall, the same sign he had read earlier today on first entering.

Somehow, the sign had changed:

> TYME SEFARI INC.
>
> SEFARIS TU ANY YEER EN THE PAST.
>
> YU NAIM THE ANIMALL.
>
> WEE TAEK YU THAIR.
>
> YU SHOOT ITT.

Eckels felt himself fall into a chair. He fumbled crazily at the thick slime on his boots. He held up a clod of dirt, trembling. "No, it *can't* be. Not a *little* thing like that. No!"

Embedded in the mud, glistening green and gold and black, was a butterfly, very beautiful, and very dead.

"Not a little thing like *that*! Not a butterfly!" cried Eckels.

It fell to the floor, an exquisite thing, a small thing that could upset balances and knock down a line of small dominoes and then big dominoes and then gigantic dominoes, all down the years across Time. Eckels' mind whirled. It *couldn't* change things. Killing one butterfly couldn't be *that* important! Could it?

His face was cold. His mouth trembled, asking: "Who—who won the presidential election yesterday?"

The man behind the desk laughed. "You joking? You know damn well. Deutscher, of course! Who else? Not that damn weakling Keith. We got an iron man now, a man with guts, by God!" The official stopped. "What's wrong?"

Eckels moaned. He dropped to his knees. He scrabbled at the golden butterfly with shaking fingers. "Can't we," he pleaded to the world, to himself, to the officials, to the Machine, "can't we take it *back*, can't we *make* it alive again? Can't we start over? Can't we—"

He did not move. Eyes shut, he waited, shivering. He heard Travis breathe loud in the room; he heard Travis shift his rifle, click the safety catch, and raise the weapon.

There was a sound of thunder.

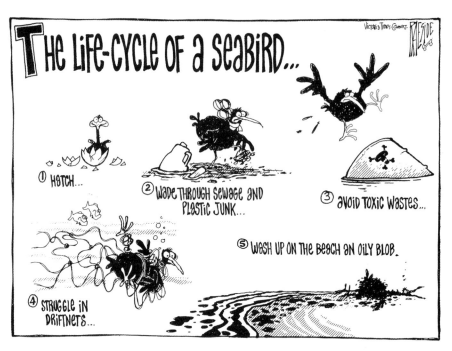

In the Jungle

Annie Dillard

Like any out-of-the-way place, the Napo River in the Ecuadorian jungle seems real enough when you are there, even central. Out of the way of *what?* I was sitting on a stump at the edge of a bankside palm-thatch village, in the middle of the night, on the headwaters of the Amazon. Out of the way of human life, tenderness, or the glance of heaven?

A nightjar in deep-leaved shadow called three long notes, and hushed. The men with me talked softly in clumps: three North Americans, four Ecuadorians who were showing us the jungle. We were holding cool drinks and idly watching a hand-sized tarantula seize moths that came to the lone bulb on the generator shed beside us.

It was February, the middle of summer. Green fireflies spattered lights across the air and illumined for seconds, now here, now there, the pale trunks of enormous, solitary trees. Beneath us the brown Napo River was rising, in all silence; it coiled up the sandy bank and tangled its foam in vines that trailed from the forest and roots that looped the shore.

Each breath of night smelled sweet, more moistened and sweet than any kitchen, or garden, or cradle. Each star in Orion seemed to tremble and stir with my breath. All at once, in the thatch house across the clearing behind us, one of the village's Jesuit priests began playing an alto recorder, playing a wordless song, lyric, in a minor key, that twined over the village clearing, that caught in the big trees' canopies, muted our talk on the bankside, and wandered over the river, dissolving downstream.

This will do, I thought. This will do, for a weekend, or a season, or a home.

Later that night I loosed my hair from its braids and combed it smooth—not for myself, but so the village girls could play with it in the morning.

We had disembarked at the village that afternoon, and I had slumped on some shaded steps, wishing I knew some Spanish or some Quechua so I could speak with the ring of little girls who were alternately staring at me and smiling at their toes. I spoke anyway, and fooled with my hair, which they were obviously dying to get their hands on, and laughed, and soon they were all braiding my hair, all five of them, all fifty fingers, all my hair, even my bangs. And then they took it apart and did it again, laughing, and teaching me Spanish nouns, and meeting my eyes and each other's with open delight, while their small brothers in blue jeans climbed down from the trees and began kicking a volleyball around with one of the North American men.

Now, as I combed my hair in the little tent, another of the men, a free-lance writer from Manhattan, was talking quietly. He was telling us the tale of his life, describing his work in Hollywood, his apartment in Manhattan, his house in Paris . . . 'It makes me wonder,' he said, 'what I'm doing in a tent under a tree in the village of Pompeya, on the Napo River, in the jungle of Ecuador.' After a pause he added, 'It makes me wonder why I'm going *back*.'

The point of going somewhere like the Napo River in Ecuador is not to see the most spectacular anything. It is simply to see what is there. We are here on the planet only once, and might as well get a feel for the place. We might as well get a feel for the fringes and hollows in which life is lived, for the Amazon basin, which covers half a continent, and for the life that—there, like anywhere else—is always and necessarily lived in detail: on the tributaries, in the riverside villages, sucking this particular white fleshed guava in this particular pattern of shade.

What is there is interesting. The Napo River itself is wide (I mean wider than the Mississippi at Davenport) and brown, opaque, and smeared with floating foam and logs and branches from the jungle. White egrets hunch on shoreline deadfalls and parrots in flocks dart in and out of the light. Under

the water in the river, unseen, are anacondas—which are reputed to take a few village toddlers every year—and water boas, sting-rays, crocodiles, manatees, and sweet-meated fish.

Low water bares grey strips of sandbar on which the natives build tiny palm-thatch shelters, arched, the size of pup tents, for overnight fishing trips. You see these extraordinarily clean people (who bathe twice a day in the river, and whose straight black hair is always freshly washed) paddling down the river in dugout canoes, hugging the banks.

Some of the Indians of this region, earlier in the century, used to sleep naked in hammocks. The nights are cold. Gordon MacCreach, an American explorer in these Amazon tributaries, reported that he was startled to hear the Indians get up at three in the morning. He was even more startled, night after night, to hear them walk down to the river slowly, half asleep, and bathe in the water. Only later did he learn what they were doing: they were getting warm. The cold woke them; they warmed their skins in the river, which was always ninety degrees; then they returned to their hammocks and slept through the rest of the night.

The riverbanks are low, and from the river you see an unbroken wall of dark forest in every direction, from the Andes to the Atlantic. You get a taste for looking at trees: trees hung with the swinging nests of yellow troupials, trees from which ant nests the size of grain sacks hang like black goiters, trees from which seven-coloured tanagers flutter, coral trees, teak, balsa and breadfruit, enormous emergent silk-cotton trees, and the pale-barked *samona* palms.

When you are inside the jungle, away from the river, the trees vault out of sight. It is hard to remember to look up the long trunks and see the fans, strips, fronds, and sprays of glossy leaves. Inside the jungle you are more likely to notice the snarl of climbers and creepers round the trees' boles, the flowering bromeliads and epiphytes in every bough's crook, and the fantastic silk-cotton tree trunks thirty or forty feet across, trunks buttressed in flanges of wood whose curves can make three high walls of a room—a shady, loamy-

aired room where you would gladly live, or die. Butterflies, iridescent blue, striped, or clear-winged, thread the jungle paths at eye level. And at your feet is a swath of ants bearing triangular bits of green leaf. The ants with their leaves look like a wide fleet of sailing dinghies—but they don't quit. In either direction they wobble over the jungle floor as far as the eye can see. I followed them off the path as far as I dared, and never saw an end to ants or to those luffing chips of green they bore.

Unseen in the jungle, but present, are tapirs, jaguars, many species of snake and lizard, ocelots, armadillos, marmosets, howler monkeys, toucans and macaws and a hundred other birds, deer, bats, peccaries, capybaras, agoutis, and sloths. Also present in this jungle, but variously distant, are Texaco derricks and pipelines, and some of the wildest Indians in the world, blowgun-using Indians, who killed missionaries in 1956 and ate them.

Long lakes shine in the jungle. We travelled one of these in dugout canoes, canoes with two inches of freeboard, canoes paddled with machete-hewn oars chopped from buttresses of silk-cotton trees, or poled in the shallows with peeled cane or bamboo. Our part-Indian guide had cleared the path to the lake the day before; when we walked the path we saw where he had impaled the lopped head of a boa, open-mouthed, on a pointed stick by the canoes, for decoration.

This lake was wonderful. Herons, egrets, and ibises plodded the sawgrass shores, kingfishers and cuckoos clattered from sunlight to shade, great turkey-like birds fussed in dead branches, and hawks lolled overhead. There was all the time in the world. A turtle slid into the water. The boy in the bow of my canoe slapped stones at birds with a simple sling, a rubber thong and leather pad. He aimed brilliantly at moving targets, always, and always missed; the birds were out of range. He stuffed his sling back in his shirt. I looked around.

The lake and river waters are as opaque as rain-forest leaves; they are veils, blinds, painted screens. You see things only by their effects. I saw the shore-line water roil and the sawgrass heave about as thrashing *paichi*, an enormous black fish of these waters; one had been caught the previous week weighing 430 pounds. Piranha fish live in the lakes, and electric eels. I dangled my fingers in the water, figuring it would be worth it.

We would eat chicken that night in the village, and rice, yucca, onions, beets, and heaps of fruit. The sun would ring down, pulling darkness after it like a curtain. Twilight is short, and the unseen birds of twilight wistful,

uncanny, catching the heart. The two nuns in their dazzling white habits—
the beautiful-boned young nun and the warm-faced old—would glide to the
open cane-and-thatch schoolroom in darkness, and start the children singing. The children would sing in piping Spanish, high-pitched and pure; they
would sing 'Nearer My God to Thee' in Quechua, very fast. (To reciprocate,
we sang for them 'Old MacDonald Had a Farm'; I thought they might recognize the animal sounds. Of course they thought we were out of our minds.)
As the children became excited by their own singing, they left their log
benches and swarmed around the nuns, hopping, smiling at us, everyone
smiling, the nuns' faces bursting in their cowls, and the clear-voiced children
still singing, and the palm-leafed roofing stirred.

The Napo River: it is not out of the way. It is in the way, catching sunlight
the way a cup catches poured water; it is a bowl of sweet air, a basin of
greenness, and of grace, and, it would seem, of peace.

Plenty

Jean Little

I have plenty of everything
     but want.
I try to imagine hunger,
Try to imagine that I have not eaten today,
That I must stand in line for a bowl of soup,
That my cheekbones angle out of my hollowed face;
But I smell the roast in the oven.
I hear the laden refrigerator hum.

I think of people whose walls are made of wind.
I stand outside in the cold.
I tell myself I am homeless and dressed in rags;
But my shiver lacks conviction.
I stand in fleece-lined boots and winter coat.
Home is a block away.

I leave my wallet at home.
Pretending I have no money,
I walk past stores and wish.
"I have no money, no money at all, no money—"
I turn my head in shame as I pass the bank.

I pay for a parcel of food. I gather clothes.
I adopt a child under a foster parent plan.
I do what I can. I am generous. I am kind—

I still have plenty of everything
     but want.

What's the Youth?

TEXT: KAREN BENOIT
ILLUSTRATIONS: EMMANUELLE ROUSSEAU

IT **WORKS**! NOW, CONTINENT BY CONTINENT, I WILL RID THE WORLD OF EVERYTHING YOUTHFUL. HA! HA! HA!

FIRST, AFRICA -- TWO-THIRDS OF THE POPULATION IS UNDER 25. READY, AIM, **FIRE**!

POOF

WHAT! A MALFUNCTION? BACK TO THE OLD DRAWING BOARD.

AS THE HUMAN BODY AGES -- INERTIA INCREASES. HHMM.... YOUNG PEOPLE DO HAVE A CERTAIN ENERGY, ENTHUSIASM AND INITIATIVE.

HUH? THEY SEEM TO HAVE A HEIGHTENED SENSE OF IDEALISM, OPEN-MINDEDNESS AND CREATIVITY -- HHHH -- ENOUGH TO CHALLENGE THE STATUS QUO.

YOUTH... OVER HALF OF THE WORLD'S POPULATION! PERHAPS A VITAL ELEMENT TO ALL COUNTRIES? HHMM... WITH EDUCATION AND OPPORTUNITY, THEY COULD BRING CHANGE AND IMPROVEMENT.

IT SEEMS YOUNG PEOPLE HAVE ENORMOUS VALUE WHICH FAR OUTWEIGHS THEIR FEW ANNOYING HABITS.

MAYBE I CAN PUT THE AGE RAY IN REVERSE AND USE IT ON MYSELF!

EXCELLENT!

Growing Up Touareg

Donna Douglas

Idrissa is a 16-year-old Touareg. He lives with his parents, his brother and four sisters in a small village of 5000 inhabitants called Timia, in Niger on the edge of the Sahara. Their village is made up of a series of small adobe houses or mud-huts, without any electricity or running water.

When Idrissa reached the age of 13, his father offered him a job as shop-keeper. Since then, Idrissa has been making a living out of it. He sells fabric, foodstuffs, sandals and his monthly take-home pay is equivalent to $20 Canadian. This trade is quite different from the nomadic life of caravaneer and shepherd led by his ancestors and some of his seniors still today.

The Touaregs, a people of Sahelian Africa, are also known as the "blue men of the desert." Is it because their skin is blue? Not quite. It's the dye from the indigo blue (used to give colour to their traditional turbans) made from plants that run on their skin. This silk or cotton turban-veil is called a _chèche_ and measures 5 to 6 meters long. It protects them from the sun, cold nights, the sand and some even say that it protects them from evil spirits.

Touaregs practise the Muslim faith. Contrary to other Muslim societies where the women wear the veil, it is the Touareg men who wear it. They start veiling themselves as soon as their beards appear. The indigo _chèche_ is only worn for special occasions, such as weddings. The everyday _chèche_ comes in assorted colours.

Every year, the men leave on caravans. For 1300 years, they have been crisscrossing the desert east, west, north and south. They exchange the salt that they collect in Bilma for millet (a type of grain), money and clothing. No planes, no trucks. Everything is done on camels' backs.

This way of living, however, is threatened. In the last few years, the Niger government has passed drastic laws forcing Touaregs to settle. In addition, very serious droughts have destroyed a large part of the camel herds and forced caravaneers to change jobs and become tradesmen. This is how Idrissa's father became a tailor.

Today, young people like Idrissa no longer participate in caravans as much as before. So they make do with listening to the more experienced explain how to orient oneself in the desert. Did you know that in the desert, the wind always blows in the same direction? In the daytime, one can orient oneself by the touch of the wind on one's body and by the lines drawn on the sand by the wind. At night, the stars lead the way. It happens, sometimes, that travellers lose their way or their camels. The camels sometimes return home six months later!

Idrissa's parents, like the majority of Touaregs, refuse to send their children to the French school for fear that they would lose their traditions and want to settle in the big city. The Touareg people think that attending school is futile (only about 5% of them attend school) since it does not teach them how to survive in the desert. Therefore, Idrissa receives lessons from the village priest. He is the spiritual chief and healer who passes on the traditions, so

dear to the Touareg people. With him, Idrissa reads the Koran (the religious scriptures of Islam) and learns Arabic.

Idrissa must also conform to what we could call the moral code of Touaregs: the *Ashek*. For example, he cannot address himself directly to his father but must wait until his father speaks to him first. When his father speaks, Idrissa cannot ask him to repeat. His mother acts as go-between when Idrissa has any requests. *Ashek* means never to forget one's traditions or do something which might bring disgrace. It means being generous, helping those in need, greeting people.

Idrissa tries to put *Ashek* into practice and seems very respectful towards his parents. He says his mother is the most important person in his life. She raises goats with the help of two of her daughters and sometimes it's necessary to lead their flock more than 50 km away from their house. Idrissa would like some day to be able to earn enough money so his mother would not have to work.

When you're 16, you want to see the big city, go to the movies, something Idrissa likes very much to do once in a while. So he dresses up and sets off to tour the city. City life is a totally different world. There are all those products that are sold and lots of water. Also, in the city, one can earn more money and, to Idrissa, money means freedom. He even believes that money is more important than love. "If you're in love and have no money, what will you do? Someone who suffers from hunger and poverty doesn't think of love."

Idrissa has certain fears, just like we do: he is afraid of war, poverty and changes such as participating in caravans. "Anything unknown brings a certain fear . . ." says Idrissa.

His dreams? To become the village priest or chief. To have children some day, perhaps a couple of wives as his religion permits, and make enough money to buy a car. But will he want to swap his camel for a car?

Reprinted with permission by TG Magazine and Adobe Foundations, 4519 Marquette, Montreal, PQ, H2J 3Y3, 514-526-5031.

Canada's Undefended Border

"... you want to know what Canada is all about ... I'll tell you what it's all about ...
it's YOU reading and listening to all these media people in Toronto
telling you what Canada is all about ... THAT'S what it's all about ..."

The Enchanted Apple-tree

translated by M.C.O. Morris

Once upon a time there lived an old woman whose name was Misery.

Her one and only possession was an apple-tree and even this caused her more pain that pleasure. When the apples were ripe, the village urchins came and stole them off the tree.

This went on year after year, when one day an old man, with a long white beard, knocked at Misery's door. "Old woman," he begged, "give me a crust of bread."

"You, too, are a poor miserable creature," said Misery, who, although she had nothing herself, was full of compassion for others. "Here is half a loaf, take it; it is all I have, eat it in peace, and may it refresh you."

"As you have been so kind," said the old fellow, "I will grant you a wish."

"Oh!" sighed the old woman, "I have only one desire, that is, that anyone who touches my apple-tree may stick to it until I set them free. The way my apples are stolen from me is past all bearing."

"Your wish is granted," said the old fellow, and he went away.

Two days later Misery went to look at her tree; she found hanging and sticking to the branches a crowd of children, servants, mothers who had come to rescue their children, fathers who had tried to save their wives, two parrots who had escaped from their cage, a cock, a goose, an owl, and other birds, not to mention a goat. When she saw this extraordinary sight, she burst out laughing, and rubbed her hands with delight. She let them all remain hanging on the tree some time before she released them.

The thieves had learnt their lesson, and never stole the apples again.

Some time passed by, when one day someone again knocked at old Misery's door.

"Come in," she cried.

"Guess who I am," said a voice. "I am old Father Death himself. Listen, little mother," he continued. "I think that you and your old dog have lived long enough; I have come to fetch you both."

"You are all-powerful," said Misery. "I do not oppose your will, but before I pack up, grant me one favour. On the tree yonder there grow the most delicious apples you have ever tasted. Don't you think it would be a pity to leave them, without gathering one?"

"As you ask me so graciously, I will take one," said Death, whose mouth was watering as he walked towards the tree. He climbed up to the topmost branches to gather a large rosy apple, but directly he touched it, the wretch remained glued to the tree by his long bony hand. Nothing could tear him off, in spite of his struggles.

"There you are, old tyrant, hanging high and dry," said Misery.

As a result of Death hanging on the tree, no one died. If persons fell into the water they were not drowned; if a cart ran over them they did not even notice it; they did not die even if their heads were cut off.

After Death had hung, winter and summer, for ten long years on the tree, through all weathers, the old woman had pity on him, and allowed him to come down on condition that she should live as long as she liked.

This, Father Death agreed to, and that is why men live longer than the sparrows, and why Misery is always to be found in the world, and will doubtless remain until the end of time.

Credits

Every effort has been made to trace the original sources of materials contained in this book. The publisher would be pleased to hear from copyright holders to rectify any errors or omissions.

"Self-employment: A Dream that Can Become a Reality." Reprinted from *Canada Prospects*, Volume 1, Issue 1, Fall 1992, by permission of Canadian Career Information Partnership.

HANS CHRISTIAN ANDERSEN: "The Ugly Duckling" from *The Fairy Tale Treasury* by Virginia Haviland and Raymond Briggs. First published by Hamish Hamilton Children's Books, 1972. Reprinted by permission of Hamish Hamilton Ltd.

JUDIE ANGELL: "Dear Marsha." Copyright © 1989 by Judie Angell. From *Connections: Short Stories* by Donald R. Gallo, Editor. Used by permission of Delacorte Press, a division of Bantam Doubleday Dell Publishing Group, Inc.

BARRON (cartoon): "You want to know what Canada is all about." Reprinted with permission—The Toronto Star Syndicate.

ROBERTA BEECROFT: "Ending the Blame Game." Reprinted with permission by *TG Magazine*, 202 Cleveland Street, Toronto, ON, M4S 2W6, 416-487-3204.

KAREN BENOIT and EMMANUELLE ROUSSEAU: "What's the Youth?" Reprinted from *Under the Same Sun* by permission of the Canadian International Development Agency.

SADHU BINNING: "Neighbour." Reprinted with permission from *East of Main*, edited by Calvin Wharton and Tom Wayman (Arsenal Pulp, 1989).

RAY BRADBURY: "A Sound of Thunder." Reprinted by permission of Don Congdon Associates, Inc. Copyright © 1952, renewed 1980 by Ray Bradbury.

DIONNE BRAND: "Market Day" from *Earth Magic*, Kids Can Press, 1979.

MARTHA BROOKS: "What I Want To Be When I Grow Up" from *Paradise Café and Other Stories* (Thistledown Press Ltd., 1988). Used with permission.

CHRISTY BROWN: "A Look of Pity" from *My Left Foot*. Reprinted by permission of the publisher, Martin Secker & Warburg.

ROCH CARRIER: *The Boxing Champion*. Text © 1991 by Roch Carrier, translated by Sheila Fischman, published by Tundra Books.

DON CAYO: "Televising the Three R's in New Glasgow." First published in *Canadian Geographic*, August/September 1991. Reprinted by permission of the author.

YVONNE CHANG: "A New World." Reprinted with permission by *TG Magazine*, 202 Cleveland Street, Toronto, ON, M4S 2W6, 416-487-3204.

NATHAN LEE CHASING HIS HORSE: "Dances with History." Reprinted from *Seventeen*, August 1991.

SUZANNE CHAZIN: "Another Shot at Life" was reprinted with permission from the November 1992 *Reader's Digest*. Copyright © 1992 by The Reader's Digest Assn., Inc.

VAL R. CHEATHAM: "Sherwood Forest Revisited." Reprinted by permission from *Skits and Spoofs for Young Actors* by Val R. Cheatham. Copyright © 1976, 1977 by Val R. Cheatham. Publishers, Plays, Inc., Boston, MA, USA.

JENI COUZYN: "Specimen 2001, Probably 21 C." From the book *Specimen 2001, Probably 21 C* (Douglas & McIntyre), by permission of the author and Andrew Mann Ltd.

FRANK DAVEY: "The Piano" from *The Arches: Selected Poems*, Talon Books, 1980. Reprinted by permission.

ANNIE DILLARD: "In the Jungle." Reprinted by permission of Russell & Volkening as agents for the author. Copyright © 1982 by Annie Dillard.

DONNA DOUGLAS: "Growing Up Touareg" and "Sonam . . . serenity and concentration." Reprinted with permission by *TG Magazine* and Adobe Foundations, 4519 Marquette, Montreal, PQ, H2J 3Y3, 514-526-5031.

ELIZABETH ELLIS: "Flowers and Freckle Cream." Reprinted by permission of the author.

DELIA EPHRON and EDWARD KOREN: "How to Hide a Pimple," from *Teenage Romance: Or How to Die of Embarrassment* by Delia Ephron, illustrated by Edward Koren. Copyright © 1981 by Delia Ephron. Illustrations copyright © 1981 by Edward Koren. Used by permission

ADRIAN RAESIDE (cartoons): "What a beautiful spot", "Aerosol dinosaur", "Seabird", and "Inside Quickly." Reprinted by permission of Adrian Raeside.

JEFFREY REED: "Can We Make Basketball Canada's National Sport?" Reprinted with permission by *TG Magazine*, 202 Cleveland Street, Toronto, ON, M4S 2W6, 416-487-3204.

MARY WALTERS RISKIN: "I Want To Be Beautiful So Bad, It Makes Me Sick." Reprinted from *Zoot Capri, The Magazine*, Spring 1992 issue, copyright the Alberta Alcohol and Drug Abuse Commission.

SAKI: "The Open Window" from *The Complete Short Stories of Saki* (The Bodley Head).

CHRISTOPHER SHULGAN: "What Cool Is." Reprinted by permission of the author.

PETER D. SIERUTA: "25 Good Reasons for Hating My Brother Todd" from *Heartbeats and Other Stories* by Peter D. Sieruta. Copyright © 1989 by Peter D. Sieruta. Reprinted by permission of HarperCollins Publishers.

LOIS SIMMIE: "A Sliver of Liver" from *Who Greased the Shoelaces* by Lois Simmie. Reprinted by permission of Stoddart Publishing Co. Limited, Don Mills, Ontario.

SCOTT STEELE: excerpt from "A Dream in Gold", from "The Power of Youth", *Maclean's Magazine*, Maclean Hunter Ltd., February 22, 1993.

ANNE TYLER: "Teenage Wasteland." Copyright © 1983 by Anne Tyler. Reprinted by permission of Russell & Volkening as agents for the author.

W.D. VALGARDSON: "A Matter of Balance" © W.D. Valgardson.

BILL WATTERSON (cartoon): CALVIN AND HOBBES copyright 1993 Watterson. Reprinted with permission of UNIVERSAL PRESS SYNDICATE. All rights reserved.

BUDGE WILSON: "The Metaphor" from *The Leaving* by Budge Wilson, 1990, Stoddart Publishing Co. Limited, Don Mills, Ontario. Reprinted by permission of the publisher.

JIM WONG-CHU: "Equal Opportunity." Reprinted with permission from *East of Main* edited by Calvin Wharton and Tom Wayman (Arsenal Pulp, 1989).

VALERIE WYATT: profile of James Naismith. Text by Valerie Wyatt reprinted from *Inventions: An Amazing Investigation* with permission of the publisher, Greey de Pencier Books.

JANE YOLEN: "Happy Dens or A Day In the Old Wolves' Home." Reprinted by permission of Curtis Brown, Ltd. Copyright © 1984 by Jane Yolen.